Adoption For Dummies®

Cheat Sheet

Basic Steps to Adoption

For more detailed information on the steps involved in adoption, head to Part II.

For domestic adoptions:

1. Find an agency or attorney.
2. Fill out an adoption application; then do the home study and paperwork, including writing a profile and a Dear Birthmother letter.
3. Wait for a placement.
4. Make it through the supervision period.
5. Finalize in court.

For international adoptions:

1. Find an agency.
2. Fill out an application and undergo a home study.
3. Prepare your dossier and other necessary paperwork.
4. Work with the BCIS (Bureau of Citizenship and Immigration Services, formerly the Immigration and Naturalization Service) to secure your visa approval.
5. Wait for a child to be assigned to you.
6. Wait for your paperwork to clear all the necessary checks so that you can be cleared to bring your child home.
7. Travel to your child's birth country to finalize the adoption and bring her home, *or* prepare for your child's arrival in the United States.
8. If necessary, re-adopt your child back home.

Important Questions to Ask the Attorney

For the right answers, head to Chapter 7.

- How long have you been in practice?
- What is your legal specialty?
- Do you belong to any professional organizations that relate to adoption?
- What's your familiarity with adoption laws in your state?
- What types of adoption (domestic, international, interstate) do you handle?
- How many adoptions do you facilitate each year?
- Have you ever had a complaint filed against you, and if so, what action was taken?
- What's your experience with contested adoptions?
- What are your fees and when are they paid?
- Can you give me the names of references?
- What services do you offer birthmothers?
- Who's responsible for securing background and medical information from the birthmother?

Important Questions to Ask an Agency

For the right answers, head to Chapter 7.

- Is the agency licensed in the state?
- What are the agency fees, what are they for, and when do I pay them?
- What are your agency's specific requirements for families?
- What type of adoptions (open, semiopen, infants, special needs, and so on) does your agency facilitate?
- What type of preparation or education do you offer to families?
- What does the home study process entail?
- What is the estimated length of time for the process — that is, from application to placement?
- What kind of post-placement supervision will be required?
- What services does the agency offer birthmothers?
- What happens when a birthmother we have connected with changes her mind about the adoption?
- How many adoptions did the agency complete last year?
- How many adoptive families are waiting for a placement?
- Can the agency provide a list of references of former clients?

For Dummies: Bestselling Book Series for Beginners

P9-CNC-200

Adoption For Dummies®

Cheat Sheet

Your Home Study To-Do List

As soon as you make the decision to adopt, you can begin to amass info that you'll need for the home study (explained in Chapter 9). Gathering this information early can save you time once the home study begins.

- Your birth certificates for parents and possibly birth certificates for your other children
- Your marriage certificate
- Any divorce decrees
- Your latest tax return documents and/or check stubs (usually three months worth)
- Your regular monthly expenditures, with totals
- The amount of any child support obligations you have
- Your total amount of debt (including credit card balances, mortgage, and so on)
- The value of your home and other properties, savings, and other accounts
- Names, addresses, and phone numbers for at least four personal references
- Names, addresses, and phone numbers for employer references

Tip: You can also schedule appointments for physicals for everyone in the family (but don't go until you have the proper agency form for the doc to fill out).

Positive Adoption Language (PAL)

Part of the stigma associated with adoption comes from the language that people have traditionally used when speaking about it. The following lists examples of positive adoption language that you should use and negative language you should avoid.

Positive Language	Negative Language
Birthparent	Real parent or natural parent
Birth child	Own child, real child, natural child
My child	My adopted child
Born to unmarried parents	Illegitimate
Make an adoption plan	Give up, put up for adoption
Decide to parent her baby	Keep her baby
International adoption	Foreign adoption
Adoption triad	Adoption triangle
Child in need of a family	Unwanted child
Unplanned pregnancy	Unwanted pregnancy
Could not conceive or could not carry pregnancy	Could not have children, barren
Parent	Real parent
Search	Track down

For Dummies: Bestselling Book Series for Beginners

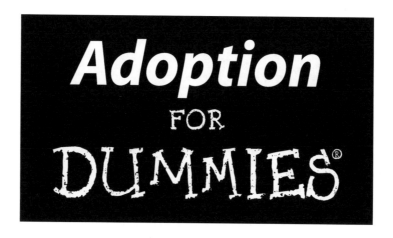

Adoption FOR DUMMIES®

by Tracy Barr and Katrina Carlisle

WILEY

Wiley Publishing, Inc.

Adoption For Dummies®

Published by
Wiley Publishing, Inc.
111 River Street
Hoboken, NJ 07030
www.wiley.com

Copyright © 2003 by Wiley Publishing, Inc., Indianapolis, Indiana

Published by Wiley Publishing, Inc., Indianapolis, Indiana

Published simultaneously in Canada

For general information on our other products and services or to obtain technical support, please contact our Customer Care Department within the U.S. at 800-762-2974, outside the U.S. at 317-572-3993, or fax 317-572-4002.

Wiley also publishes its books in a variety of electronic formats. Some content that appears in print may not be available in electronic books.

Library of Congress Cataloging-in-Publication Data:

Library of Congress Control Number: 2003105677

ISBN: 0-7645-5488-3

10 9 8 7 6 5 4 3 2 1

About the Authors

Tracy Barr has been a part of the Dummies phenomenon for almost a decade. In that time, she has served as editor, editorial manager, writer, and consultant to the folks who write and edit *For Dummies* books. Most recently, she helped write *World War II For Dummies* with Keith D. Dickson, *Latin For Dummies* with Clifford Hull and Steven Perkins, and *Religion For Dummies* with Rabbi Marc Gellman and Monsignor Thomas Hartman. Her most challenging and rewarding role, however, is a personal one. She built her family through adoption and is the mother of four rambunctiously wonderful children. Her personal experience with adoption did not begin with her own children, however, but with her family of origin, which itself was built through adoption. As one of six children in an interracial family and as an adoptive mother, she is well aware of the issues that adoptees and their parents face.

Katrina Carlisle, BSW, LSW, is currently the executive director of Coleman Adoption Services, Inc., in Indianapolis, Indiana. Her duties include providing direct services to birthparents prior to placement and post-placement, conducting home studies and post-placement supervision visits for adoptive parents, providing search and reunion services for adult adoptees and birthparents, and leading transracial adoption seminars and other types of community education. She has three years of experience as a social worker in adoption and child welfare agencies. Two of her four children were adopted.

Dedication

From Katrina:
In loving memory of my son,
Bryce Ryan Carlisle
October 16, 1979–November 23, 2000
"Always remembered, forever loved"

From Tracy: To my husband, Larry, who has given my life happiness, and to my children — Adam, Sarah, Mary, and Alex — who have given it meaning.

Acknowledgments

From Katrina: I would like to thank the following people: My coauthor, Tracy, for asking me to do this project and then for having the patience to guide me through it. My husband, John, for his love and support in everything I do. My children, Derrick and Kara, for teaching me about adoption and allowing me to share their stories. My son Reid for understanding that his stories are not about adoption and, therefore, not in the book. My grandchildren for sharing their energy with me and my daughters-in-law for their encouragement. My mom and dad for their enthusiasm for this book and for telling everyone they know about it. My personal cheerleaders, Kenan and Mary. All my co-workers at Coleman Adoption Services, Inc., for believing in me and to all the wonderful birthmothers, adoptive parents, and adoptees who have taught me everything I know.

From Tracy: I would like to thank the following people: My coauthor, Katrina, for trusting me when I said that, together, she and I could actually write this book. My husband, Larry, for his love, support, and too many other things to list here. My children, for interrupting me regularly enough to remind me exactly why I took on the task of writing this book. And the people in the family I grew up in: my parents, Lanny and Mary Carmichael; and my siblings, Kelly, Sandy, Billy, David, and Wendy, just because.

From both authors: Several people helped create this book: Natasha Graf, Norm Crampton, Alissa Schwipps, and Tina Sims, the Wiley acquisitions and editing team that pulled everything together; Melitta Payne, of Bethany Christian Services, who graciously provided information on international adoptions; Kathy Gallop, of Lutheran Social Services, who took time from her busy schedule to read the manuscript and offer always helpful suggestions; and to all the people who shared their own adoption stories with us: Laura and Brian Allen, Sherry and Bill Frazer, Amy Young-Gray, Jon and Jennifer Kirkman, Charlotte Ottinger, Christine and Maurice Rembert, Leon and Tonna Thomas, Ilene Watson, and Carl and Vicki Witmer.

Publisher's Acknowledgments

We're proud of this book; please send us your comments through our Dummies online registration form located at www.dummies.com/register/.

Some of the people who helped bring this book to market include the following:

Acquisitions, Editorial, and Media Development

Senior Project Editor: Alissa D. Schwipps

Acquisitions Editor: Natasha Graf

Senior Copy Editor: Tina Sims

Acquisitions Coordinator: Holly Grimes

Technical Editor: Kathy J. Gallup

Editorial Manager: Jennifer Ehrlich

Editorial Assistant: Elizabeth Rea

Cover Photos:
©SuperStock/SuperStock/PictureQuest

Cartoons: Rich Tennant, www.the5thwave.com

Production

Project Coordinators: Nancee Reeves and Kristie Rees

Layout and Graphics: Jennifer Click, Seth Conley, Carrie Foster, Stephanie D. Jumper, Jacque Schneider

Proofreaders: TECHBOOKS Production Services, Brian H. Walls

Indexer: TECHBOOKS Production Services

Publishing and Editorial for Consumer Dummies

   Diane Graves Steele, Vice President and Publisher, Consumer Dummies

   Joyce Pepple, Acquisitions Director, Consumer Dummies

   Kristin A. Cocks, Product Development Director, Consumer Dummies

   Michael Spring, Vice President and Publisher, Travel

   Brice Gosnell, Publishing Director, Travel

   Suzanne Jannetta, Editorial Director, Travel

Publishing for Technology Dummies

   Andy Cummings, Vice President and Publisher, Dummies Technology/General User

Composition Services

   Gerry Fahey, Vice President of Production Services

   Debbie Stailey, Director of Composition Services

Contents at a Glance

Table of Contents

Introduction

*Y*ou hear all sorts of things said or implied about adoption. Some info comes from people who know a lot about it; some comes from people who don't know jack about it but make assumptions anyway. Some comes from people whose experiences have been good; some from those whose experiences have been bad. The result? Enough conflicting information to make your head spin.

The truth is, the adoption experience is as varied and unique as the people who are touched by it. What may be true for some, based on their unique circumstances and influenced by their own perceptions, may not be true for others.

So when everybody has an opinion and most of the books on the market deal with specific aspects on adoption or particular types of adoptions, where do you go when you don't know enough to know what you need to know more about? To a general reference, and that's what *Adoption For Dummies* is.

One thing you should know is that everyone who writes about adoption has a bias, and so do we. We're all for it. Our own personal and professional experiences with adoption have only reaffirmed for us that adoption is a wonderful and natural way to build families. Having said that, you also need to know that we don't try to "sell" you on the idea of adoption. Why? Because adoption isn't the right choice for everyone. But for those for whom adoption *is* the right choice, we can say that you're in for the ride of your life.

About This Book

No adoption book — or at least no adoption book that you can carry around without a hydraulic lift — can tell you everything there is to know about adoption. In this book, we don't even try. What this book does is tell you what you *need* to know. How does adoption work? How much can it cost? How do you decide whether adoption is a good choice for your family? What kinds of things do you need to be prepared to deal with if you build your family through adoption? And more. And all in an easy-to-use reference.

Each chapter is divided into sections, and each section contains information about some part of understanding adoption, like

- What you can expect during your home study and what to include in the profile you'll be writing
- Who the people involved in your adoption are (birthparents, social workers, and so on) and what roles they play
- Adoption laws and guidelines you need to be aware of
- Questions to ask when you start hunting for a reputable adoption agency or attorney
- How to deal with the issues that adoptive families face

The great thing about this book is that *you* decide where to start and what to read. It's a reference you can jump into and out of at will. Just head to the table of contents or the index to find the information you want.

Conventions Used in This Book

To help you navigate through this book, we've set up a few conventions:

- *Italic* is used for emphasis and to highlight new words or terms that are defined.
- **Boldfaced** text is used to indicate the action part of numbered steps.
- Monofont is used for Web addresses.

What You're Not to Read

We've written this book so that you can 1) find information easily and 2) easily understand what you find. And although we'd like to believe that you want to pore over every last word between the two yellow covers, we actually make it easy for you to identify "skippable" material. This information is the stuff that, although interesting and related to the topic at hand, isn't essential for you to know:

- **Text in sidebars:** The sidebars are the shaded boxes that appear here and there. They share personal stories and observations, but aren't necessary reading.
- **Anything with a Technical Stuff icon attached:** This information is interesting but not critical to your understanding of adoption.

✔ **The stuff on the copyright page:** No kidding. You'll find nothing here of interest unless you're inexplicably enamored by legal language and Library of Congress numbers.

Foolish Assumptions

Every book is written with a particular reader in mind, and this one is no different. As we wrote this book, we made a few assumptions about you:

✔ You haven't had much experience with adoption — beyond what you see on TV — and want to find out whether it's really as perilous an endeavor as some people would lead you to believe.

✔ You're thinking about adopting but aren't sure whether it's the right choice for your family. Or you want to adopt, but you don't know where to start or what to expect.

✔ You want basic information, but you don't want to become an expert in adoption law or to have to spend inordinate amounts of time scouring through legal journals.

✔ You've decided to adopt but are facing objections from family members or friends, and you want an adoption book that's hefty enough to have an impact when you hit them upside the head with it.

How This Book Is Organized

To help you find information that you're looking for, this book is divided into five parts. Each part covers a particular aspect on adoption and contains chapters relating to that part.

Part 1: Everything You Ever Wanted to Know about Adoption but Didn't Know Whom to Ask

Many people starting the adoption journey have a zillion questions: What's it mean? How much does it cost? Who's involved? How long does it take? What do I need to know that I don't know to ask? And more. If you have the same questions, welcome to Part I. Here you can find the answers to basic questions that rattle around the brains of just about everyone who first considers adoption as an option in family planning.

Part II: Getting Started and Moving Forward, One Milestone at a Time

Let's face it. Filling out an application on which you state both your weight and your income is not as fun as having sex. As a result, many people, when they first think about adoption, don't think, "Goody. We get to conjure up a family." They think, "How many painful, silly, embarrassing things am I going to have to do to get a child?" This part sets aside the fact that this is *exactly* the same question that people who conceive their children should be asking and explains, in detail, what steps you have to take.

Part III: Birthmothers and Birthfathers

All adoptions involve birthparents. These are the people who created the child you love and whom you may fret the most about, especially during the early stages of your adoption. "Will they like and select us?" "Will they follow through with the adoption plan?" "Will they challenge the adoption?" "How involved will they be after the placement?" are all questions that adoptive parents ask themselves at one time or another. To help alleviate your concerns, this part explains who the birthparents are, the roles they have in your adoption plans, and why, even though they may not be part of your life, they're still important to you.

Part IV: Issues Adoptive Families Face

As an adoptive family, you're going to face issues that parents who give birth to their children don't have to face. These issues include things like deciding whom to tell what about the adoption, how to share the adoption story with your child, how to help your child deal with questions or emotions she has about her birthmother, how to shut up rude strangers who focus on the ways in which your family is different, or how to handle family members who treat your kids differently than their cousins. This part explains what issues you should be prepared to face and offers suggestions on how to deal with them when they arise.

Part V: The Part of Tens

Want to know what adoption books are great to read to your kids? How about resources that you, as an adoptive parent, can use? Think you need a support group? This part offers lists of things — books, resources, and support groups — that you may find helpful.

Icons Used in This Book

The icons in this book help you find particular kinds of information that may be of use to you:

You see this icon anywhere we offer a suggestion or bit of advice — like how to save time or who to use as a resource — that can help you with the task at hand.

This icon points out important information that you want to remember.

Most people you work with in adoption are ethical, honest, and competent, but some aren't. Whether the problem is one of intentional wrongdoing or just plain ignorance, the implications for your adoption can be disastrous. This icon serves as your warning to beware of certain people or situations.

This icon appears beside information that is interesting but not necessary to know. In fact, feel free to skip the info here if you want. Doing so won't impair your understanding of adoption.

The best people to hear from are the people who've gone through what you're going through (or thinking about going through). So we include personal stories from people who have adopted or been adopted. To help you easily find these anecdotes, we highlight them with this icon.

Where to Go from Here

This book is organized so that you can go wherever you want to find complete information. Want to know about birthparent searches, for example? Head to Chapter 19. If you're interested in how to create your profile, go to Chapter 9 for that. You can use the table of contents to find broad categories of information or the index to look up more specific things.

If you're not sure where you want to go, you may want to start with Part I. It gives you all the basic info you need to understand adoption and points to places where you can find more detailed information.

Part I
Everything You Ever Wanted to Know about Adoption but Didn't Know Whom to Ask

The 5th Wave   By Rich Tennant

"Adopting a child as a single parent requires many skills. This next part of our screening process is designed to determine your sense of humor."

In this part . . .

*I*f you're like most people first considering adoption, you may have a few basic questions swirling around in your brain that you want answered before you go much further. What does it require? How much does it cost? How long does it take? Whom do I contact or work with? And how will my past affect my chances? This part answers these questions for you, and then it asks one more: Is adoption the right choice for *you?* Although you won't find the answer to that question here, you do find things to think about as you decide.

Chapter 1

Adoption Basics

· ·

· ·

Some cultures believe that children visit their parents in dreams before they are born — that the child's soul somehow recognizes its parent's soul and is drawn to it, despite the boundaries of time and space and even physical existence. Whether you accept this belief or not, it is a compelling idea, don't you think? That something other than conventional ties — genetic ties, historical ties, racial or ethnicity ties — joins people together and that this connection exists beyond time. Maybe adoption is simply what this mystery looks like after bureaucrats get hold of it.

Part of adoption is the practical stuff: the filling out of papers, the home studies and interviews, the things you cross off your list and store away in your closet as you wait. But the other part is the indefinable thing that makes adoption — having a child who is so completely yours that your heart seems to beat in time with his or hers — as mysterious and miraculous as conception and birth.

The mechanics are slightly different, true. After all, sex is optional in adoption (but then, nowadays, it is in some conceptions, too), the wait may be a few weeks or a few years, and your child may come to you in the gangly body of a preteen or the teetering one of a toddler. But in the end, your child is your child. This chapter gives you a quick tour of what adoption is, what you do when you adopt, what you need to know, and where to go to get more detailed information.

Defining Adoption

Most dictionaries define adoption, in more or fewer words, as the creation of a parent-child bond where one wouldn't exist naturally. In other words, when you adopt, you legally become the parent of a child born to someone else. That means, in the eyes of the state, you assume legal and custodial responsibility for the child, and the child has the same legal rights (inheritance and so on) as any child born to you.

Of course, the legal aspect of adoption is important because it confers rights and responsibilities where none would have existed otherwise. And this definition is technically accurate, as far as it goes. But it doesn't go far enough. When you adopt, you become more than the legal parent of a child. You become that child's mom or dad — in your heart, in your mind, in your body, and in your soul.

Conceiving and bearing children is one way to build a family. Adoption is merely another way to accomplish the same goal. In that way, adopting a child is different only in the process, not in the result.

Exploring common myths

Many people have misconceptions about adoption. And who can blame them? If you form your opinion about adoption from how it's often portrayed on sitcoms or in film or — heaven forbid — on daytime talk shows, you'd think that the whole enterprise is filled with a bunch of crazy adults, confused kids, and annoying social services personnel. The following sections cover some of the more potent presumptions about adoption. Of course, these explanations are no match for Jerry Springer, but then, what is?

Myth 1: It's a lesser relationship

Flesh of my flesh, bone of my bone.

Blood is thicker than water.

Blood will tell.

He's blood.

All of these phrases speak to one thing: the presumed primacy of the connection between people who share the same bloodline. The concept that a genetic link is one of the main, if not *the* main, foundation of human relations leads to one of the biggest misconceptions people have about adoption: that it is, in some way, a lesser relationship because the parents didn't conceive and bear their child. Without the physical link, the thinking goes, the same deep bond can't exist between adoptive parents and their children.

Yes, adopting a child is different from bearing a child, but not in the ways you may think. True, adoptive parents don't share a genetic link with their child, but don't mistakenly assume that this is the only physical bond between parents and their kids. Tell an adoptive mother that she didn't labor for her child, for example, and she can probably rattle off reams of things she had to do, publicly and privately, to bring her child home. Or tell an adoptive father who falls asleep with his baby on his chest that he doesn't have a physical connection to that child. Or dare to suggest to the woman standing at the bus stop on the first day of kindergarten or the father who watches his daughter walk across the stage at her graduation that the tears they're holding back are less real or less genuine or in some way less heartfelt because the only thing they haven't shared with their children is DNA.

It's not genetics that creates the parent-child bond. It's love and shared experience and commitment.

Myth 2: It's a secret

Once upon a time you didn't talk about adoption. It ranked right up there with unwed mothers and extramarital affairs as a taboo topic. Not only did you *not* talk about it, but sometimes you didn't even share the information with the most important person involved: the child. And if you did share it, you waited until he or she was old enough to "take" the news. The reason for the secrecy? Fear of the stigma of being "illegitimate" and the whole notion of the sins of the fathers tainting the sons.

Adoption arrangements themselves often were closed — that is, the birthmother and the adoptive families were kept absolutely separate and their identities secret. Birth moms had no say in adoptive placements, and adoptive parents who wanted personal information, beyond what the agencies provided, had little or no recourse. Court records on adoptions were sealed, making it difficult even for the child to discover the identity of his birthparents.

Thankfully, things today are a lot different:

> ✔ The stigma of adoption is, if not dead, hopefully taking its last painful breath. First, the idea of illegitimacy — of a child somehow not being "right" because the people who conceived him weren't married — is going by the wayside. Also becoming outdated is the notion that children somehow are receptacles for their parents' sins. These changes are good because every child should be able to embrace his life story, however it began.

✔ Most adoptions in the United States are open or semi-open, meaning that birthmothers and adoptive parents can arrange to have the contact that they feel comfortable with. (To find out more about open and semi-open adoptions, head to Chapter 2; Chapter 15 covers the types of contact that can be arranged.) In addition, all adoption professionals and nearly anyone else who knows anything about it agree that children have the right to know about their adoption, and the adoption story — the story you share with your child about how she came into your family — is a great way to share that information.

✔ Many states have taken steps to help adopted children find out information about their birthparents. Some have opened all adoption records; others provide registries for people wanting to be reconnected. For details on how to conduct a search for birthparents and the type of information you can get, head to Chapter 19.

Myth 3: It's a competition

Adoption is both happy and sad. One family's loss is another family's gain. One woman will have empty arms, and another's will be full. Because of this paradox, many people mistakenly assume that the birthparents and the adoptive parents are, in some way, competing or at cross-purposes. Who is, after all, the "true" parent — the one who bears the child or the one who raises her?

Before you answer, think about this: All parents — birth and adoptive — want the same thing: for their children to grow up happy, healthy, safe, and loved and for their children to fulfill the potential within themselves. The only possible answer, then, is that true parents are the ones who give that opportunity to their children. If you recognize that birthparents and adoptive parents achieve this goal together, then you understand the nature of adoption.

Getting the language right, PAL

The phrases that people commonly used in the past (and that less informed people still use today) to describe or define adoption have negative connotations. How would you feel, for example, if someone asked, "Why didn't your real mom want you?" The language in this question implies that 1) the mother you have isn't the one you really belong to and 2) that you weren't placed for adoption because your birthmother wasn't prepared to be a parent; you were placed for adoption because she didn't want *you*.

So in comes PAL, which stands for Positive Adoption Language. This is the language you'll hear when you talk with adoption professionals, and it's the language you should use when *you* speak about adoption. Table 1-1 lists some phrases and terms that you should use and that you should avoid.

Table 1-1	Positive Adoption Language
Positive Language	*Negative Language*
Birthparent	Real parent or natural parent
Birth child	Own child, real child, natural child
My child	My adopted child
Born to unmarried parents	Illegitimate
Make an adoption plan	Give up, put up for adoption
Decide to parent her baby	Keeping her baby
International adoption	Foreign adoption
Adoption triad	Adoption triangle
Child in need of a family	Unwanted child
Unplanned pregnancy	Unwanted pregnancy
Could not conceive or could not carry pregnancy	Could not have children
Parent	Real parent
Search	Track down

Distinguishing between adoption and foster parenthood

Many people mistakenly assume that adoption is like foster care, in that the role of the adoptive parent is to care for the child until he or she is grown or until the "real" parent can resume that responsibility. Although there are some similarities between adopting a child and fostering a child (both result in people caring for children born to others and both are arrangements based on love), the goals are different.

In adoption, the child's legal relationship with the birthparents has been ended, either voluntarily or by court order (see Chapter 11 for details on how children become available for adoption). The adoptive parents become the child's parent in every way and permanently. The goal is the creation of the adoptive family.

In a foster relationship, the foster parents care for a child in need while the state agency works with birthparents toward reunifying the family or, barring that, toward terminating the parents' rights. Foster parents care for the child's physical and emotional needs with the understanding that the state's goal, if all goes well, is to return the child to his or her birthparents.

Many states require or recommend that people adopting through state agencies first become foster parents for the following reasons:

✔ The arrangement helps state agencies, many of which are in dire need of loving homes for children in the child welfare system.

✔ If you're interested in adopting an older child, as the foster parent, you may be able to adopt the child in your home if he or she does become available for an adoption.

✔ Remaining in the home they've already adjusted to, rather than being taken to another placement, is much better for the older children who become available for adoption.

✔ You may be more comfortable committing to an adoption of an older child if you've already parented that child as a foster parent.

If you're interested in adopting from state agencies or fostering children in their care, call your local welfare office for information. Keep in mind, though, that fostering isn't a substitute for adoption. It takes a special mind-set to foster a child. You have to be able to put aside your needs as a parent so that, if the time comes, you can let that child go.

Looking at the Adoption Process: What Happens When?

One big question people have when they begin the adoption process is "How do things work?" — meaning, what happens when? Basically two important things happen separately:

✔ You decide you want to adopt and take the steps necessary to qualify and prepare yourself for a child.

✔ A child becomes available either because the state has terminated the birthparents' parental rights or because the birthparents have voluntarily relinquished those rights.

In all U.S. adoptions (both domestic and international), those processes remain separate and don't converge until the end, when a child is actually placed in your home.

Although in open and semi-open adoptions and in many attorney-facilitated adoptions (explained in Chapter 2), you may have an agreement or an understanding with a particular woman that she will place her child with you when that child is born, *nothing* can compel or force her to follow through. So, although you may be very involved with her and feel connected to the child she carries, her decision is her own, and you have no legal or moral say in what she decides. And she could very well decide to parent her baby herself.

The following sections briefly outline the process you follow when you adopt, and explain what makes a child available for adoption.

You: Working toward adoption

Obviously the first thing you need to do when you adopt is to make the decision that adoption is a good choice for you. It isn't for everybody (head to Chapter 6 for things you should think about before you decide to pursue adoption). Some people, in their heart of hearts, don't want to or don't believe that they can truly be the parents of children born to someone else. That's okay. All people have a right to their own dreams of a family. But if this describes you, don't adopt.

Once you decide that adoption is a good choice for your family, you need to hook up with people who can help you bring that dream to fruition. That means that you need to find an agency or an attorney to work with. Choosing an agency or attorney to help you is one of the most important decisions you make because these people have such a huge impact not only in how the process goes but in how you feel about what happens. For these reasons, you need to shop around, do research on the options available, and make an informed decision. Chapter 7 explains what you need to look for in the agencies and attorneys you're considering.

After you find an agency or attorney to work with, you're going to find yourself very busy with the process (see Chapter 9). If you're working with an agency, you have the home study to look forward to, the assignments (like putting together a profile of your family, filling out all sorts of necessary forms, and amassing all the documentation you'll need). If you're adopting internationally, you'll also be preparing for your trip to your child's birth country. You also have the wait — the time you spend waiting for the call that your child has been born or is available and ready to come home. (Chapter 10 suggests ways to keep your sanity and use the time wisely during the waiting period.)

All this work and waiting eventually lead to placement for domestic adoptions (when the child is actually placed in your home) or the referral of a child in international adoptions (when the child is assigned to you and is waiting for all the government paperwork to clear so you can bring her home). In both scenarios, your child is yours, but the adoption isn't done yet. If you're adopting domestically, you have the supervision period ahead of you. During this time, the social worker checks in to see how things are going with you and your new family member. If you're adopting from another country, you're waiting for the time when you can travel to your child's birth country and bring her home.

The finalization hearing follows the supervision period (see Chapter 12). Finalizing your adoption is exactly what it sounds like: the end of the adoption process, when your child legally becomes your child forever. After your finalization hearing, which takes place in a county within your state (for domestic adoptions) or in the child's birth country (for international adoptions), the adoption is done — that is, unless you're adopting internationally and have to re-adopt back in the States (Chapter 3 explains when re-adoption of a foreign-born child may be necessary).

This process can take anywhere from a couple of months to a few years. The length of the process depends on several factors. Some of these things you can control (like whom you work with and how open you are in what you'll consider), but others you can't (like whether a birthmother follows through with her adoption plan). But one thing is certain: Once you make the decision to adopt (and are approved by an agency), your chances of getting a child are practically guaranteed.

Your child: Becoming available

While you're busy preparing yourself for a family (or an addition to your family, as the case may be), other events are going on absolutely outside of your control.

Before you can adopt domestically, the parental rights of your child's birthparents have to be relinquished voluntarily by the birthparents or terminated by the state.

In most cases, if you adopt an infant domestically, the birthparents (usually the birthmother, but occasionally the birthfather, too) have voluntarily relinquished their rights. That means that they've made an adoption plan and have contacted an agency or lawyer to help them. Keep in mind, though, that they can't actually give up their parental rights before the child's birth. Despite all the work they may do to prepare themselves for the culmination of their decision (the counseling, the selecting of an adoptive family, and so on), they can't actually sign the consent forms (the legal forms that end their status as the child's parents) until after the child is born.

In most adoptions of older children, the state has terminated the birthparents' rights because of abuse, neglect, or abandonment. Before taking this step, the state generally works with the birthparents in the hopes that they'll be able to acquire the parenting skills they need in order to reunite the family. Failing this, the state begins termination hearings. The termination process, from beginning to end, can take years. Chapter 11 explains this topic in more detail.

If you're adopting internationally, your child has to meet both his birth country's criteria for orphan status *and* the U.S. criteria for orphan status. Although the definition of an orphan may differ in the specifics from country to country, basically, the following criteria have to be met:

✔ The birthparents, if they're living, have voluntarily ceded their rights to the child or have had their rights terminated according to their country's laws.

✔ If the birthparents are dead or incapacitated, no other relative is available to raise the child.

Most people assume (rightly) that adoption laws differ from country to country. What many people don't know is that adoption laws differ from state to state within the United States, too. Because a lot of legalities have to happen for a child to be cleared for adoption, either domestically or internationally, make sure that the agency or attorney you're working with knows all the adoption laws that apply.

It Takes (Half) a Village: Meeting the Folks Involved

Building a family through adoption is practically a community effort. You can't do it alone. You need the help and services of several different people. The following sections identify who's involved and what role they play.

The birthparents

Obviously, other than you, the birthparents are the most significant people in your adoption. Without them, you wouldn't have your child. Whether you ever have contact with your child's birthparents or not, they'll be important to you:

✔ First, their decisions during the adoption process directly impact your family, and when all is said and done, those decisions made it possible for you to have your child.

✔ Second, these people may someday be important to your child. Most children who've been adopted have questions about their birthparents (who they were, what they looked like) and the decisions they made (mainly, why did they make an adoption plan?). Even if your child isn't particularly interested in finding his birthparents (some kids aren't), he may still want medical information that can only come from them.

Head to Part III for a complete discussion about birthparents: who they are, how they can impact your adoption, and the type of contact you can have with them during the adoption process and beyond.

The social worker

When you adopt, expect to work, at some point, with a social worker. Although the media have a tendency to portray social workers as Mary Kay ladies channeling Torquemada, don't believe it. If you adopt through a public or private agency, the social worker is your best friend in the business. She's your advocate and your information source. She's also the one who leads you through the sometimes labyrinthine process of adopting a child in the United States, performs your home study, and keeps you informed as your adoption progresses. (For information on working with an agency, go to Chapter 2. To find out what to look for in the agency you work with, head to Chapter 7.)

If you work with an attorney or a facilitator (Chapter 7 explains how to find reputable ones), your only contact with a social worker may be during your home study. The social worker evaluates whether your home is a suitable one for a child and makes a judgment about whether you'd make good parents. Even if your relationship with her is short-lived, it's still an important one because her impressions can impact your adoption.

The attorney

All adoptions require the services of an attorney. If you work through an agency, you still need an attorney to do the legal work associated with the adoption (filing the adoption petition in court, being present to represent you on your finalization day, and so on).

Many families choose to work solely with attorneys in their adoptions. In these situations, the attorney does more than the legal work. She also acts in the role of an adoption agency, often locating birthmothers or children available for adoption or guiding you in finding a birthmother who wants to place her baby for adoption.

For information on attorney-assisted adoptions, head to Chapter 2. To find out how to locate a reputable attorney, go to Chapter 7.

Da judge

You can't finalize an adoption without going to court, standing (or sitting) before a judge, and swearing, under oath, that you know what you're doing. Actually, the court proceeding requires a little more than that (head to Chapter 12 to find out what). Nevertheless, the judge is the sweetheart of the whole deal because he's the one who makes everything final. No matter how long you've waited, no matter how many detours your adoption journey included, when the judge stamps those papers with the official seal, your child is your child forever. In fact, you very well may decide that the judge, on your finalization day, is your very favorite person in the whole world.

A myriad of other people

If you're adopting internationally, in addition to the people in the States who you're working with (see the preceding sections), you have contact with a whole cadre of other people in your child's birth country. These people usually include

- ✔ The attorney in your child's birth country
- ✔ The person who meets you at the airport and takes you everywhere you need to go and translates for you (sometimes this person is the attorney; sometimes it's someone else)
- ✔ Orphanage personnel or foster parents (referred to as *nannies* in some countries, including Chile and Guatemala)
- ✔ The other families you'll probably travel with, stay in the same hotel with, get your child with, and go through the whole process with
- ✔ Possibly a social worker in your child's birth country

Spending Time and Money: You'll Probably Need Both

Two big concerns that folks have about adoption are the amount of money it costs and the amount of time it takes. With the common perception being that you have to have thousands of dollars at your disposal and years to wait, many people think of adoption as a luxury they can't afford or aren't young enough to pursue. The following sections outline basic information about the cost — time- and money-wise — of adoption.

Fees, fees, and more fees — and then some

Unfortunately, the perception that adoption costs a load of money isn't entirely wrong. American adoptions — particularly the adoption of healthy infants — does cost money. The amount varies, depending on the fees your agency or attorney charges and the expenses you may need to cover for the birthmother during her pregnancy, and it can range from a few to several thousand dollars.

The important thing to know is that adoption is possible for most people, even those of modest means. Many private agencies (who place primarily infants) base their fees on income. So although the total amount still isn't chump change, it can be manageable. Adopting older children (who are often placed by state welfare agencies) costs only a nominal fee, if it costs anything at all.

Head to Chapter 4 for more detailed information on the money matters: what you *have* to pay for, what you *may* have to pay for, and what you *can't* pay for, as well as some creative ideas on how to raise the money you need.

Some day, our prince (or princess) will come

When the subject of time and adoption comes up, you generally hear two typical scenarios: the "we put our application in on a Friday and got the call on a Monday" scenario, and the "we've waited so long for our first child that now we're too old for number two" scenario. Although either is possible, most adoptions fall between those two extremes. Typically, you can expect to wait anywhere from six months to two years for a placement.

The hardest part, of course, is not knowing whether your adoption falls into the six-month category or the two-year category. Here are some factors that affect how long you wait:

- **How open you are in your stated preferences:** You certainly can specify that you will only consider a healthy newborn boy with dark curly hair and blue eyes and a dimple on his left cheek. Doing so, however, will automatically take you out of consideration for any child who doesn't fit that description.

- **Whether you want a healthy infant or an older child or child with special needs:** Many adoptive parents specify healthy infants. If you're one of them, you're in a popular crowd and can expect the wait to be longer. Because fewer families are open to older children or children with special medical needs, those who are usually get placements more quickly.

- **Whether you go with an attorney or an agency:** Although not a hard-and-fast rule, adoptions through attorneys generally take between six months and a year, and can be impacted by how aggressive you are in locating a birthmother if that isn't a service your attorney provides. Agency adoptions usually can take a little longer (between six months and two years), the time often depends on how many adoptive families the agency has on its waiting list and how many children the agency places every year, on average.

- **How much money you have:** More money usually means more options. And options give you a leg up in the adoption world. No, it's not fair. And no, people with money don't deserve those options any more than other people do. But the fact is, the more money you have to invest in building your family, the more quickly it usually happens.

- **Dumb luck:** Who knows why things happen the way they do? Never discount the "it was meant to be" mentality, and be prepared for anything.

Examining Adoption Issues You and Your Child (ren) Will Face

People commonly refer to the finalization hearing as the time when the adoption is over. Actually, to be technically accurate, the *process* is finished, but the adoption lasts a lifetime. Your child will always be a child born to someone else. And, as an adoptive family, you're going to face issues that people who give birth to their children don't.

Common worries

If you're just beginning to consider adoption, you may have a few concerns. Most people do. Many of these worries tend to fall into two categories: the genetic stuff (everything that has to do with the fact that you and your child don't share the same genetic background) and the birthparent stuff (everything to do with the fact that someone else out in the world has a connection to your child that you don't). Here are some of the highlights:

✔ **Fear of unknown health issues:** If you had given birth to your child, you may think that you'd know what conditions may lurk in his or her genes. When you adopt, if you don't know the family history — or if the one you get is sketchy, to say the least — how can you know that everything will be okay? The truth is, you don't (of course, you don't know with birth children either). But remember that reputable agencies make you aware of any risk factors that they know about so that you can make a decision that's right for you.

Your healthy infant may develop a lifelong condition; your child who was born addicted to cocaine may flourish without any long-lasting effects. When you adopt, you must accept the unknowns and commit to your child no matter what — just as any parent would do.

✔ **Worries about bonding:** A lot of press has been given to bonding and how important it is to a child's development. You may wonder whether, if you weren't there to bond with your child during the first days or weeks or even years of his life, can the two of you bond now? The answer is almost always yes. Once you begin to care for your child and your child responds to you and grows to rely on you for the care and love she needs, you'll bond. If you're adopting an older child, bonding may take more time (and you'll probably have to do it without the warm fuzzies that make you feel good), but it still happens.

✔ **Fears that the birthmother will change her mind and reclaim your child:** Who hasn't seen news stories detailing some horrible adoption scenario in which the birthparents and adoptive parents end up in court fighting over the child? The story is so compelling because it speaks to every parent's biggest fear: losing a child. For adoptive parents, these scenarios are particularly frightening. But keep these things in mind:

• Nearly all adoptions end successfully.

• A reputable agency counsels a birthmother on all her options (not just adoption) and then helps her make a decision that is right for her. Because the birthmother isn't pressured or coerced into making an adoption plan, chances are she'll follow through because, as difficult as it is, she made the decision for herself. Furthermore, if the agency has reason to believe that a birthmother will change her mind or that a birthfather will challenge the placement, it won't place that child in an adoptive home.

- In most states, after the birthmother signs the consent forms, she can't simply reclaim her child. She must prove that she was forced to sign, lied to, or not in her right mind.

Common questions and topics

If you adopt, the adoption issue will always be a part of your life. You're going to face it whenever your child asks you a question about her birthmother or birthfather, whenever a stranger feels compelled to speculate about why your child doesn't share your race, and whenever the anniversary of the placement day rolls around and you get teary-eyed from remembering what it felt like to behold your child for the first time.

One of your jobs as an adoptive parent is to help your child understand adoption in general and her adoption in particular in such a way that she's comfortable with her history and confident of her place in her family and in the world. Here are some ways you can accomplish this goal:

- Share your child's adoption story with her in a positive way and from the very beginning. You want her first encounter with word *adoption* to be a positive one, and you want her adoption story to be one that she enjoys hearing.

- Answer your child's questions honestly and in an age-appropriate way and don't interpret curiosity or longing for the birthmother (which is common to children who've been adopted) to be a rejection of you. You're the one she looks to make her feel safe. When your child is old enough and if she expresses an interest in finding her birthparents, help her. Who better than you to help her deal with the feelings and emotions that a birthparent search can bring to the surface?

- If you've adopted an older child, first realize that your child may not feel the same way about the adoption that you do — and may even resent you for it. That's normal. But regardless of your child's feelings, your commitment shouldn't waiver.

- Respond to other folks' inappropriate comments or questions in such a way that your child comes away from the encounter feeling okay. You'll be surprised at the stupid and thoughtless things people say — often with the best intentions — and heartbroken that these comments have the power to hurt your child. Chapter 17 has suggestions for what you can do when people say thoughtless things.

You're going to encounter a bunch of other situations and issues that are unique to adoptive families (Part IV is devoted to just such topics). These situations will challenge you, exasperate you, warm your heart, and — no kidding — sometimes make you laugh out loud. Through all of it, remember that you have a special role in your child's life, a role that is yours and yours alone: Mom or Dad.

Your Child and You

So many children are already available for adoption, and so many other children are going to be born to women who aren't prepared to parent them. What this means is that there is no shortage of adoptable children — not in the United States and not in the world. In fact, there are more children available than there are adoptive homes for them. There are babies and toddlers and preteens and teens. There are healthy children and children with medical issues. There are singles and sibling groups. There are children born in the United States and children born elsewhere. There are children of every race and every ethnicity. If you're adopting, your child is somewhere in this mix.

So the question isn't so much "Where are the children?" They're everywhere. The question is "What child do you want to parent?" Finding the answer for this question can be hard, mainly because saying that you're open to a particular type of child feels like you're rejecting all the other children.

But, hard or not, this is one question you can't dodge. At some point in the adoption process, you're going to have to actually state your preference — about age, about race, about challenges or special situations, about whatever — to another person. And you must be honest, for your sake and for your child's. Head to Chapter 8 for the details on describing the child you want to adopt.

The best thing we have ever done

Before we became involved in our adoption efforts, we used to think that adoption was something extraordinarily expensive that only rich people could afford. But that was really not the case. You don't necessarily have to go someplace like China or Russia to adopt a child. There are children right here in the United States who need families, too. Once you hold that little child in your arms for the first time, you won't care at all if it's a boy or a girl, or what color his or her skin happens to be.

We also used to think that it would be difficult raising "someone else's child," but these two boys we have adopted are not someone else's children. They are *our* children. We can honestly say, without any doubt, that we love them just as much as we love our older biological child. Adoption has definitely been the best thing we have ever done.

Jon and Jennifer Kirkman

When you're done answering the question "What kind of child do I want?" then you need to ask yourself a follow-up question: "What kind of parent does that child deserve?"

Obviously, all children deserve good parents. Forthright. Honest. Loving. Gentle. Consistent. Stable. Committed. As an adoptive parent, however, you have to add another descriptor to that list: fearless.

You may not have brought your child into the world, but you have to help him navigate his way through it: through the ignorance of people who assume that, because he doesn't look like you, he can't be yours. Through the presumption of those who think that, because she doesn't do laps in the same gene pool as your forebears, her tie to you is somehow diminished. Through the questions that rankle (Is she your own?) to the compliments that chafe (He's so lucky that you took him from that place!), you must be a fearless advocate for the integrity of your child and your family.

In a world that too often defines who belongs together by things like race or genes or culture, your family is a testament to the fact that some people aren't bound by those limitations. When all is said and done, the person this will matter the most to is your child, your very own child, the one who, some-day, will walk fearlessly through the same world on his own.

Questions to Ask Yourself

We suppose that having an entire book devoted to the topic of adoption implies that adoption is pretty difficult. Lots of stuff you need to know. Even more stuff you need to do. And all sorts of things to watch out for and be prepared to handle. The process itself *is* pretty formidable. But when it comes to deciding whether adoption is right for *you*, it's really pretty simple. Ask yourself these questions:

- ✔ **Why do I want a child?** You can come up with a lot of good answers to this question. One of the best — and the one you'll hear most often from most people — is also the simplest: I want to be a parent.

- ✔ **Am I ready to love a child who I didn't give birth to?** If you want to adopt, the *only* answer to this question is a resounding *yes!*

- ✔ **Am I ready to commit to a child "until death do us part"?** You can disown your parents. You can divorce your spouse. But your child will be your child forever. You can no more toss away a child you adopt than you can toss away a child you give birth to. If you think differently, get goldfish instead. They, unlike children, can survive quite nicely being accessories in your life.

> ✓ **Am I prepared to discuss adoption openly and honestly with my child?** All people have a right to their personal history. Your child has a right to hers. How you discuss it has a lot to do with how your child feels about herself and her place in the family. So the answer here is, Yes, I'm prepared. If you're not (or need advice on how to discuss the adoption positively), head to Chapter 16.

The preceding questions are the nutshell questions: the most important indicators of whether adoption is right for you. And if it is, you better get hoppin'. Somewhere out there, your child — born or unborn — is waiting for you.

Chapter 2

Sorting It All Out: Types of Adoptions

. . . .

In This Chapter

▶ Working with an agency or an attorney

▶ Adopting domestically or internationally

▶ Infants, older kids, and special-needs kids: Beginning to think about your child

▶ Choosing between closed, semi-open, and open adoption arrangements

. . . .

What type of adoption do you want to pursue? The answer to that question is a no-brainer: "a fast and easy one." As you'll find out when you begin the adoption process, though, there's no such thing as a simple question. Even the simple questions are just openers for more in-depth questions that require more introspective answers.

In the adoption world, the seemingly simple question "What type of adoption do you want to pursue?" is actually a four-parter. The questions that are really being asked are these:

✔ Would you feel more comfortable working through an agency or an attorney — or one of the other available options?

✔ Do you want to adopt children from the United States or children from other countries, and are you open to adopting children of another race?

✔ Are you open to children of any age or do you have a preference? Similarly, are you interested in only healthy children, or are you open to kids with special needs?

✔ How much information would you feel comfortable sharing with the birthmother — none, some, a lot? — and how long do you want this contact to last?

If you don't know how to answer these questions, don't feel bad. Most people just beginning the adoption journey don't, either. This chapter can help. It introduces and explains the different categories so that you can make informed decisions about which options best meet your needs.

Agency, Attorney, or Other: Ways to Connect to Your Child

Open the phone book, turn to the As, and search for *Adoption*. A whole slew of ads for agencies, attorneys, and hybrids of the two jump out at you. Your first thought may likely be "Holy cow! Where do I start?" soon followed by the next thought: "How do I choose?"

You begin by figuring out which avenue you want to promenade down. Would you be more comfortable with an agency adoption or would you prefer to work through an attorney? Another option — facilitator adoptions — seems to be a growing trend in the United States. Maybe that's the path you'll choose.

The following sections explain each of these options so that you know the types of things you can expect, regardless of the route. Here are two things to remember:

- ✔ **Your choice is your choice.** Most people have opinions about the right way to go about adopting a child: Some see attorney and facilitator adoptions as profit industries and dislike the idea of advertising for a baby. Others see agency adoptions as needlessly intrusive and judgmental. You decide what's right for you.

- ✔ **You have to be comfortable with what you choose.** That means you have to trust the people you're working with. They have a tremendous impact on whether, when all is said and done, you can look back fondly on the time you spent waiting for your child. Head to Chapter 7 to find out how to find reputable agencies, attorneys, and facilitators.

Different resources have different categories for types of adoption. Some define *agency adoptions* as adoptions arranged by a licensed child-placing agency, while adoptions arranged through an attorney or facilitator are called *independent adoptions*.

Agency adoptions

When you begin to look at adoption agencies more closely, you find that they fall into two different categories: state agencies and private agencies. Whether you go with one or the other depends on things like the type of child you want to adopt. If you're looking for older kids or want to parent a child with special needs, you're more likely to make a connection through your state agency. If you want a healthy infant, your chances are better if you go through a private agency. Another factor, unfortunately, may be your financial resources. Adoptions through the state are less expensive than adoptions through private agencies.

State agencies

State agencies are the agencies that your state government runs. Many of these offices are called things like the Division of Family and Children (in Indiana, for example) or the Department of Social and Health Services (in Washington state). These agencies, whatever they may be called in your state, offer many services to families in need. Finding homes for available children is just one of the services they provide.

Children available through state agencies are *wards of the state,* kids whom a state court has determined to be *children in need of services* (CHINS). Often, these children have been removed from their homes because of abuse or neglect. Sometimes, they were orphaned, or their parents are no longer able to care for them because of some catastrophic illness or event.

When you work through a state agency, you'll find that the available kids are usually older, not infants. The reason for this is that state agencies try to reunite kids with their parents before making them available for adoption. And they can only be placed in an adoptive home after the state terminates the rights of the birthparents. The termination process can take years. (For more information on how kids become available through state agencies, head to Chapter 11.)

Finding suitable adoptive homes for these kids is harder, too. Often, the children who have been taken into custody are part of a sibling group, and the state makes every effort to place the kids together. In addition, the children have usually been abused or neglected and, as a result, may have behavioral issues to deal with, as well as attachment difficulties that stem from the abuse and from possibly being moved from foster home to foster home. (For more information about some of the issues older or special-needs kids face, head to Chapters 8 and 16.)

My Forever Family

Indiana has a statewide adoption program called My Forever Family, which is administered by the Indiana Foster Care and Adoption Association in collaboration with Indiana Family Social Services Administration. The goal of the program is to get kids out of foster care and into homes. Interested adoptive parents go through special-needs adoption training and receive a monthly magazine that has information and photos of waiting children, as well as a number you can call if you're interested in a child.

Your state may offer a similar program or resources you can tap into if adopting an older child or a child with special needs is something that interests you. Contact your local Office of Family and Children to find out more.

If you're interested in adopting through your state agency, here are a couple of other things to keep in mind:

✔ The wait can be long because of the bureaucracy and because state agencies are often understaffed, and workers are overwhelmed. Don't be surprised if the process, from start to finish, takes a year, and keep in mind that some could happen faster and some much slower.

✔ In pursuing a state adoption, you generally contact the *case manager,* the person who handles a caseload of children in the system (in your state, this person's title may be something else), submit your home study, and wait. The more flexible you are as to what you will accept and the more children you express an interest in, the better your chances.

✔ You may be one of several families being considered for the same child. If so, the case manager (or sometimes a committee) will interview you and the others to determine what each family's strengths are and to see what each can offer the child. After you're selected as the final family, a meeting with the child is planned. After that first meeting, a visitation schedule is set up so that the child can be eased into your family.

✔ Most states charge little or nothing for adoption services. In fact, many states offer adoption subsidies after the adoption is finalized. These subsidies help offset the costs of raising a child who may have special needs due to abuse or neglect or having spent years in the system.

If you're interested in adopting a child through your state agency, contact your local Office of Family and Children. You can also head to the Internet: Many state agencies now offer photos of waiting children and info about them on their Web sites. National resource exchange groups also circulate info and photos of waiting kids around all the states. In the search box, type in **adoption** and the name of your state to access a list of adoption resources. An alternative that can link you directly to adoption agencies and attorneys in your state and others is the Adoption.org Web site (www.adoption.org).

Private agencies

Private agencies are typically full-service adoption agencies that the state licenses to place children for adoption. These agencies provide all the services necessary to facilitate adoption: They typically have a staff of social workers who provide supportive counseling and services to the birthparents, perform home studies, and educate and prepare adoptive families. They also have an attorney on staff or an attorney to recommend, who can handle the legal aspects of finalizing the adoption.

Birthparents (usually the birthmothers) contact these agencies on their own and ask for their services to help them understand their options and to plan an adoption that suits their needs. The birthparents rely on the agencies to properly screen the adoptive families and prepare them for adoption.

Here are some things to know about private agencies:

✔ Most usually place newborns. Some agencies prefer to place healthy infants, and other agencies may specialize in special needs. Some do both. Some agencies are medical-condition-specific, such as an agency with the sole purpose of finding homes for kids with Down syndrome.

✔ If you adopt through a private agency, expect to pay an application fee, a home study fee, a fee at placement, and legal fees. A typical range for all these fees is $7,500 to $15,000. Of course, some adoptions through private agencies cost more, and some cost less. Some private agencies may require you to pay other expenses as well, such as any medical costs not covered by insurance or Medicaid and some of the birthmother's living expenses. Head to Chapter 4 for information on fees.

✔ Private agencies have different criteria for whom they'll accept as prospective adoptive parents. Some church-affiliated agencies, for example, accept applications only from people affiliated with that religion. Other agencies may have a marriage or age requirement. Be sure to find out what criteria the agency has before you submit an application.

✔ For an adoption through a private agency, the average time from start to finish is between six months and two years. That time range can vary, though, depending largely on two things:

• **How flexible you are.** The more conditions and situations you'll consider, the more frequently the agency will offer your profile to birth moms. Waits for minority infants, for example, are usually shorter than waits for white infants.

• **The number of people the agency serves.** Obviously, if the agency has lots of birthmothers and few adoptive families, your wait will be shorter. Conversely, an agency with few birthmothers and lots of adoptive families translates into a longer wait.

✔ Private agencies can be nonprofit agencies or for-profit agencies. To qualify for nonprofit status, an agency's purpose must be not to make money, but to fulfill some religious, charitable, educational, literary, or scientific purpose. In addition, no money that the organization makes can go to enrich people. (Nonprofits have other rules; head to Chapter 4 to find out what they are.) This distinction may be important to you as you select an agency to work with.

✔ The important thing is the agency's license. All child-placing agencies must undergo annual license reviews to ensure that they're following the state adoption laws and facilitating adoption in an ethical manner. Before you select an agency, make sure it's licensed and that the license is current.

Attorney adoptions

You always need an attorney to finalize an adoption, but the attorneys we talk about here do more than just help you with finalization. Some attorneys actually act in the role of an adoption agency. That means they work for adoptive families to locate an expectant birthmother or an available child. Most attorneys work with infant adoptions; many limit the arrangement even further to include only healthy infants.

Because attorneys aren't qualified to provide home studies, you have to work with an agency for that, but the attorneys handle the rest of the adoption themselves. They may guide you to place ads for birthmothers to read and respond to, or they may connect you with a birthmother who responded to their advertising.

Here are some things to know about attorney adoptions:

✔ Although attorney adoptions can be more expensive than some private agency adoptions, you often receive a placement faster, usually within a few months, most within the year.

✔ In addition to the attorney fees (commonly between $8,000 and $15,000), you can also expect to pay for

- Birthmother expenses (how much depends on the laws in your state)

- Medical expenses relating to the pregnancy

- Any advertising and other costs you incur to locate a birthmother yourself

- Any additional services, like counseling for the birthmother prior to placement

Chapter 4 has more information on what adoptions cost and what the money goes for.

✔ Adoption laws vary by state. If you decide to pursue adoption through an attorney, be sure to get one who *specializes* in adoption, not one who dabbles in it. Chapter 7 explains how to find a reputable adoption attorney.

Facilitator adoptions

Facilitators are individuals who charge a fee to adoptive parents to locate or find a birthparent. Facilitators usually place only healthy newborns.

When you work with a facilitator, you pay an upfront fee (usually between $4,500 and $8,000, although occasionally much more) to begin the process. This fee goes toward the advertising used to find birthmothers and the facilitator's expenses and profit. After the facilitator locates a birthmother, you meet with or talk to the birth mom by phone. You also pay the birthmother's living expenses, as well as any medical expenses. If the birthmother asks for counseling, you have to pay for that, too. In addition, you're responsible for attorney fees (you still need to find an attorney to do the legal work associated with the adoption), as well as a home study fee (legitimate facilitators require that you complete a home study with a licensed agency). When all is said and done — and if the birth mom follows through with her adoption plan — you adopt the baby when it's born.

Some things to keep in mind about facilitator adoptions:

✔ The facilitator you work with may not be in your state. In fact, the facilitator could be in one state, the birthparent in another, and the adoptive family in yet another. So you don't necessarily get the chance to have face-to-face contact with the birthmother or the person who connects you to her.

✔ Because facilitators find birthmothers all over the United States, you're more likely to deal with interstate adoption issues. Basically, the adoption laws of the state where the birthmother lives are the laws you have to abide by. To protect yourself and the progress of the adoption, make sure that everything you do meets the legal requirements of the state where the birth mom lives.

✔ A facilitator doesn't have to be a social worker, nor does he or she have to have any special training or experience. Find out what the facilitator's credentials are; some may just be entrepreneurs.

✔ Currently, most states don't license adoption facilitators, and no government agency regulates or oversees how they conduct their business. If you believe that your interests can best be served by going this route, do your homework and investigate the facilitator you plan to work with. Chapter 7 tells you how.

The Internet twins – a cautionary tale

When you hear talk about the buying and selling of babies, your first reaction may be "Oh, that couldn't happen" or "Oh, that couldn't happen *here*." The truth is it happens everywhere and more often than you may think.

One well-known case involved twin girls, born to a birthmother who made an adoption plan and promised her infants to not just one set of adoptive parents but two different sets of parents — possibly three, depending on what news account you believe. Each adoptive couple paid the California-based facilitator, who conducted her business over the Internet, several thousands of dollars. The first couple, with whom the babies were initially placed, paid $6,000; a British couple, who got the babies next, paid $12,000.

When the story came to light, the birthmother had already regained custody of the girls from the first adoptive parents (she had the right to do that under the deal) and then placed them in their second adoptive home — in England — where the British courts took jurisdiction. Meanwhile, back in the States, the first adoptive family waged a court battle to have the babies returned to them; the birth mom decided that she wanted to parent the girls herself and filed a petition to have custody returned to her; and the birthfather did the same in a separate petition.

Of course, the first adoptive family believed that the girls should be returned to them, and many reasonable people who followed the story believed likewise. The second adoptive family believed that the girls should remain with them, an opinion that other reasonable people shared. Nearly everyone believed that the facilitator (and possibly the birthmother) had acted unethically and wanted to profit financially from the placement of the twins.

Then more investigations followed, and a couple other important tidbits came to light:

- The first adoptive father had been accused of molesting his child's baby sitter and, possibly, her sister.

- The home of the second adoptive family was unsuitable for children. The British courts determined that the girls shouldn't remain with the British couple and should be returned to the United States.

In other words, the adoptive families themselves hadn't been adequately screened. An unfit home and a past history of molestation are huge red flags — the kinds of things that would have stopped reputable agencies, attorneys, and facilitators from placing children with those families.

The lesson you should learn from this: Do your homework! As hard as it may be to force yourself to think objectively and dispassionately when you want a child so desperately that you actually ache, you have to, to protect yourself and your child. Examine the claims being made, think about the amount of money that changes hands, and investigate the practices against your own sense of ethical conduct.

Making a choice

Most adoptions in the United States — both domestic and international — are agency or attorney adoptions. In deciding which option is better for you, you need to think about a few things:

How involved you want to be in finding a birthmother

In agency adoptions, the agencies often offer a layer of separation between you and the birthmother, usually informing you after the birthmother selects your profile, or in some cases, after the child becomes available. True, you may not get to share in the pregnancy and you may never meet or have contact with the birthmother, but you also are less likely to attach to a child who isn't yours yet. Given that a large number of birthmothers (sometimes as many as 50 percent) who originally make an adoption plan decide to parent their children after birth, this separation can save you a lot of heartache. In attorney adoptions, you're much more involved in locating a birthmother and often have the opportunity to be more involved emotionally and financially with her, too.

The services you want

Accredited adoption agencies have professional social workers and counselors who lead you through the adoption process and help you deal with issues and situations that may come up. In agency adoptions, social workers provide the following help:

- ✔ If you do have contact with the birthmother prior to placement (and most private agency adoptions fall into this category nowadays), the social worker is present at your meetings with the birthmother and guides you on how to proceed.
- ✔ The social worker monitors the progress of the relationship you form and acts as an intermediary.

Some of the most important services that social workers provide, though, are to the birthmothers. That's fine, you may be thinking, but what does that have to do with me? *A lot.* In addition to counseling before the placement, agencies often provide counseling to birthmothers after the placement. During those first few weeks and months, while you're basking in the bleary-eyed glow of your new or expanded family, birth moms are experiencing their most intense grief. And the social workers are there to help them deal with their feelings of loss and feel at peace with their decisions. In attorney and facilitator adoptions, counseling for the birthmother is often an extra that you can choose to pay for or not. Often most of the counseling comes before the placement, not after.

Your finances and how long you're willing to wait for a child

As a rule, attorney and facilitator adoptions are more expensive than agency adoptions, but you'll probably get a placement earlier, too. On average, these adoptions are usually completed within a year. Agency adoptions, depending on the agency, can take from a few months to a few years.

Unlike adoption agencies, attorneys don't have to be licensed to work with adoptive families. Most states don't require facilitators to be licensed, either. Although an agency has to submit to an annual license review to ensure that it's ethically facilitating adoptions, attorneys and unlicensed facilitators don't.

Your personality

If you're a real go-getter and have the time and the energy and no qualms about doing the search for and selling yourself to a birthmother on your own, an attorney adoption may be a good fit for you. Agency adoptions plod along a little more slowly, but you have professionals making the connections, screening the adoptive families, working with the birthmothers, and offering the necessary counseling.

At Home or Abroad: Where the Children Come From

Some people believe that no children are available for adoption in the United States, but that's certainly not true. Many children — infants and older kids — are being placed for adoption in the States. More and more children are also being adopted from other countries. What this means is that another decision you have to make before you truly begin your adoption pursuit is to decide whether you want to adopt a child born in the United States or elsewhere. The following sections give you some things to think about regarding this issue.

In the good ol' USA: Domestic adoptions

Most adoptions within the United States each year are domestic adoptions. Many people adopt domestically simply because doing anything else never occurs to them. Nevertheless, you may prefer a domestic adoption for the following reasons:

- ✔ **The United States has many children who need loving families.** Although the number of infants available for adoption has declined because of legalized abortion and increased contraceptive use, many women who find themselves unexpectedly expecting still choose adoption over abortion. And, unfortunately, some kids always end up in the child welfare system because their families couldn't parent them.

- ✔ **A healthy infant is usually exactly that.** Because of access to health care and the resources available in the United States, most women have access to prenatal care, and after delivery, infants receive basic health tests and necessary help.

- ✔ **You're more likely to have more information about and possible contact with the birthmother.** Agency social workers meet with the birth mom and gather important information from her: her medical history, her social history, and even information regarding her hobbies and interests. They also gather information about the birthfather, which is very important for adoptive families.

- ✔ **Infants are often placed with you shortly after they're born.** When the birthmother signs adoption papers following the delivery of her child (usually at least 24 hours after the delivery), the child is available for adoption. For this reason, many adoptive parents bring their children straight home from the hospital.

Process at a glance

Once you decide to adopt within the States, you need to decide on an agency, attorney, or other method. See the section "Agency, Attorney, or Other: Ways to Connect to Your Child," earlier in this chapter, to figure out which of these options you'd be more comfortable with. All domestic adoptions follow the same basic stages:

1. **You fill out an application and undergo a home study.**

2. **You're matched with (and possibly meet) a birthmother.**

3. **After the birthmother signs the consent forms, the child is placed with you.**

   The birthmother usually signs the consent forms (in which she voluntarily terminates or relinquishes her parental rights) within days of the child's birth. To find out more about consent forms, head to Chapter 13. For information about the role the birthfather plays in all this, see Chapter 14.

4. **You finalize the adoption in court.**

For a more detailed explanation of the adoption process, hop to Chapter 3. For tips and suggestions on how to make it through each step, see the chapters in Part II.

Money issues

Typical expenses for domestic adoptions may include the following:

- ✔ The adoption fee, which you pay to the adoption agency, attorney, or facilitator

- ✔ The home study fee and legal fees for finalizing the adoption

- ✔ Birthmother expenses during the pregnancy

Understanding "special needs" in the United States

In the United States, children who have minor, correctable medical problems — like a club foot that might require surgery, for example, or a dislocated hip requiring a special sling — aren't usually considered special-needs placements. That's because many families welcome the opportunity to parent these kids. Demand for children is so high in the States, in fact, that these problems make little difference in these kids' opportunities to find homes.

Children classified as special-needs are kids with more serious problems, such as Down syndrome and spina bifida, or children whose difficult family histories have put them at risk. The label "special needs" comes into play when families waiting for a healthy infant aren't comfortable with the child's condition or situation, and special families must be sought out for the child. For more information about special-needs placements, see the section "Opening your heart to special-needs children," later in this chapter.

Some states have strict regulations on what and how much you can pay in domestic adoptions. Not only do you need to know the adoption laws in your state, but, if you're paying expenses for a birthmother in another state, you need to know the laws in that state, too, so that you can avoid doing anything illegal. Indiana law, for example, stipulates that you can't pay any expenses until the second trimester of the pregnancy, and you can't pay more than a total of $3,000 for the whole pregnancy, not counting medical costs. Reputable agencies and attorneys who know their stuff can lead you through the labyrinth of adoption laws.

It's a wonderful world: International adoptions

A growing number of American families adopt internationally every year. Some of the most popular countries for international adoptions are China, Guatemala (as well as other Central and South American countries), Russia, Kazakhstan, Korea, Vietnam, and Haiti. Many people adopt infants from these countries, but older children and special-needs children are also available.

Some families prefer international adoption for the following reasons:

 ✔ **They feel adopting internationally is easier than adopting domestically.** China, for example, prefers older couples, who may have more difficulty adopting domestically because of their age. Singles are also able to adopt more readily internationally.

✔ **They see international adoption as a humanitarian act.** A few years ago, for example, when images of Romanian orphanages hit the airwaves, and people saw and learned about what transpired during the collapse of the Romanian government, they flocked to help these children in desperate need. More recently, in response to press reports of infant girls in China being abandoned because of the cultural preference for sons, many American couples turned their attention there.

✔ **They feel that adopting internationally is a way to avoid having to deal with the birthmother.** If this is your main reason for wanting to pursue an international adoption, consider this: You're going to be dealing with the birthmother whether she's in the next county over or the next country over. Why? Because the birthmother will very likely be an important issue for your child as he or she grows and matures. For more information on birthmothers and the unavoidable role they play in your child's life, head to Chapter 13.

A few things to ponder

If you're thinking about adopting internationally, you need to consider and be comfortable with the following things:

✔ The children available in these countries are rarely newborns. If you request an infant, your child would probably be between 6 and 12 months old before you could bring him or her home.

✔ Because of the sometimes extreme poverty or the lack of resources in the child's birth country, poor nutrition, malnutrition, and untreated medical problems, such as unrepaired cleft lips and palates, are not uncommon.

✔ You usually have to travel to the country at some time during the adoption process. Sometimes you have to make two trips: once when your child is assigned to you and again to bring your child home.

A few countries let you arrange for an escort to bring your child to the United States. However, after you pay the expenses for the escort, the cost is about the same as if you traveled to the country yourself to bring your child home.

✔ In an international adoption, the birthmother is not available as an important resource for your child. As your child asks questions and exhibits curiosity about his or her birth family, you'll have very little info to share. In a domestic adoption, you may have continued contact with the birthmother, which can be an avenue you use to secure information your child feels is important.

My (Katrina's) daughter from Korea longed for information about her birth family throughout her life. She wondered what her birth mom looked like, who she herself looked like, why she was placed for adoption, if her birthmother thought about her, and if she loved her. I couldn't answer any of her questions satisfactorily. Thankfully, she was able to locate her birth family in Korea when she was 22 years old, and she finally had some answers to her questions.

✔ Although some countries, such as Guatemala, place the babies in individual homes similar to foster homes in the United States, other countries, such as China and Russia, house available children in orphanages. Depending on the region's resources and stability, the quality of these orphanages and the level of care and attention the children receive vary a great deal. Trustworthy international agencies do their best to work with reputable orphanages and to make adoptive families aware of any issues that may result from the child's time in these environments.

Children raised in orphanage settings don't receive the love and nurturing all children need. Even with dedicated orphanage staffs, the adult-child ratio is often so high that the kids don't receive the individual attention they crave.

A very brief description of the process

The process for international adoptions is more complicated than domestic adoptions because you're dealing with two governments, two cultures, a distance of usually thousands of miles, and — gird your loins — the Bureau of Citizenship and Immigration Services (BCIS), formerly known as the United States Immigration and Naturalization Service (INS), which you have to convince to let you bring your child into the country. And that means *a lot* of paperwork and, usually, quite a bit of time.

After you convince the United States that the adoption is a go, you have to convince the other country to let the child leave. And that means more paperwork and more time. In general, here's what you can expect (head to Chapter 3 for a blow-by-blow account of the steps you need to take):

1. **You hook up with an international agency and have a home study done.**

   The agency you work with may not be in your state. If that's the case, you have to find a local agency to do your home study.

2. **You prepare a dossier.**

   The dossier is the packet of information you need to adopt the child. It includes things like the BCIS documents, as well as notarized copies of other important documents (like your birth certificates, marriage license, health reports, and so on).

3. **You're matched with a child.**

4. **After a period of time, during which the birth country issues a visa to the child, enabling him or her to leave, the adoption is finalized.**

5. **Your child comes home.**

6. **You re-adopt the child in the United States.**

Adopting internationally sounds intimidating, but many people do it and have wonderful stories to tell about how their child came to them. Just make sure that you hook up with a reputable agency, which can help you through the steps and all the forms that you'll be filling out, and buy lots of pens. You'll need them.

More money issues

When you adopt internationally, you generally have the same expenses as you would in a domestic adoption, in addition to travel expenses, translation costs, and possible orphanage "donations," which are not optional. Go to Chapter 4 for a complete rundown of what you have to pay for.

Infants, Older Children, and Special-Needs Kids: The Children You Adopt

Although many adoptive families seek healthy infants, healthy infants aren't the only kids in America who are being adopted. Many folks open their hearts and their homes to kids who are older, and children and infants who have — or may have — special medical or behavioral problems.

When you begin the adoption process, you're going to be asked about the type of child you think you can — and want to — parent. The following sections give you some food for thought about your options.

Oh, baby, baby! Adopting newborns and toddlers

Many families prefer to adopt infants and toddlers for these reasons:

- ✔ They feel that bonding will be easier with a younger child.
- ✔ They believe that a younger child will be unscathed from negative experiences.
- ✔ Families who haven't parented before are hoping to have the full experience from the very beginning.

For these reasons, infants are the most sought-after children in adoption. As a result, the demand for babies — and the competition for them — is higher.

If you're willing to wait whatever time is necessary and to pay the necessary expenses, you should be able to adopt an infant in the United States or an infant or toddler internationally.

Toddlers are rarely available in the United States because birthmothers are more likely to make an adoption plan for a child they've never parented. If the baby goes home with the birthmother, making a decision to place that child for adoption is that much harder. Even if birth moms do decide that placing their toddler for adoption is best, other family members often step in to prevent the placement of the child.

Beyond babyhood: Adopting older children

Children are usually considered "older" when they reach school age. (Before that age, finding adoptive homes for them is still fairly easy.) In the United States, older children are usually available only through state agencies; the reason is that they've been removed from their homes because of neglect or abuse. (See the earlier section "State agencies" for more information about the children available for adoption through your state's Division of Family and Children.)

Many older children are readily available, but before you pursue adopting an older child, be sure that you know what you're getting into. These children require mature and committed families who are willing to learn and prepared to go the long haul. After all, you don't want to be just one more in a (possibly) long line of people who've failed them. Following are a few of the things you need to think about (Chapter 16 has more information about some of the special issues that families who adopt older children face):

- ✔ Older children in the United States may have serious behavior problems — or not. Some typical behaviors include lying, stealing, temper outbursts, sexual acting out, and so on, depending on the type of abuse they suffered. They may also have attachment disorders (see Chapter 18 for information about that condition). They often require long-term counseling.

- ✔ In the United States, most state agencies require that you attend special-needs adoption training before you can adopt these kids. The training covers the behaviors you may encounter and appropriate methods of discipline.

- ✔ Older children overseas are also at high risk for behavioral problems. (Many may have been raised in orphanages or brought to an orphanage at an older age due to family circumstances, such as the death of a parent.) The issues these kids face and the behavior problems they exhibit are similar to those of the U.S. kids, but you must also factor in the language barrier.

✔ Unfortunately, families who adopt older children experience a greater rate of adoption disruptions. A *disrupted adoption* is one in which the adoption falls apart and the child is, again, removed from the home. To find out what you can do to prevent this from happening to you and your family, head to Chapter 18.

✔ Another factor to consider in older children adoption is the sibling connection. Many of these children have siblings, and the sibling bond is a strong one. For this reason, most adoption professionals believe that keeping the children together is important. The ongoing connection with a sibling may also ease the child's adjustment to the adoptive family.

Older children can bring great rewards to adoptive families, but years may pass before those rewards are evident. That's why, if you're interested in adopting an older child, you should be motivated by your desire to help a child rather than by your need for a loving/reciprocal relationship.

These children are in desperate need of loving families but do a thorough self-evaluation before making the decision to adopt these kids. If you're willing to make a commitment to an older child, contact your local Office of Family and Children and ask how to proceed in your county.

Opening your heart to special-needs children

Although older children may be considered special needs because of the issues they may face, this section focuses on medical-needs children and at-risk children.

✔ **Medical-needs kids:** These children are born with heart-wrenching conditions such as spina bifida, Down syndrome, blindness, and so on. With many of these conditions, the prognosis is available when the diagnosis is made. The advantage for these families is they know upfront about what to expect and can make an informed decision and prepare in advance.

✔ **At-risk kids:** These children have been exposed to drugs (such as alcohol, cocaine, and heroin) before they were born, which could cause damage to the developing baby. An infant exposed prenatally to alcohol, for example, is at risk for fetal alcohol syndrome. Although in many cases, the child develops normally with no signs of the condition, a family needs to understand the risk and be willing to commit to the child without knowing what the future holds. Other at-risk situations include infants born to parents with mental illnesses or children conceived through rape or incest.

Sometimes the birthmother was considering adoption before her child's condition was known. Other times, she considers adoption because she has learned of her child's condition. Either way, agencies are available to help her make an appropriate placement for her child. (As a rule, attorneys and facilitators, who work in adoptions of healthy infants, don't usually get involved and may refer her to an agency that will.)

Agencies that place special-needs babies for adoption are always looking for interested families. And thankfully, many families want to adopt special-needs kids. You may be one of them. If you are, keep some things in mind:

✔ When you apply at agencies, you'll be asked if you would consider special-needs children. Before you answer, educate yourselves: Talk to doctors and developmental therapists, visit Web sites, hook up with other parents who have children in these situations, and read everything you can get your hands on.

   When you talk with a physician, make sure that the doctor you question has had experience with the situation you're describing. Although no doctor can tell you for sure what will happen and how things will progress with your child, doctors who've dealt with a specific condition have a better understanding of what you may be facing.

✔ Adopting special-needs children can bring you all sorts of rewards, not the least of which is the opportunity to love a very special child. One thing that families of these children have in common is the ability to rejoice at small victories and focus on their child's progress rather than the delays.

✔ Support groups are available for families dealing with many different conditions. These groups offer support, friendship, comfort, and education for families.

✔ In the United States, many services are available to families of special-needs children. The kids may qualify for an adoption subsidy, Social Security Disability Insurance, or ongoing Medicaid. To find out whether the child you're considering is eligible for these kinds of services, talk to your social worker or contact your local Office of Family and Children.

Closed, Semi-Open, and Open: The Adoption Arrangement

How much, if any, contact you have with the birthmother before and after placement determines how open your adoption arrangement is. Some families prefer to have little or no contact; other families practically adopt the birthmother, too. Many families find a happy middle ground. The following sections describe these different arrangements.

Every adoption agency or attorney has its own definition of the terms *open, semi-open,* and *closed adoption.* Be sure that you understand your agency's definition before you state which type of adoption arrangement you prefer.

Closed adoptions: A preference of the past

A closed adoption is an adoption in which the birthparents prefer not to select a family or have contact with them. No identifying information is exchanged, and the agency chooses the family for the birthparents. After the child is placed in the adoptive home, the family doesn't correspond or have any contact with the birthparents. Years ago, closed adoptions were the norm. Today, very few birthmothers choose this type of adoption.

Semi-open adoptions: Contact with confidentiality

In a semi-open adoption, the birthmother (and sometimes the birthfather) selects the adoptive family after reading the profiles of available families. After selecting an adoptive family, the birthmother may decide that she wants to meet the family in person. Additional meetings may take place as well, and adoptive parents may participate in things like doctor visits and the labor and delivery. In semi-open adoptions, however, identifying information (last names, addresses, and phone numbers, for example) isn't exchanged, and no face-to-face meetings are scheduled following placement. The adoptive parents and the birthmother can correspond through the agency, if they choose, exchanging letters, photos, and gifts.

Open adoptions: Everybody knows everybody

Open adoptions usually proceed similarly to the semi-open adoptions (see the preceding section), but at some point, the two parties do exchange identifying information. Following the placement, the adoptive family and the birthmother have direct contact with one another, without the agency acting as the intermediary.

An open adoption usually includes regular meetings between the adoptive family and the birthmother. What constitutes "regular meetings" depends on what the adoptive parents and birthparent agree on. For some families, it means one or two meetings a year in places like the zoo or a park. For other families, it may mean that the birth mom is a regular visitor in the family's home and participates in holiday gatherings and birthday celebrations.

Note: Many agencies do only fully open adoptions, believing that they're healthier for the child, as well as for the birthmother and the adoptive family. If you're working with such an agency, be sure that you're comfortable with this arrangement.

An open adoption story

When I first heard the term "open adoption," I was working at a crisis pregnancy center. I thought the idea sounded like a good one, but at the time, my husband and I hadn't even thought about adoption. I would soon learn that an open adoption would become a very big part of our lives.

The agency we chose did semi-open adoptions. If our birth mom wanted to meet us, and ours did, then we would meet with her, and we all would decide how much information we wanted to share. Our first meeting went very well. We took pictures of our home and extended families to share with the birth mom, and she did the same. Our birth mom was very open and honest about her situation. She just wanted to be sure she was making the right decision. By the end of the meeting, we had agreed to send her pictures often, with possible meetings in the future.

When the agency called to tell us our birth mom was expecting again and wanted us to have this child as well, we didn't hesitate to tell them yes. This adoption was going to be very open. We exchanged telephone numbers with our birth

mom, and I planned to go to doctor visits with her, as well as be there for the birth. She and I talked on the phone often, and I was able to go to one doctor visit with her to see an ultrasound to find out we were having a boy. My husband and I didn't make it to the hospital for the birth, but neither did the birth mom! She had the baby, who decided to come seven weeks early, on her couch while the ambulance was on its way!

We talk on the phone with the birthmother at least once a month, and we send tons of pictures. We hope that sometime in the future we can all get together for maybe a day at the zoo.

My husband and I have been blessed with two beautiful little boys. We are thankful to be able to know our sons' birth mom and learn more about her each time we talk so that we can share these things with our boys one day.

Many people are afraid of open adoptions because they think it may be too risky, but there is risk involved with every adoption. Things don't always go as planned. For us, open adoption has been a wonderful experience.

Jon and Jennifer Kirkman

Chapter 3

The Adoption Process from Beginning to End

*Y*ou want to start a family or add to your family. Where do you begin? You can begin with candlelight, wine, and romantic music, if you like. Many people do. Then you get down to business — and, in adoption, *business* ain't a euphemism for sex. It really is business: You have to find an agency or attorney to work with, you have to fill out all sorts of paperwork, and then you have to make all sorts of decisions and take all sorts of steps under the scrutinizing eye of all sorts of professionals. All the while, you keep your fingers crossed and hold your breath until a judge bangs the gavel and says the legal equivalent to "Remember, folks, you asked for this."

Getting to that moment can be intimidating. When you're at the beginning, looking down the tunnel, what you see are a million things that have to be done before you can even get a glimmer of the light. Although a lot does have to happen, the process is pretty predictable. Knowing what to expect may not make the time go any faster, but it can make the time pass more easily. Because the process is slightly different for domestic and international adoptions, this chapter explains both.

Adoption has a great beginning: when you make the monumental decision to share your love and life with a child. And it has a wonderful end: your family. The stuff in between — the stuff covered in this chapter — is the process. Don't get hung up in it. Take it a step at a time, and keep in mind what you have to look forward to.

Born in the USA: Adopting in America

Most adoptions in the United States each year are domestic adoptions. That means that the children are born and placed in the United States. Whether you go through an agency, an attorney, or a facilitator, the steps you follow in a domestic adoption are pretty much the same.

If you're looking at an interstate adoption (in which the child you want to adopt is in another state), head to the later section "Dealing with out-of-state adoptions" for important information you need to know about that option.

Finding an agency or a lawyer

Families trying to decide whether to pursue an adoption through an agency or a lawyer are usually interested in three things: *How much* will it cost? *How long* will it take? And *what* do I have to do? All these questions are important, but you need to consider other things as well.

The first step in finding an agency or lawyer is to decide whether you want to pursue domestic or international adoption (see Chapter 2 if you need help with that one). Once you make that decision, then you're ready to make calls to local agencies and attorneys who provide the type of adoption you select, and ask for information packets. You can usually rule some out right away when you read the listed requirements (length of marriage, number of children in the home, age, religion, and so on).

After you've narrowed the number of agencies down to the few you're interested in, you need to take a closer look. You should be looking for specific things (head to Chapter 7 for more info on finding a reputable agency or attorney):

- Is the agency nonprofit or for profit and how do you feel about that?

- How much experience has the agency or attorney had? If the agency was recently established, you may want to move on to one with time-proven success. If the attorney specializes in real estate law, you may want to find one who focuses on adoption.

- What services are offered? Do the services include counseling for the birthmother? Do the services — to both the adoptive family and the birthmother — end when the adoption is finalized, or do they continue through the ups and downs of the years to come?

- Does the agency offer different levels of openness? Specifically, does it offer the level of openness that you're comfortable with?

✔ Does the agency expect you to pay birthmother expenses? Does it expect you to locate your own birthmother?

✔ Do you believe that this agency/attorney practices adoption ethically? When looking at an agency, ask for proof that the agency license is current (the license means that the agency meets or exceeds the state requirements). When looking for an attorney, check with the local Better Business Bureau and the local bar association to see whether complaints have been filed.

Most agencies and some attorneys offer public information meetings about adoption. These meetings are an excellent, pressure-free way to get many of your questions answered, and they often include an adoptive family describing its experience with that agency.

Head to Chapter 7 for information on how to locate a reputable agency or attorney.

Filling out the application, if necessary

Filling out the application and submitting it (along with any necessary application fee — or retainer, if you're going with an attorney) is what really gets the ball rolling in an adoption.

Application and retainer fees vary by agency and attorney. You can expect application fees to range between $100 and $600 and retainer fees to range from $500 to $1,000, on average. Although the fee or retainer is usually non-refundable, many agencies and attorneys deduct the amount from the adoption fee.

Don't stress out over the application. It's just a series of questions that you already know the answers to:

✔ **Identifying information:** In addition to things like your name, address, and phone number, you usually have to provide your Social Security number and birth date, as well.

✔ **Brief summary of personal information:** Here, you identify things like your race, your religion, and your level of education. If you have other children in your home, you list their names and ages, too. You also generally have to provide basic information about your parents and siblings.

✔ **Employment status:** Here, you indicate your occupation, the name of your current employer, and your annual income.

✓ **Information about your home:** In addition to directions to your home (which the social worker will need for the home study; see the following section), you also indicate whether you're buying or renting. (Don't panic: You don't have to own your home to adopt.)

✓ **The type of child you're interested in:** Here you identify the race (Caucasian or minority) and age (infant or older child) of the child you want to adopt. You also indicate whether you'd consider a child with special medical needs.

✓ **References:** You'll be asked to provide names, addresses, and phone numbers of about four personal references. Your employer may have to give a reference for you as well.

As soon as you send in your completed application, you're telling the agency that you've definitely decided to use its services, which gets it moving. The first thing the agency does is to start checking your criminal history and contacting your references. You'll also be assigned a social worker — one of the most important people in your life for the next few months (or years).

Doing the home study

The home study is the intensive period of investigation and preparation that comes after you turn in your application. During this period, you'll have a series of interviews with your social worker, both as a couple (if you're married or have a partner) and individually. During these interviews, expect to focus on the following topics (remember that the required information varies for different agencies and attorneys):

✓ Your childhood

✓ The way you were disciplined as a child and your views on discipline

✓ Your dreams for your child

✓ Your religious beliefs and how you practice them

✓ Your spouse and your marriage (positives and negatives)

✓ Your hobbies and interests and how you spend your time

✓ Your educational background

✓ Your views on adoption as a way of forming a family

✓ Your views on birthparents

✓ The type of adoption and the amount of openness you're comfortable with

✓ The type of child you're hoping for

- ✔ Any criminal history, any marital separations, or previous divorces
- ✔ Your family's attitudes toward your adoption plans

You'll also fill out enough paperwork to give yourself writer's cramp. This paperwork includes

- ✔ Questionnaires regarding your individual views on parenting and discipline
- ✔ Your individual autobiographies (one for you and one for your spouse or partner, for example)
- ✔ Health forms completed by your family physician
- ✔ Financial forms stating your annual income, your debts, and the amount of your savings, as well as other information

The last part of the home study is the visit to your home. During this visit, the social worker walks through and verifies the number of rooms in your house. Of course, if you're like most people, you'll probably spend the days leading up to the visit cleaning like a maniac, but the worker isn't doing a white glove test — and he certainly won't notice how clean the grout behind the toilet is. He simply wants to determine that you can provide a safe and adequate home for your child (and no, the child doesn't have to have his or her own room).

After the interviews, when all the paperwork is completed, and if everything looks okay, the social worker types up and signs the home study report, and you're approved for a child. The fee for a home study, which varies by agency but is usually between $700 and $2,500, is generally due when the home study is done.

Writing a profile

A *profile* is the packet of information you prepare to introduce yourself to the birthmothers considering you. Often, the profile includes a letter to the birthmother and photos of you and your family, your pets, your home, and so on. The letter and photos are placed in a notebook that the social worker gives to a birth mom to read.

If you don't know where to begin or how to put your profile together, a lot of help is available. First, many agencies usually give written guidelines and show you some examples of profiles other families have put together. And Chapter 9 has plenty of information to get you started. You can also find helpful hints and suggestions about writing the birthmother letter and creating a profile on the Internet. Just type in **adoption profiles** (or something similar) to begin your search.

If you're like a lot of families, you may worry that you'll never be selected from a profile — that if you aren't a doctor married to a lawyer and if you don't live in a mansion, you'll never measure up. The truth is, birthmothers choose families for different reasons. Some are looking for the "perfect" couple; others may be suspicious of the perfect couple. Some want a family similar to the one they grew up in, and others want something different. One birthmother may love the idea of a family living in the country, and another may feel that country life sounds boring. I (Katrina) once had a birthmother choose a family because its dog had the same name as her childhood pet. There's a match for everyone.

Making contact with a birthmother

When you work with an agency, a social worker arranges your initial contact with the birthmother — assuming, of course, that she wants to meet you (occasionally, she may not want any contact).

The first meeting, which includes you, the social worker (who acts as a mediator), and the birth mom, may take place at the agency or in a restaurant or other neutral location. This is your opportunity and the birth mom's opportunity to ask and answer questions. The birthmother, for example, may ask why you want to adopt or how you'd raise her child. You might ask about the birthfather, her pregnancy, her due date, and whether she knows the baby's gender. Often, during this meeting, you'll discuss how much contact you both want in the future. Will you be attending any doctor visits? Will you be at the hospital when she delivers? Does she want letters, pictures, and/or videos following placement?

Meeting the birthmother is usually a frightening thought for the family, but the birthmother is almost always equally nervous to meet them. A funny thing happens, though: Despite their initial nervousness, after the visit, families are almost always very happy they met the birthmother. They feel more compassion for her and see her as a real person doing a courageous thing. Similarly, the birthmother is usually more comfortable with her adoption plan after meeting the family. She has a clearer picture of the life her child would live in that home, and she is less fearful that her child will be hurt or abused (a common fear of birthmothers).

With an attorney adoption, you're often responsible for initiating your own contact with the birthmother. You can meet with her alone or just talk with her by phone. Occasionally, you may not have any contact with her; in this case, all arrangements are made through the attorney.

Surviving the waiting period

The waiting period is the hardest time for families. During the paperwork/home study stage, you're so busy that you don't have time to stew. But when you're waiting for your child to arrive, you have plenty of time on your hands.

If you have a more open adoption arrangement, you can remain in contact with the birthmother and keep tabs on her doctor visits, ultrasounds, and so on. If you aren't in touch with the birthmother, you can call your agency for updates. (Just make sure that you aren't driving the agency staff crazy with multiple calls. Early in the pregnancy, monthly calls are appropriate; toward the end of the pregnancy, weekly calls are acceptable.)

You can put this waiting time to good use. Decorate the nursery, read parenting books, and attend classes on child care. Many hospitals offer classes on newborns, and some even have classes specifically for new adoptive parents. Join a support group of other adoptive families (you don't have to wait until you have the child to join). Pick out the perfect birth announcement; many announcements are available for adoptive parents. Most importantly, sleep! It won't be long before that's no longer an option. Chapter 10 has more information on how to spend your time waiting.

Making it through the placement period

The placement period is a whirlwind of activity. Your baby is here. You're getting adjusted to each other and trying to develop a schedule that works for everyone. Your mother won't leave. You're tired of the endless stream of baby showers and have enough baby monitors to set up surveillance around your whole neighborhood. You're sleep deprived and ecstatically happy. You're parents! But you also may have some fears and issues because, although you have your child, the adoption isn't finalized yet. In fact, it won't be finalized until after the placement period, which can last anywhere from a couple of weeks to a few (usually around three) months. How long your placement period is depends on a few things:

- The laws in your state.

- Whether you're working with an agency (many agencies require a three-month supervision period before the adoption is final) or attorney (many attorneys don't require a supervision period prior to finalization).

- The judge who issues the adoption decree. Some judges are sticklers that a certain amount of time pass between placement and finalization; others aren't.

The fear factor

The placement period can be an emotional roller coaster. In addition to the usual fears of having a new child — like how to get those spindly little Gumby arms and legs into the jumpsuit without dislocating something — you also may be dealing with other issues related specifically to the adoption. Following are three of the biggest fears adoptive parents have:

✔ **That a legal-risk adoption will fall through:** If your adoption is a legal-risk adoption (which usually means that the birthfather hasn't consented to the adoption), you may be on pins and needles worrying something may go wrong. Although birthfathers do have rights and can challenge an adoption plan they don't agree to, most legal-risk adoptions end successfully. Skip to Chapter 14 to find out what role birthfathers can play in an adoption and what their legal rights are.

✔ **That the birthmother will change her mind:** Just about any adoptive parent you talk to has had this fear. For those who live in states where birthmothers can change their minds after they sign the adoption consent form, the fear is especially sharp. (If you've developed a good relationship with the birthmother, this possibility may not be as frightening.)

✔ **That you won't bond with the child:** Sometimes you'll bond immediately and intensely with your child. Other times, it may take a little time. If you're in the "this is taking a little time" group, you may worry that you'll never bond with your child or that you aren't feeling as connected as you should be. Don't worry. The bonding experience is different for every parent and every child, regardless of whether the child was born or adopted into the family. Parents who have given birth to their children don't always bond immediately with them, either.

Unfortunately, no one can make these fears go away. They're legitimate concerns, and nobody can pooh-pooh them into oblivion. You just have to live with them until the placement period is over, and your adoption is finalized. If it helps, talk to someone close to you or go to an adoption support group. You can also find more information on common concerns of adoptive parents in Chapter 6.

And remember, even though it feels like it lasts forever, the placement period does actually come to an end.

So if you're working with an agency, you still have that darn social worker hanging around. She'll make a couple of visits to check on the baby and your adjustment. She'll ask you all sorts of questions about how you're bonding with the baby, how your family members have accepted your new child, how you're handling your new responsibilities, and so on. Remember, the social worker isn't expecting to find anything wrong; she's just assuring the agency of the child's safety and well-being.

Following this period of supervision, the worker submits a report recommending that you be allowed to finalize the adoption in court.

Finalizing in court

Shortly after your child is placed with you (placement is explained in the preceding section), your attorney files a Petition to Adopt in court. This petition basically states that you want to adopt the child and what you want the child's name to be. The court hearing, which occurs after the placement period is over, is scheduled.

You, your attorney, and maybe someone from the agency will attend the court hearing to finalize your child's adoption. (You can also invite other people with whom you want to share the day.)

During the hearing, you'll be sworn in and have to provide information such as the following (if you're married, your spouse has to testify, too):

- ✔ Your name and address
- ✔ The child's birth date and placement date
- ✔ The date of your marriage
- ✔ Whether you realize that this child will have all the rights of any child born to you and will inherit equally from you
- ✔ Answers to questions that the judge decides to ask (this doesn't happen very often, and the attorney will let you know if you should expect additional questions)

If you make it this far — and nearly all adoptions do — finalization is practically assured. The reason is that your agency or lawyer should make you aware of any problems significant enough to prevent the finalization from occurring.

After the judge hears the testimony, he or she signs the papers granting the adoption and (usually) graciously agrees to be the center figure in a family photo with two ecstatic parents, one oblivious baby, and anybody else you want to drag behind the bench to say "Cheese!" When all is said and done, you'll get an adoption decree proving that you've adopted the child.

For a blow-by-blow account of what you can expect at the finalization hearing, head to Chapter 12.

The Wide World of International Adoption

Every year, a growing number of Americans pursue international adoptions. Although the process for international adoption has many similarities to domestic adoptions (you still need to find an agency or attorney, fill out an application, go through a home study, and so on), international adoptions have a few extra steps that you need to be aware of.

The application and home study

For the most part, the application and home study process is the same for international adoptions as it is for domestic adoptions (see the earlier section "Doing the home study"). You will find a few differences, however. One of the main differences is that the international agency may not be the agency that does your home study. The home study has to be done locally (that is, by an agency within your state). If your international agency is in another state, you'll have to work with a local agency to complete the paperwork. Here are some other differences you can expect:

- The application fee and home study fee may be slightly higher to accommodate the extra work required of the agency.

- During the interview process, your social worker will spend time discussing the issues involved with adopting a child from another country and will also offer suggestions for how you can incorporate your child's culture into your family life.

- If the child you're adopting isn't the same race you are, the social worker will discuss all the aspects of a transracial adoption. You also may have to answer additional questions that address the issues that interracial families face. Head to Chapter 16 for information on these issues.

- Some countries have specific information they want covered in the interviews that may not be covered in a domestic home study. You may be asked, for example, to formally identify who would raise your child in the event of your death.

- Additional interviews may be necessary. Although most domestic home studies usually require three interviews (one with the couple together and then one with each spouse individually), you'll find that some countries require more. China, for example, requires four or five.

- Your home study report may need to be translated. The agency personnel usually makes these arrangements. (Although a local agency — and not the international agency you're working with — usually conducts the home study, the international agency arranges for the translation of the documents.)

Dossier preparation

The *dossier* is the set of documents you have to compile to adopt a child internationally.

Preparing the dossier can be overwhelming. When you first see the list of things you have to provide, you may think that you're facing a nearly impossible task. You aren't. Once you accept the challenge and dive in, checking the items off the list is pretty darn satisfying. You can begin to compile the documents for your dossier immediately. The dossier includes things like the following:

- ✔ **Birth certificates:** You need three certified copies of your birth certificate from your state Board of Health. (You need three copies for each person adopting.)

- ✔ **Marriage certificate (if you're married):** You need three certified copies of your marriage certificate from your Bureau of Vital Records. To find out where to write for vital records in your state, head to the National Center for Health Statistics Web site at www.cdc.gov/nchs/howto/w2w/w2welcom.htm.

- ✔ **Any divorce decrees:** If you've been divorced, you need to provide three notarized copies of any divorce decrees from your Bureau of Vital Records.

- ✔ **An assortment of financial statements:** Often, you need to provide a one-page, typed description of the family assets, bank balances, and so on, in addition to three notarized copies of the same information. Your agency has guidelines.

- ✔ **Employment information:** This information includes letters from your employer, on company letterhead, stating your position, how long you've worked there, and your salary. You need three notarized copies of this letter.

- ✔ **Medical information:** After you have a basic physical, your doctor has to write a letter, using his practice's letterhead, saying that you're in good health. In addition to this, your doctor may need to fill out a specific health form, which you'll provide three notarized copies of.

- ✔ **Fingerprint clearance and approval from the U.S. Bureau of Citizenship and Immigration Services (BCIS):** See the following section, "Visa approval: Step 1," for information on getting this clearance.

- ✔ **Your home study report:** Again, you need three notarized copies of the completed home study report, typed by your social worker and provided by the agency.

Each agency and country may have slightly different requirements. Some countries, for example, require the additional step of having documents authenticated by having the state seal added to them. Your agency can give you a complete and detailed list of what you need to provide.

Once you have your documents together, your international agency sees to any necessary translations and mails them where they need to go.

Visa approval: Step 1

Every child entering the United States needs to have a visa approval. To get this approval, you begin the process by submitting the I-600A form, the "Application for Advance Processing of Orphan Petition." Essentially, with this petition, you're asking the BCIS to okay you as an adoptive parent of a child born in another country. The BCIS makes this decision based primarily on your home study and on FBI fingerprint clearance. If it decides that you'd make a suitable parent, it sends you the I-171H, the "Notice of Favorable Determination." You want the I-171H because it allows you to proceed with your adoption plans.

To get a copy of the I-600A, contact a local office of the U.S. Bureau of Citizenship and Immigration or download the form from the BCIS Web site, www.immigration.gov.

You file the I-600A with the BCIS before a specific child is assigned to you. You send a fee of $460 with the application plus a $50 fingerprinting fee for each person adopting (meaning $100 for a couple). (*Note:* The BCIS won't accept a personal check and will send your whole packet back to you. Send a money order or cashier's check.) When the BCIS receives the application, it'll contact you with specific instructions regarding the appointment time and location for the fingerprinting. Your fingerprints go to the FBI for clearance.

The time period between filing the I-600A (the application for the visa approval) and receiving the I-171H (the approval itself) can be long and tedious. To speed things along, send your completed I-600A application before your home study is finished. Just include a letter stating you'll provide the home study as soon as it's done. By beginning the process even before your home study is complete, the adoption isn't delayed.

Once the BCIS has the I-600A form, the fingerprint clearance from the FBI, and a copy of your completed home study, it can make a determination about granting the visa approval.

The I-600A form is just the beginning of getting your child a visa. Head to the section "More BCIS stuff: Visa approval, Step 2" to find out what you need to do after you adopt your child.

Assignment of a child

When the international agency receives all your necessary paperwork (the visa approval, the completed home study, and all the documents in the dossier), it begins looking for your child. Your name may be added to a list of waiting families. If that's the case (and it usually is), the agency has to work its way down the list to your name before it can seek your child.

In its search, the agency will meet your requirements for age, gender, and medical conditions. When it identifies a child as an appropriate referral for you, the agency sends a packet of information about that child along with photos and/or a video. The packet of information includes the child's name, information about the child's birth family, and the child's medical condition and developmental abilities.

When you receive this packet, you'll be given a specific length of time to make a decision to accept this referral or wait for another.

Although most families accept their first referral, agencies expect that some families won't. If you decide to pass on one referral and wait for another, the agency won't consider it a negative strike against you. However, if you continue to reject child after child who fits your criteria, your motives will be questioned.

Here's the great thing about the assignment process: Once you receive your referral and agree to accept it, you've just become a parent! You have a child! The not-so-great thing is knowing that your child is being cared for by strangers and not knowing under what conditions. So although having a child assigned to you is when the excitement really begins, it's also when the worry starts.

This is also the time when your friends and family may begin to avoid you because you're driving them crazy. Try to remember that your friends and family have lives outside of your adoption experience and don't be too disappointed when those close to you get a little tired of hearing about what color you've painted the nursery.

The waiting period

For international adoptions, the waiting period refers to the time between the assignment of a child and the time when the child comes home. Following are some of the many things you can do while you wait for the magic phone call that alerts you it's time to travel to pick up your child:

✔ Join a support group that includes families adopting from the country you have selected. If a support group isn't available, ask your agency to connect you with other families that have traveled to that country for their adoption.

✔ Read all the literature available because you may not have time available later.

✔ Make sure that your passport is in order and get all your necessary travel immunizations out of the way.

If you have questions about getting a passport, turn to the Web:

- To download a passport application off the Web, go to `http:// travel.state.gov/download_applications.html`.
- For instructions on how to apply for a passport, go to `http:// travel.state.gov/passport_obtain.html`.
- To apply for a passport in person, you may need to go no farther than your local U.S. Post Office; many accept passport applications. To find an office near you that offers this service, go to `http://iafdb.travel.state.gov`.

✔ Shop for the items you need to take with you.

✔ Make advance arrangements for mail collecting, plant watering, pet care, and so on so that when you get the call, you can just put your travel plan in motion.

✔ Prepare your child's room.

✔ Select a pediatrician and tell her of your adoption plans. She'll usually arrange to see your child within days of your arrival home.

And try not to worry. You do have a child out there, even though your child isn't with you. It's a difficult time, but your wait will soon be over.

Traveling (if necessary) to the birth country

Most countries require at least one of the adoptive parents to travel to collect their child. Of course, this travel adds to the expense of the adoption, but many families look at the trip as a sort of extra special vacation. It may not be a luxury cruise, but traveling to your child's country has many benefits:

✔ Experiencing your child's country and culture firsthand makes sharing the information later that much easier.

✔ Seeing the conditions your child lived in can make you better prepared to meet his or her needs.

✔ Meeting your child's caregivers may give you an opportunity to gather additional information regarding the child's history, daily routine, diet, and so on.

✔ You may have the opportunity to meet the child's birthparent and, as a result, have an accurate description or photos to offer your child later on.

Most agencies make the travel as stress free as possible. They usually arrange for all the transportation and a translator, and in most cases, you travel with other adoptive families. Someone will meet you and the other families at the airport, and you'll travel as a group to meet your children. An agency representative will guide you through the necessary legal quagmire and the court process for finalizing the adoption. You'll also probably have free time for sightseeing.

Finalization in the birth country

Most countries allow you to adopt your child before you leave the country. If you're a married couple, the country may not require that you both be present for the finalization. Some countries may not require your presence at all, and you can adopt the child by proxy. Other countries grant you only legal guardianship so that you can take the child from her birth country. In these cases, you actually adopt your child after you get back in the United States.

To grant the adoption (or legal guardianship), foreign courts usually require proof of the child's identity and his orphan status, proof that your family is an appropriate one (this is where the home study comes in), and evidence that your own government (the U.S. government, in this case) has cleared you for adoption.

Each country's laws and requirements can vary greatly. The actual process — things like the number of times you appear in court, whether the birthmother is required to appear in the court, and so on — is different in each country as well. Again, your agency will prepare you and guide you through the process so that you know what to expect.

More BCIS stuff: Visa approval, Step 2

After the adoption has been finalized or after you've been granted legal guardianship, you have to make another trip to the BCIS. This time, you head over to the U.S. embassy or consulate in your child's birth country and submit Form I-600, the "Petition to Classify Orphan as an Immediate Relative." With this form, the BCIS determines whether your child meets its definition of an orphan. If so, then the BCIS grants your child a visa (what kind of visa depends on the adoption situation), and you're free to bring your child home.

You'll get one of the following visas:

✔ **IR-2 Immigrant Visa:** The BCIS issues this visa if you adopted a child overseas and have had full legal and physical custody of her, in the birth country, for at least two years. This is the visa you get if, for example, you've lived in the other country for a significant period of time and, during your time there, adopted a child from that country.

✔ **IR-3 Immigrant Visa:** You get this visa if

- You've seen your child before or during the adoption process.

- You finalize the adoption in his birth country.

- Your child meets the U.S. definition of an orphan.

✔ **IR-4 Immigrant Visa:** You get this visa when, for whatever reason, you've only been granted legal guardianship of your child and must re-adopt her in the United States.

Re-adoption at home

Most agencies and attorneys recommend that families re-adopt the kids in the United States after their return so that U.S. law recognizes the adoption. Follow your attorney's advice. If you decide to re-adopt, you can begin preparations soon after you return to the United States. You'll have some additional legal costs, but these should be minimal in comparison to other costs you've already incurred.

In some cases, you *must* re-adopt in order for the adoption to be considered valid in the United States:

✔ **If your child entered the United States on an IR-4 Immigrant Visa:** You get this visa if, instead of adopting the child in the birth country, you are only granted legal guardianship. See the preceding section for details.

✔ **If you haven't seen your child prior to her arrival in the United States:** Not all countries require that you be present to adopt. In cases where you adopt by proxy or where, if you're a couple, only one of you goes, you must re-adopt back in the United States.

✔ **If you're a resident of Iowa:** Sounds like a joke, but it isn't. States don't have to recognize international adoption decrees, and Iowa is the only state that requires all children adopted internationally to be re-adopted at home.

Securing U.S. citizenship for the children

The Child Citizenship Act of 2000 became effective on Feb. 27, 2001. This law allows for the automatic acquisition of U.S. citizenship for all adopted children of U.S. citizens. What that means is that, if you're a U.S. citizen, any child you adopt from any country automatically becomes a U.S. citizen, too. Your child acquires his U.S. citizenship as soon as the adoption decree is final. You don't need to take any other steps.

Countries open to adoption

Many countries are open to international adoption; the following list includes just a few. But before you pick one, here's some advice: Although you may be tempted to pick a country first and then find an agency, we recommend that you hook up with a reputable international agency first. Find a good agency that you'll feel comfortable working with, look at the programs and countries that agency offers, and *then* select the country you want to adopt from.

Bolivia	Ethiopia	Russia
Brazil	Guatemala	South Korea
Bulgaria	Haiti	Sri Lanka
Cambodia	India	Thailand
China	Kazakhstan	Ukraine
Columbia	Philippines	Vietnam
Ecuador	Romania	

Keep in mind a couple things about international adoptions:

✔ The key to a successful international adoption is to find a reputable agency. Reputable agencies work only in countries that are considered safe, and they keep you informed of the status of adoptions in the region.

✔ Countries regularly open up new programs, close programs, and change requirements for their programs. Although you'll want to research the country you select, you can count on your agency to notify you of problems, challenges, or changes that arise. Most international agencies have programs in several different countries. If you begin working in one country and that program closes, your agency can transfer you to begin working with a different country.

Extra Prep for Special Situations

Most adoptions — domestic or international — proceed pretty much the way we describe in the earlier sections. You fill out an application, you have a home study and submit yourself to all sorts of excruciatingly personal questions, you wait for people to approve you for a child and then for a child to become available, and then you count down the days until your child comes home and the adoption is finalized.

In a few cases — like when you adopt older kids and kids with special needs or when you adopt a child who lives in another state — you need to do a little more preparation and jump through a couple more hoops.

For special-needs and older child placements

The process for adopting an older child or a child with special needs — whether domestic or international — is the same as other adoptions of that type. However, because of some special issues you'll face, some extra preparation can be beneficial.

Kids with special needs

If your child has medical needs, get all the information you can and tap into the resources available in your area:

- ✔ **Find out everything you can about the condition:** Talk to doctors, get on the Internet, or visit a medical library if you have one nearby.

- ✔ **Immerse yourself in information about the medical community.** Research your local hospitals and the specialists practicing in your area. Find one that you'd be comfortable working with.

- ✔ **Join a support group of parents dealing with the same issues you are.** You can find support groups for parents of children with all sorts of medical conditions. These people can be excellent resources for finding your way through the maze of Social Security disability and adoption subsidies. For help in finding support groups, head to Chapter 22.

Older kids

If you're adopting an older child, the adoption process may be slightly different. An older child will be eased into your family through get-togethers and visits that precede placement, for example. Here are a few other things that you'll want to do to help your child adjust to her new family:

- ✔ **Immediately prepare for family counseling.** Counseling can ease the transition and help your child deal with some feelings she may be having. It can also help you communicate. So don't wait until you have significant issues to deal with. Remember, getting counseling for your child doesn't mean that you aren't capable or good parents; it just means you recognize that your child has a world of beliefs, habits, thoughts, and fears you know nothing about.

- ✔ **Share the family rules and expectations.** Explain how things work in your family and be specific:
  - "In our family we sit at the table each evening for dinner, but we usually sit in the family room at lunch time."
  - "You may open the refrigerator anytime you want to get a juice box."
  - "This is where you put your clothes when you take them off."

Be very patient. I (Katrina) once worked with a family that was upset because their child never flushed the toilet. Come to find out, the child was *punished* in a previous home for flushing the toilet. Imagine visiting a country where the language, culture, and customs are unfamiliar to you. This is how your child feels.

✓ **Be prepared for the language barrier.** Although most parents, at some point, will say that they and their kids don't speak the same language, with an older child from another country, you and your child *really may not* speak the same language. If this is the case, as your child learns your native tongue, try to learn his.

Dealing with out-of-state adoptions

Adopting a child from another state (called an *interstate adoption*) is very doable, but it does require a few extra steps. In an interstate adoption, the child you're adopting doesn't live in your state. Essentially, it's not enough that you and the birthmother agree to the adoption. Before you can take the child home, the two states have to agree, as well.

Basically the sending agency (the agency in the state where the child is born) has to submit a request to its state to allow the child to leave the state's jurisdiction. The birth state then communicates with your state (where the child will be living after the adoption). Several offices handle the paperwork before the sending agency receives the final approval to allow the child to leave.

An interstate adoption requires loads of paperwork and many supporting documents. Your agency or attorney should handle all the paperwork for you.

You have two jobs through all this:

✓ **Find a hotel in the child's birth state.** Pick someplace comfortable because you and your child will be there awhile.

✓ **Enjoy your new child and your stay in the hotel while you wait for the final approval to travel home.** This approval can take a week, a month, or more. The agency or attorney you work with can give you a good estimate on the amount of time your specific case is likely to take.

The laws you have to follow are those in the state where the child is born or resides. So, before you do anything, make sure that you're familiar with the adoption laws in that state and know how these laws apply to you. You don't want to pay birthmother expenses, for example, in a state where doing so is illegal.

The Interstate Compact on the Placement of Children

The Interstate Compact on the Placement of Children (ICPC) is an agreement between states designed to facilitate adoptions across state lines and offer protection to the children involved. The arrangement is between the *sending* agency (the agency in the state where the child is born) and the *receiving* state (the state where you live). This compact allows for the sending agency to retain jurisdiction (and financial responsibility) for the child until the adoption is final. Both states have to agree to the terms and the transfer of the child's residency.

Beyond Finalization

Most adoptive parents heave a huge sigh of relief when the adoption is finalized. It means that the social worker is out of your life, your child is yours forever and no one can take her away, and you're done with the paperwork and questions and interviews and inspections — all the stuff you had to do to build your family. It's over. Finally.

But it isn't. Your child will be an adopted child her whole life. And how you deal with that impacts how your child feels about herself and her place in your family. Adoptive parents and their children have to deal with all sorts of issues that children born into a family don't have to deal with. Following are just a few of the issues that will come up (Part IV explains these and other issues in more detail):

✔ **The adoption story:** You can't lie to your child and not let him know he's adopted. First, many in your family, in your church, and in your community know that you adopted this child. Someone will say something sometime. I (Katrina) encountered a woman who, when she was 35 years old, was told by her hairdresser that she was adopted. The hairdresser, who didn't know the parents had kept the adoption a secret, innocently commented that she remembered the adoption. Finding out that way can be devastating.

You have to decide what to tell and when to tell it. In case you're not sure *whether* to tell, let us help you: tell. How? From the very beginning. Tell your child about the adoption from the time he's a baby. That way, he won't remember being told; he'll just grow up with the knowledge. Chapter 16 has tips and suggestions for sharing the adoption story with your child.

✔ **Feelings of rejection:** You know that you love your child and that he certainly was wanted: After all, how long did you wait and how many hoops did you jump through to bring him home? You also know that the birthmother made the adoption plan because she wanted her child to have what she wasn't able to provide. What your child sees is that he isn't in the family he was born into because the woman who carried him for nine months gave him away.

✔ **Questions of belonging:** For children born into a family, the question of belonging doesn't come up in the same way it does for adopted children. Sure, a birth child may not be anything like her mom or dad, but people will attribute the difference to the latent genes of some ancestor. Not so with a child who's been adopted. For adopted children, the question "Why am I in this family?" is a real one and, if the adoption is transracial or transcultural, one they'll have to think about whenever anyone decides to point out that they're not the same race or ethnicity as their parents.

✔ **Grief for the birthmother:** Some adoptees deal with feelings of grief directly connected to their adoption. As an adoptive parent, I (Katrina) wasn't prepared for that grief. I was caught completely off guard when my 3-year-old daughter told me she was sad because she never got to see the lady that grew her in her tummy. We talked about it, and thinking that I had handled it quite well, I was again caught off guard when she told me she "just wanted to die" when she was 5 years old. She expressed to me that she loved her birth mommy and she missed her. Many adopted children, whether they can — or are willing to — articulate it, share this feeling of loss.

In dealing with these and other issues, a good place to start — and the easiest — is to love your child fiercely enough that the depth of your love alone gives him or her a sense of security. Your child belongs to you: Nothing — no person, no event, no feeling or question your child may have — can change that fact. From there, you need to understand that your love alone isn't enough. It won't stop the questions about the people who "gave them up"; it won't stop the feelings of not being wanted; it won't make your child feel less conspicuous when someone — a friend, a teacher, a stranger — asks questions like "Is he adopted?" or "Why didn't your real mom want you?"

What you want is for your child to feel secure enough in your love that she can explore and express her feelings without fear of hurting you. And though your heart will break when your little one is in tears because some bozo felt the need to explain the difference between "real kids" and "adopted kids," you need to acknowledge how your child feels as truth, without minimizing or explaining her feelings away.

Chapter 4

The Gasp Factor: What You Can Expect to Pay

*W*hen you talk about money and adoption, all sorts of thoughts may come to mind:

"It's so expensive. There's no way we can afford it on our income."

"It's not fair: If I were pregnant, insurance would pay for it."

"Some people are just in this to get rich."

"I want a child, but I don't want to 'buy' a baby."

Yes, those thoughts may be valid, but we're here to dispel some of the myths that often surround adoption. First, adoption does cost money, and it can be expensive, but not always. Many private agencies, for example, base their fees on your income. State agencies often charge only a nominal fee; some don't charge a fee at all. This chapter includes advice and suggestions on how you can get together the money you need to finance your adoption, as well as information on some government programs that help offset the costs.

Second, adoption and pregnancy are different paths to the same destination. Neither is better or more special or less personal than the other one. So stop comparing them. Embrace the path you're on. If you find that you're having a hard time accepting the ways in which adoption is different from pregnancy, you may not be ready to adopt.

Finally, buying a baby is illegal. Profiting from the "sale" of a child is illegal. The best way to protect yourself financially — and emotionally — from people who are out to get rich through adoption is to have a general idea of what different types of adoptions can reasonably cost, to know the types of services that reputable agencies and attorneys provide, and to know what you're allowed to pay for and what you aren't.

This chapter gives you a general idea of what you can expect to pay when you adopt through the public agencies, through private agencies, and through lawyers. But keep in mind that these numbers are averages. What you pay for your adoption may be more or less, depending on the circumstances in your particular situation and the laws in your state.

Money's Role in American Adoption

What makes a good home for a child? Annual trips to Europe, an Olympic-size pool at the west end of the estate, and a closet full of Tommy Hilfiger and Wooden Soldier clothing? No, but many people think that adoption is only for the rich — for the ones who can afford to pay sometimes tens of thousands of dollars to become parents.

What makes a good home are loving parents, a stable environment, and the necessary resources to provide life's necessities. Yet many couples and individuals who can provide *that* feel like they've run headlong into a brick wall when the topic of adoption fees comes up. And who can blame them? Money does play a role in American adoption, especially in the adoption of healthy infants.

More resources mean faster placements (usually)

The unfair but unavoidable fact in America is that the more resources you have — that is, the more money you have to spend on adoption — the more quickly you are likely to get a child. Here's why: The only public agencies dealing in adoption are those in the individual states' department of Family and Social Services (otherwise known as State Welfare Departments); this office rarely has infants to place (see Chapter 2 for why this is so). If you want an infant (that is, a child under age 2), your only real option is to contact a private agency or an attorney. In many cases, which of these you choose often depends on how much you can afford to pay and how long you're willing to wait for a baby.

Some private agencies, for example, base their fees on the families' ability to pay: Lower-income families have lower fees; higher-income families have higher fees. Either way, the fee often doesn't exceed a certain amount. For this reason, more families can afford to adopt through these agencies, but they also have a longer wait for a child (sometimes several years) because of the long list of waiting parents. Other agencies have a set (and usually higher) fee for healthy infants and, possibly, a sliding scale fee for special-needs (and sometimes minority) babies. Because of the higher fee, fewer people can afford these agencies, and for this reason, placements happen more quickly (between one and two years is pretty average). For attorneys who arrange adoptions directly between a birthmother and a family, the average wait is around six months — and the total, after you've paid for the birthmother expenses, the lawyer's fees, and any incidentals that get added to your bill, can often be higher than many private agency adoptions.

What all this means is that people with money tend to get babies faster (often within a few months, if they go with an attorney); people without money can wait years. So although it's not true that only rich people can adopt, it is true that how much money you have to spend on the adoption process can have a direct impact on how long you have to wait for a child.

Unfair? You bet. But as long as private adoptions are legal in the United States, families with more resources have more options. That doesn't mean that adoption isn't an option for middle-income families, however. You just have to be more creative with getting the money together. The section "Financing an adoption," later in this chapter, gives you some ideas.

The profit motive

Private adoptions aren't legal in all countries. In England, for example, all adoptive placements go through the government agencies, not private agencies or individuals. In this way, the English have eliminated the motive of financial gain from the adoption process. That's not the case in America. Private adoptions are legal here, and they account for a large percentage of all adoptions. And some folks make a pretty penny in facilitating adoptions.

So after you get past the link between how much money you have and how that impacts how quickly (and even if) you can build a family, you have to decide whether you're comfortable with the amount of money legally changing hands in American adoptions. When you choose an agency or an attorney, you need to be okay with what your money is being used for. Paying $15,000, for example, for services to birthmothers, salaries to a staff of qualified social workers, and operating expenses for the organization may be more acceptable to you than paying the same amount of money for quarter-page ads in the Sunday paper and a luxurious office with a giant neon stork in the foyer.

You have a right to know where your money is going — how much for services rendered and how much for profit — and an obligation to make sure that you work with people who act in an ethical way. So ask. If you can't get straight answers or you don't like the answers you hear, go elsewhere.

Nonprofit versus for-profit celebrity smackdown

Some people will tell you that there's very little difference between nonprofit and for-profit agencies, and in many cases, that's true. Several for-profit agencies, for example, conduct their businesses in much the same way that nonprofit agencies do; in fact, many agencies that are currently for profit are actively working on achieving nonprofit status. Conversely, many nonprofit agencies actually turn a profit — that is, they bring in more money than they spend. So you shouldn't pick an agency — or reject an agency — just because of its nonprofit status.

Having said that, the requirements and limitations placed on nonprofit agencies are important to know about — especially if you're someone who thinks that adoption should be about service and not money. Here are some things to know about nonprofit agencies:

✔ By definition, a nonprofit organization can't exist to make money; it must fulfill some religious, charitable, educational, literary, or scientific purpose. If the organization begins to extend its business beyond its stated purpose, the organization can lose its nonprofit status (and the tax exemptions that go with that status).

✔ The organization must be incorporated, adopt a set of bylaws (rules governing the organization), and have a certain number of directors (how many depends on the state law) to oversee how the organization conducts its business.

✔ Although nonprofit organizations can take in more money than they spend (that is, they can make a profit from the work they do), they must use this money to further the organization's mission. It can't go to the organization's members, directors, or corporate officers. In addition, if the organization is ever dissolved, the assets have to go to another tax-exempt organization.

In short, nonprofit adoption agencies, by law, can't exist for the purpose of enriching the people who run them, the people who work for them, or the people who turn to them in a time of need. The fees they charge are for the work they do in adoptions, and if they want to keep their nonprofit status, any money they do make must go to further that mission.

You may wonder how people can profit from adoption and *not* be selling babies. The fees you pay are for *services* that facilitate adoption, not for the delivery of a baby. Nevertheless, private agencies, attorneys, and facilitators can charge whatever they want — and whatever you're willing to pay — for these services. And therein lies the rub. When profit enters into the equation of who gets kids, the answer, if profit is the primary motive, is those who can pay. This is one reason we recommend that you find a reputable nonprofit agency to work with.

The Cost of Private Agency Adoptions

Private agencies are agencies licensed by your state to place children for adoption. They typically provide services to both adoptive and birthparents, and they're allowed by law to provide all the services necessary to help you with adoption.

In almost all cases, private agencies place infants. (If you're interested in adopting an older child, contact your local Office of Family and Children and see the section "State Agencies: Your Government at Work," later in this chapter, for information on the cost of adopting through your state agency.)

When you pay

When you work with a private agency, you generally have some relatively minor upfront expenses for things like the application fee and the home study. In general, though, you don't pay the bulk of the fee itself until after you receive a placement — that is, until your child is actually in your home. This type of payment schedule protects you in a couple of ways:

- ✔ If you don't pay until after the fact, you still have the resources to pursue another placement if the placement you were counting on doesn't happen. Remember, even if a birthmother has selected you, met you, told you she's absolutely, positively at peace with her decision, and invites you to the hospital to participate in the delivery of her baby, she can't relinquish her parental rights until after the baby is born and she can sign the consent forms. And between the time she goes into delivery sure of her decision and the time when she can sign the consent forms, she has every right to change her mind. And many birthmothers do.

  Every state has different rules regarding when birthparents can relinquish their parental rights. Sometimes hospital policy figures into the equation as well. See Chapter 11 for information about consent forms.

- ✔ Many agencies have a policy stipulating that, if anything catastrophic happens to disrupt the adoption before finalization — the birthmother challenges the placement, and the child is removed from your home, for example, or some unforeseen health issue results in the death of the child — they will make another placement without charge.

The financial protection we outline in the preceding list doesn't help diddlysquat with the emotional toll these situations can take on you. A child lost to you is a child you've lost. But it can keep your dream of becoming a parent alive, especially if you think that you can afford to adopt only once.

The agency fees and what your money goes for

Fees vary by agency. Some agencies charge a set fee; others base their fees on your income. In many cases, fees for a child with special needs may be less than those for a healthy child.

When you work with a private agency, you're probably looking at spending anywhere from $7,500 to $15,000 total, depending on how the agency assesses its fee, the agency's policies regarding extra expenses, and your particular situation. Following is a rundown of what you pay for an adoption through a private agency:

The application fee

The application fee generally runs between $100 and $600. You submit the fee when you turn in your application. The money goes for the paperwork and background checks that begin the adoption process. This money is usually nonrefundable, but many agencies deduct this amount from the final cost of the adoption.

The home study fee

This fee can range from $700 to $2,500. You usually pay this fee after the home study is completed. Most agencies consider the cost of the home study to be part of the overall fee. So, for example, if the agency fee is $10,000 and the home study fee is $1,000, you would owe $9,000 (minus the application fee if that's deducted as well) at the time of placement. (Home studies for international adoptions are usually a little more than those for domestic adoptions because of the extra paperwork and the translation costs.)

The home study itself is the investigation the social worker performs to make sure you're ready to be a parent. In reputable agencies, the home study also has an important educational purpose: preparing you for the adoption. By the time you're done, you should know a lot more about birthmother issues, adoption issues, how to talk to your child, and so on. All in all, the home study requires a lot of paperwork, a lot of questions, and a few visits. Head to Chapter 9 for the juicy details of what you have to look forward to during your home study.

The agency fee

Agency fees pay for the agency's operating expenses (rent and utilities, advertising, office supplies, transportation and mileage costs, and salaries for staff, for example), as well as the services the agency provides to its clients: the adoptive families and the birthmothers. You pay the agency fee, minus any deductible expenses (like the application fee and the home study fee), when the agency places a child with you.

The services that the birthmothers receive are the most important — and most vital — component of the agency fee, and it's where, in reputable agencies, most of the money goes. All birthmothers who contact these agencies receive services, but not all place their children for adoption afterwards. So even though the agency's social workers may have spent agency time and resources giving transportation to the birthmothers, providing counseling, helping with Medicaid applications, and offering an assortment of other services, the birth mom is under no obligation to place her child.

Receiving services and then not placing a child *isn't* a scam. The agency's role is to help women understand their options and make the best decisions for themselves and their children. It is not to "pay" them, through services, for unborn babies. When a woman decides to parent her child, the agency absorbs the cost of the services, without reimbursement.

When you pay the agency fee, your money doesn't go toward a particular birth mom's expenses; it goes toward the services that the agency provides to all its birthmothers.

Attorney fees and court costs

You need an attorney to file your adoption petition in court and to appear at the hearing with you. The attorney fees and court costs aren't usually included in the agency fee.

Each attorney charges at his or her own rate, and what you pay can range anywhere from $500 to $10,000. Most attorneys, however, whose only role in the adoption is filing your petition and representing you in court, charge around $1,000 to $2,000 for that work. (If your attorney is acting as an adoption facilitator as well as your legal counsel, head to the section "There Oughta Be a Law! Cost of Attorney Adoptions," later in this chapter, for information on the costs associated with that.)

Although some agencies may require that you use a specific attorney, you often have the opportunity to find your own. If you do, hire an attorney who knows adoption law in your state and, if you're adopting a child from another state, the laws for that state, too. You never know when your adoption could be contested or at risk, and you don't want to be represented by an attorney inexperienced in adoption.

Other expenses you may encounter

You may be responsible for other costs in addition to the fees that the agency charges. Because some of these costs can be pretty significant, you need to be aware of your agency's policy regarding additional costs.

Birthmother's medical expenses

If a birthmother has insurance, the costs — or most of the costs — of her pregnancy are usually already taken care of. Often, however, birth moms find themselves without adequate medical coverage. In that situation, many agencies encourage them to apply for pregnancy Medicaid; they may even schedule her appointment and provide transportation to help her through the bureaucratic maze. If that option doesn't work out, however, and she finds herself without insurance or Medicaid to cover the costs of her pregnancy, you may be expected to pay those bills.

Be sure you know your agency's policy on who pays medical expenses. The going rate for vaginal births, without complications, is around $7,500. Add complications to that or extended medical stays relating to the pregnancy, and the price skyrockets. If paying for medical expenses is beyond your means, let your agency know. They can then share your profile with birth-mothers for whom medical expenses aren't an issue.

This section talks about the birthmother's medical expenses, not the baby's. As soon as the baby or child is placed with you, your insurance kicks in (or it should — be sure to check your policy; Chapter 10 has details).

Birthmother's other expenses

In addition to the medical expenses, a few agencies may expect you to help the birthmother with other expenses, including things like her rent, utilities, groceries, maternity clothes, and so on. If your agency expects you to pay the birthmother's living expenses, keep the following in mind:

✔ Some states have strict regulations regarding these expenses. A reputable licensed agency will be aware of those regulations. If you live in a state that has no restrictions, be very careful. Don't begin an open-ended arrangement where you just pay, pay, pay.

✔ Just because you pay a birthmother's expenses doesn't mean she's obligated to place her child with you. Any money you pay toward her expenses is money at risk. If she decides to parent her child, she probably won't be required to repay you the money you spent.

✔ Most birthmothers legitimately consider placing their child for adoption and legitimately need help paying their expenses. However, it is true some women try to scam families out of money. Before you enter into an agreement to pay a birth mom's expenses, ask whether your agency requires proof of the pregnancy.

I (Katrina) once went to see two "sisters" who were pregnant and wanted to discuss adoption. Their first question was "How much can we get?" They later disclosed they already had placed five children for adoption and were looking for the right "arrangement" to place numbers 6 and 7. Again, this is not the norm, but ask questions before you enter into any agreement.

State Agencies: Your Government at Work

Unlike private agencies, which help birthmothers make decisions about their children and usually *don't* become legal guardians of the children being placed for adoption, state agencies already *have* legal custody of their children. As such, states have to provide for the needs of all these kids: foster care or institutional care, medical expenses, counseling, transportation, clothing, legal representation, and so on. These costs are astronomical.

Finding permanent homes for these children relieves the state of the financial burden of their care. For that reason, states aren't looking to collect a fee for the placements of children; they're just looking for good homes for their children. As a result, adoptions through state agencies cost much, *much* less than adoptions through private agencies — if they cost anything at all. And because many children in state welfare systems are older or have special needs, states offer programs to help families offset the sometimes high costs of raising and caring for these children.

Fees in state adoptions

You won't encounter many, if any, fees when you adopt through your state agency. In fact, these adoptions are usually free, except for the following:

✔ **Possible court fees:** If you adopt through your state agency, you may have legal fees associated with finalizing the adoption. But not always. In some cases, the state or county may provide the legal representation for the adoption.

✔ **Out-of-state adoption fees:** If you adopt a child from another state, you're responsible for the travel and lodging expenses associated with out-of-state adoptions (see Chapter 3 for what to expect when you adopt kids who live in another state).

✔ **Possible home study costs:** If you're adopting a special-needs or older child, the state conducts the home study itself or contracts the home study to a private agency. In either case, the home study is performed at no charge to you. But this may not be the case if you're looking for a single, healthy child under a certain age. In these cases, you may be responsible for paying a home study fee. Ask your local Office of Family and Children for details.

Incentives to encourage adoption

Most children placed through state agencies are older or have special medical or emotional needs. Finding families who are willing and able to adopt these kids can be hard, and the costs of caring for a child with special needs can be prohibitive. For that reason, many states offer subsidies and incentives to help adoptive families.

Adoption subsidies for special-needs kids

In some cases, especially when the child has significant special needs, states offer the adoptive parents a monthly subsidy after they adopt the child. This subsidy enables the family to financially afford to raise the child (and still reduces the amount of money the state has to use for that child).

One such program is the Adoption Assistance Program (AAP), designed to help states find homes for their special-needs children. In this program, you receive a monthly check for a certain amount (usually between $200 and $500) to help offset the costs of raising a special-needs child. This subsidy usually ends when your child turns 18, although sometimes it can end when your child turns 21, depending on the severity of your child's condition. Along with the subsidy, your child also qualifies for Medicaid, the government health insurance program that provides for all your child's medical needs.

The Adoption Assistance Program is a federal program supported by Title IV-E funds. Under Title IV, the federal government gives money to states to help needy families and child welfare services. A certain percentage of the program money comes from the federal government; the rest comes from your state or county coffers. The program is usually state supervised and state administered but delegated to the county offices (that means your state oversees the program, but you go to your local Office of Family and Children to apply and receive benefits).

Until recently, all adoptions — private or public — of special-needs children could qualify for adoption assistance. Today, however, if you adopt a special-needs child through a private agency or an attorney, you don't qualify for AAP. To receive adoption assistance, you must adopt through a public agency, in your state or in another.

Reimbursement for adoption expenses

If you adopt a child with special needs, you may qualify for reimbursement of certain, one-time expenses. These expenses include things like attorney fees, agency fees, travel expenses, and so on. Each state has a maximum amount that it reimburses per adoption, ranging from $400 to $2,000. Check with your agency to see what assistance is available in your state.

This one-time reimbursement applies to you whether you adopt through your state agency or a private agency. You may still be eligible if you adopt internationally as well.

There Oughta Be a Law! Cost of Attorney Adoptions

You'll find a wide range of fees for attorney adoptions. Don't be surprised to hear anything from $8,000 to $30,000 — and more in some cases. The three factors that influence how much these adoptions cost are

- The base fee your attorney charges
- How much you spend for birthmother expenses
- What you spend for advertising

The following sections explain these factors.

Keep in mind that the fees we talk about here occur when you use the attorney not only as your legal representative in court to finalize the adoption but also as the adoption facilitator. For adoptions within families, like a relative adoption or stepparent adoption, these fees are usually much less.

Your attorney's fee

Attorneys can charge whatever they like for their professional services. In independent adoptions, your attorney's fee usually includes the legal representation and advice you get throughout the adoption process, as well as the court costs. Occasionally, it may also include the cost of locating a birthmother for you. More commonly, attorneys charge an additional fee if they have to find a birthmother for you.

In general, you make payments to your attorney as services are provided. Usually, you pay the retainer and a (sometimes) small fee for miscellaneous pre-placement expenses upfront. The remainder you pay at prearranged times during the adoption, with the final payment being made usually when a child is placed with you.

Birth mom's expenses

Often in attorney adoptions, you pay for the medical costs related to the pregnancy, as well as the birthmother's living expenses. If you want the birthmother to get any counseling, you pay for that, too. You pay these expenses as the bills come in.

How much you spend toward medical expenses obviously depends on how the pregnancy goes. How much you spend toward living expenses depends on the laws in the state where the birthmother lives.

In deciding what birth mom expenses to pay, keep these suggestions in mind:

✔ Know the laws that apply to your situation (these may be the laws in your state or another state, depending on where the birthmother lives).

   If you spend beyond the maximum allowed by state law, you're potentially placing your adoption in jeopardy. If a judge discovers that you violated the law, he could refuse to finalize the adoption and impose any legal penalties he deemed appropriate.

✔ Ask yourself, "Is this something the birthmother needs in order to deliver a healthy baby, or is this a luxury she wants?" Although you want the birth mom to receive all the medical and counseling care she needs, and you want her to eat well, you do not want her to profit from the placement of her child.

   Some people (who have the means) will agree to anything to keep the birthmother happy. Birthmothers who take advantage of this "power" are behaving unethically and immorally. Adoptive parents who accept such an arrangement are, essentially buying a baby — another unethical and immoral act. To make sure you don't find yourself in this situation, decide which things you're comfortable and willing to reimburse for, be honest with the birthmother about your limitations, and, if she's not happy with the arrangement or you begin to feel uncomfortable that she's not acting in good faith, don't proceed with this particular adoption. Head to the section "What You Can't Pay For" later in this chapter for more details about how dangerous these types of quid pro quo situations are.

✔ Always remember, the birthmother may change her mind. Just because you pay her living and medical expenses doesn't mean that she has to place her child with you. She very well may decide to parent her child herself. Whatever you give her, you give as a gift that she's not obligated to return. If she doesn't go through with her original adoption plan, you're probably out whatever you've paid thus far. (Currently, Idaho is the only state that *does* expect birthmothers to pay back money they accepted if they decide to parent their children.) Some unlucky families have had several birthmothers accept their money and then change their minds.

✔ You can't just hand a birthmother large sums of money in return for her child. That's called baby buying, and it's illegal. See the section "What You Can't Pay For," later in this chapter, for details.

Advertising costs

When you adopt through an attorney, you often have to locate a birthmother yourself. In that case, you're responsible for the advertising costs. And the broader your search — the more areas you target, the more newspapers you place your ad in, the more billboards you paste your smiling mug on — the more money you're going to spend.

In addition, some attorneys expect you to install toll-free number phone lines so that birthmothers who are interested in your ad can call. You may also need to invest in a pager at some point in order to be alerted when a baby arrives.

Not all states allow you to advertise for a birthmother. Do so only in places where it is legal.

Other stuff

Of course, the birthmother expenses, lawyer fees, and advertising costs are *in addition to* the other things you may end up paying for. The other stuff category is fairly broad, including both run-of-the-mill adoption expenses, as well as other expenses associated with independent adoptions in your state. Here are some examples:

✔ **An independent home study:** Reputable attorneys require a home study.

✔ **Travel and lodging expenses if the birthmother is in another state:** Depending on where you focused your search for a birthmother, your chances of finding a birthmother who lives in another state are fairly high. If that's the case, you'll be responsible for the travel expenses associated with an out-of-state adoption.

✔ **Possibly, a separate attorney to represent the birthmother:** Some states require that you hire a separate lawyer to represent the interests of the birth mom. Even if your state doesn't require a separate attorney, it's still a good idea. That way, you can avoid any conflicts of interest that may arise from having the same attorney.

International Adoptions: Exchange Rates Not a Factor

International adoption agency fees may range from $7,000 to $30,000. The challenge in identifying the costs for international adoptions is the variance in what the base fees cover from agency to agency. One agency, for example, may charge a higher base fee but have very few extra expenses. Another agency may have a really low base fee but have many extra expenses. International agency fees may cover the agency expenses both here and abroad, or they may charge separately for each.

The following sections outline what you can expect to pay for when you adopt internationally. To find out which of these items are included in the agency fee and which aren't, ask your contact at the agency. This person can let you know specifically what's included and what you have to budget for separately.

Agencies that work in international adoption have a lot of overhead that private agencies working solely in domestic adoptions don't have:

✔ **Offices here and abroad:** International adoption agencies often have offices both within the United States and in other countries. Each office incurs the typical administrative and operating costs.

✔ **The actual expenses incurred for each adoption:** The children must be housed, fed, clothed, educated, and treated medically while they wait for adoption. The agencies take over this responsibility.

✔ **Humanitarian relief:** Many international agencies use some of their funds for some type of additional humanitarian relief in the countries where they work. Sometimes referred to as a *relief donation,* this money goes to support programs that improve the quality of life for orphaned children. It can include things like building orphanages, schools, and play structures; installing heat or water in orphanages or schools; implementing nutrition programs; providing mattresses or beds; and so on.

Different agencies have different payment schedules stipulating when you pay for what, but, like domestic agencies, the payments are spread throughout the adoption process. One agency, for example, may require a relief donation upfront, the foreign program fee when a country is selected, postplacement fees as they are needed, and all other fees "upon request." You may a sign fee agreement as a part of the application process.

Agency services and lawyer fees

The first thing you do when you decide to pursue an international adoption is to submit an application, along with an application fee. On average, this fee ranges from $200 to $600. You also, as in all agency adoptions, have a home study fee, which can be from $1,000 to $3,500. Unlike in domestic adoptions, where the fees are usually deducted from the total amount you pay, in international adoption, this usually isn't the case because you often have a separate agency do the home study (if your international agency isn't in your state). This second agency takes the full application fee and home study fee, and then you pay another application fee to the international agency. The fee you pay the international agency may be deducted from its agency fee.

In addition to these fees, you also have the following fees:

- **An agency fee:** This is the fee, commonly between $2,000 and $5,000, that the agency charges for services it provides in the United States. This fee includes things like case management, dossier assistance, and other professional services.

- **A program fee:** Usually around $2,000 to $5,000, this fee is for the services provided by the agency's foreign affiliate in your child's birth country. For example, one agency has a China program fee of $4,565. This fee includes $565 for the China Center of Adoption Affairs (the adoption agency in China), $500 for legal expenses, $100 for the child's passport and medical exam, $3,000 for the orphanage donation, and $300 for a China host fee (the person who meets you at the airport and sticks to you like glue through the whole process). This fee is usually due when you select the country and program you plan to use.

- **A post-placement fee:** Usually between $600 and $2,000, this fee is for providing the post-placement services: making necessary visits to the home, writing the required reports on the child's progress, and so on. How many reports have to be done depends on the country you adopt from. Some countries, for example, require one report every six months for a three-year period. This fee may be due when the services begin, or you may be billed after the visits have been made.

  The post-placement fee can also include any necessary translation costs, as well as assistance toward re-adoption.

- **Legal costs:** A lawyer in the other country handles the legal work there (like preparing legal documents, attending court proceedings, doing legal work to have the child declared orphaned or freed for adoption, and so on). Many agencies include the cost of this lawyer in their fee, but ask your agency to make sure. If your agency recommends that you re-adopt your child back in the United States, you'll need an attorney here to do that. The cost of re-adoption usually *isn't* included in the agency fee.

- **Costs for finding a child:** In some international adoptions, you may be responsible for paying a fee to a child locator. This person locates children available for adoption and refers the child to the agency to be matched to a family. In South and Central American countries, the locator is often the attorney for the agency in that country. Locators generally aren't used in countries where children are housed in orphanages. The fee for the locator is generally included in your agency's regular fee. Again, check with your agency to know for sure.

Immigration and dossier preparation expenses

A lot of paperwork goes into an international adoption. You have to create a dossier that includes a long list of certified documents (marriage certificates, birth certificates, divorce decrees, and so on), as well as the home study report and your visa approval from the BCIS (Bureau of Citizenship and Immigration Services). The preceding section discusses the cost of the home study; you're gonna dish out more money to get the other stuff together:

✔ **Immigration application fee:** Every child entering the United States needs to have a visa approval. This approval costs $460. To get this approval, you can submit a preliminary petition (called the I-600A form), which lets the BCIS determine whether you'd make a suitable parent. Once you're in your child's birth country and have either adopted the child or been granted legal guardianship, you trot on over to the American embassy and submit another form, I-600, otherwise known as the "Petition to Classify Orphan as an Immediate Relative." With this form, the BCIS determines whether your child meets the BCIS's definition of *orphan.* If your child does, then the BCIS issues the visa, and you can bring your child home. Chapter 3 has all the necessary details on securing your child's visa.

✔ **Fingerprint filing fee:** Before the U.S. government approves you for an international adoption, it does a fingerprint check on you. You pay $50 for each set of prints, so that works out to $100 per couple.

✔ **Passports, passport photos, and visas:** Different passport services charge different amounts. Many online services offer to expedite the process (sometimes in as little as 24 hours), but you don't need to rush. You have plenty of time to secure your passport the old-fashioned way. If you do it the way your grandma did (through the Passport Services of the U.S. State Department), expect to pay around $85 for a new passport and $55 for a renewal — plus whatever you pay to the photographer to get a shot that doesn't make you look like a fleeing felon. (For Web site information about getting a passport, see Chapter 3.)

✔ **Marriage, birth, and any divorce certificates:** You need three certified copies of each, at $5 to 10 a pop.

✔ **Notarization and authentication costs:** Everything you send has to be notarized and/or authenticated. This will cost you around $500.

✔ **Translations of documents:** All the documents in your dossier may need to be translated and typed. If this is the case, it generally costs between $300 and $700.

Going from here to there and back again: Travel costs

When you adopt internationally, you have to prepare for travel costs whether you travel or not. Even if your child is escorted to the United States, you're still responsible for the cost of the travel, for both your child and the escort. For this reason, many families that adopt internationally decide to travel to the birth country to bring their child home themselves.

You'll probably spend between $2,500 and $6,000. Of course, how much you spend for travel depends on where you're going, who's going, and how long you plan to stay. Here are some pointers for figuring out how much you're likely to spend:

✔ Calculate the airfare for at least one adult (two if you're a couple going together) and include one child returning.

✔ Talk to your agency about the length of stay, the hotel accommodations it recommends, and so on. With that information, you'll have a pretty good idea what you need to prepare for.

Many international adoption agencies arrange for groups of adoptive families to travel together. In this way, they can provide things like transportation and translation services in a more efficient way. If that option is offered to you, take advantage of it.

✔ Find out what, if any, special fees or payments you need to make in your child's birth country. The following section outlines some additional costs you may encounter.

Special fees and other things

In some countries, it is customary or even necessary to provide gifts for the people who help you with the adoption — the attorneys in the country, the orphanage personnel, and so on. In addition, some countries require that you donate money to the orphanage. The special fees and customary payments vary from country to country. The best way to find out what types of things you'll need to have money for, and how much money is expected or considered acceptable, is to talk to your agency. Following is a list of some "incidental" expenses you may encounter:

✔ **Relief donation:** Usually between $500 and 1,000, this amount is the humanitarian relief mentioned earlier. If you're a U.S. citizen, you may be able to deduct the amount you pay from your taxes as a charitable donation.

✔ **Orphanage donation:** This fee, which can be a few to several thousands of dollars, is used to maintain and staff the orphanages. It goes toward expenses like food, clothing, utilities, and anything else needed to keep an orphanage operational.

✔ **Interpreter/translation:** Don't be surprised to pay around $1,000 for this service. The money pays for having someone interpret the conversations, legal proceedings, and so on for you when you're in your child's birth country.

✔ **Child's physical:** Before your child can enter the United States, she must have a physical that verifies she's in good health. These physicals usually cost between $40 and $100.

✔ **Child's passport:** This passport enables your child to leave the birth country and enter the United States. The passport fees vary from country to country, but expect to pay around $100. Just as a note, your child's nationality is that of his birth country. He won't acquire his U.S. citizenship until he passes through immigration in the United States.

✔ **Special "gifts," occasionally referred to in America as *bribes*.** These gifts (often money), given to clerks, judges, and others, can help move your case through the legal system and avoid lengthy delays. Your agency can let you know both who the recipients of these gifts are and how much you need to give.

What You Can't Pay For

Having spent the last several pages listing in painful detail what you can pay for, are expected to pay for, and *have* to pay for if you want a snowball's chance in purgatory of building a family through adoption, you may be shocked to discover that there are actually things you *can't* pay for. But it's true. By law, you're forbidden to pay for certain things. This section outlines those things.

And, because some folks either aren't aware of — or choose to ignore — these rules, we list things you need to watch out for so that you can protect yourself from those who view adoption more as a way to make money than as a way to build families.

Children! Duh

"It is a felony to sell or barter a child for adoption or other purposes." — Idaho

"It is unlawful to transfer or receive property for waiving parental rights or consenting to adoption." — Indiana

"A person, agency, or intermediary shall not sell or purchase any child for the purpose of adoption." — Kentucky

"It is unlawful to trade, barter, buy, sell or deal in infant children." — Pennsylvania

"It is strictly forbidden to buy or sell a child or to do so under the cloak of adoption." — China

The language of laws in different states and countries varies, but the point is the same: *Buying and selling children is illegal.* In every state in the United States. In every civilized country in the world.

A few words to the wise:

- ✔ **Stay away from the quid pro quo arrangements: You do this for me; I'll do that for you.** Even if the deal isn't as blatant as your handing over large sums of money and the birthmother handing over her child, you may still be breaking the law if the adoption arrangement is contingent upon your providing certain things in return for a baby.

- ✔ **Stay away from situations in which profit is the motivating factor in the placement plan.** How will you know? Look for clues: Requests for unnecessary items, money upfront, and so on. The section "Things to watch out for," later in this chapter, can help you figure out what things to be wary of.

Unnecessary expenses

So what's an unnecessary expense? It depends on what state you're talking about. In some states, the only necessary expenses are the birthmother's legal and medical expenses. Everything else is unnecessary. Other states add maternity clothes, living expenses, and reimbursement for lost wages to the necessary list; whatever doesn't fall within those categories is unnecessary.

What may be an unnecessary expense in one state isn't an unnecessary expense in another state. To complicate matters, some states (like Hawaii) don't have any provisions specifically regarding how much and for what a birthmother can be reimbursed; other states (like Indiana) stipulate how much, what for, and even when you're allowed to pay.

So how do you know what's allowable and what isn't? You either research your state's adoption laws yourself (not recommended for the faint of heart), *or* you hook up with an attorney or agency you can trust and let one of them guide you. Chapter 7 tells you how.

Things to watch out for

First, most people working in adoption aren't out to fleece you and break your heart. They truly have your best interests, the birthmother's best interests, and, most importantly, the child's best interests in mind. They understand adoption law, they recognize their obligation to practice in an ethical way, and they see their mission as helping birthmothers through difficult times and helping adoptive parents build families.

Unfortunately, not everyone working in adoption acts in the same spirit of service. Some may just be incompetent; others may be criminal. You need to be wary of both. Here are some things to look out for:

> ✔ **Agencies and attorneys who ask for large amounts of money upfront:** Most reputable agencies and attorneys ask you to pay certain amounts at different points in the adoption: the application fee when you turn in the application, for example, or a retainer fee when you hire the attorney to facilitate the adoption. But they don't expect you to pay the bulk of the money until the time of placement.
>
> ✔ **Birthmothers who continue to ask for more than what was originally agreed upon:** If you're paying birthmother expenses, you and your attorney or agency should outline what those expenses are, when they should be paid, and what the maximum amount is. If you're working with a birthmother directly (as you sometimes do when you adopt through a facilitator), these are things you and the birthmother need to work out before you enter into an agreement.
>
> ✔ **Attorneys, agencies, or facilitators — or their representatives — who will not or cannot meet you face to face, especially if other red flags are present:** These other red flags include large amounts of money requested upfront, your only contact having been through an Internet address or Web site, the organization is new or the person has been in business for a short period of time, and so on.
>
> Remember, if you work with an agency in another state (not uncommon, especially in international adoptions), your only contact may be through phone calls and letters, and that's normal.
>
> ✔ **A newly organized agency with no track record:** Although newness isn't necessarily a problem, inexperience is. If you go with a new agency, make sure the people you'll be working with are knowledgeable and experienced in adoption.
>
> If the organization is new, check with the Better Business Bureau. Be sure to ask about information available about the agency itself (under the agency's name), as well as the names of individuals running the business.
>
> ✔ **If the agency or individual doesn't require you to follow established adoption practice or indicates that certain checks are unnecessary:** Sure, every adoptive family would like to forgo the home study, but the home study, as big a pain as it can be, is the best way to make sure that the child is going into a safe and loving home. If the person who's helping you adopt tells you it's not necessary — because you look like nice people, because it's obvious you'd make good parents, because whatever — you shouldn't be flattered. You should be suspicious. Ask yourself, "What other shortcuts is this person taking?"

Bottom line? Trust your instincts. If something seems fishy, it probably is.

Don't Panic: You Don't Have to Be Rich to Adopt

No, we didn't add this section to provide comic relief. You *really* don't have to be rich to adopt. In terms of how you can provide for a child, the only real question agencies ask is, "Can you provide adequately?" In other words, agencies simply want to know whether you can shelter, feed, clothe, and provide medical care for your kids. If the answer is yes, whether you make $30,000 a year or $300,000 isn't important.

Having said that, if you want to adopt — especially if you want to adopt a healthy infant — you're going to have to find a way to fund your adoption. So how do you get the money together if you don't already have boatloads sitting in a bank account somewhere? You'd be surprised at some of the creative ways people have financed adoptions.

In addition, many adoptive families can take advantage of employer programs that help offset the costs of adoption, as well as state and federal programs that offer incentives and tax breaks to adoptive families.

Financing an adoption

Some families are able to pay cash for their adoptions, but many more aren't. Families can be very creative in securing the money they need for the fees involved:

✔ Some families take out loans or second mortgages or charge the adoption fees to their credit card. Some people raid their retirement accounts and then pay themselves back the money.

✔ Other families appeal to family members for loans or gifts.

✔ Occasionally, families choose to give up certain luxuries for a time. They skip the family vacation, make the family car last one year longer, and so on.

✔ Some folks add part-time jobs to their busy schedules.

One family I (Katrina) know asked its church to donate recipes and, from these recipes, created a cookbook to sell. The family even included a special section of recipes from its child's birth country. All the money raised from this enterprise went into the family's adoption fund.

Some agencies offer special assistance or grants to qualifying families. Check with your agency to see whether you qualify. In addition, some employers offer adoption benefits that may include reimbursement of some of the expenses. Check with the human resources department at your place of employment.

Qualifying for incentives and tax breaks for certain types of adoptions

All adoptive families thatearn less than $190,000 a year can qualify for an adoption credit of up to $10,000 from the federal government for expenses incurred in adopting a child. This credit is available to you regardless of whether you adopt domestically or internationally. If you adopt a special-needs child, you can receive a credit of $10,000, regardless of the adoption expenses.

Here's how the credit works: You subtract credit amounts directly from the amount of taxes you owe. If you reduce the taxes you owe to zero and still have credit left over, you can carry the credit over to the following years until you use it all up.

Being a government agency — and one with a bad reputation to boot — the IRS isn't inclined to rely solely on your assertion that there is no way on God's green earth that two ordinary people like you and your spouse could have created the most adorable child in the world. So keep accurate, complete records of all expenses you pay so that you can prove your claim for the credit.

In addition, some states offer additional tax credits or tax deductions to adoptive families. Check with a local tax professional to determine what is available in your state.

Fees have been a struggle

Before we decided to pursue adoption, my husband and I spent approximately $15,000 to $20,000 on fertility treatments: The money went for doctor bills, surgeries, fertility drugs, and grief counseling that insurance wouldn't pay for. It wiped our savings out! So for our personal circumstances, the adoption fees have been a struggle. Both my husband's mother and my mother are helping us with these fees.

We would love to have more than one child, but that probably won't happen unless we can do it on a payment plan. It's also sad to think of having to spend money to have a baby, but in reality, we would be doing the same if we weren't adopting.

Sherry Frazer

Chapter 5

Who Can Adopt?

*W*hen you make your initial contact with adoption agencies, you usually say something along the lines of "My name is so-and-so, and I (or my husband and I, or my partner and I) am thinking about adopting a child." And then the questions begin. Not yours. Theirs.

Are you married? How long have you been married? Is this the first marriage? How many children, if any, do you already have? How old are you? Do you have a history of infertility? What religion do you practice? And so on. Before you stammer out your first answer, you may have already figured out that you're going to be scrutinized and scrutinized pretty carefully.

But take note: These are the *easy* questions. Where you are in your life now — stable relationship, decent job, and so on — isn't the only thing under the microscope. Once you make it past the minimum agency requirements, the hard questions begin. People are going to be examining your past, and they're not just looking for the I-went-fishing-with-my-father stories, either. Had any legal problems? Health problems? Relationship problems? Ever suffered from a mental illness or been in trouble with the law? Ever abused drugs or alcohol? They want to know about that stuff, too.

When these questions begin to rain down on you, don't panic. Many people have an eviscerated carcass or two stinking up their pasts; fortunately, these things don't automatically disqualify you. How you've dealt with them and how you present them to your social worker, however, are vital. The key is to be honest and thoughtful about the challenges you've faced or the mistakes you've made. This chapter helps you understand how your current situation and past issues can impact your adoption and offers recommendations on how to deal with these sensitive issues in a way that won't impair your chances to adopt.

Profiling Adoptive Parents: Who Gets Kids?

Married couples have an easier time adopting, but that doesn't mean that adoption isn't an option for people who aren't married or who are part of a nontraditional couple. The truth is that anyone who can provide a loving, stable home for a child can adopt. The trick is figuring out what paths are open to you.

Married couples

Although you don't need to be married in order to adopt, obviously, married couples have more options. We can't think of any agency that won't allow a married couple to adopt. In fact, marriage is one of the first requirements many agencies have. In addition, the majority of birthmothers are hoping for a married couple to adopt their child.

Agency restrictions regarding your marriage

Of course, just being married isn't the magic ticket to adopting. Many agencies have rules regarding marriages of couples looking to adopt. Here are some of the restrictions you may encounter:

- **Length of marriage:** Some agencies require that you be married for a certain period of time (one or two years usually) before adopting. Some agencies with this type of requirement may factor in any additional time you've spent living together before marriage.

- **Restrictions regarding the number of previous marriages:** One of the key things an agency looks for is stability. A history of broken marriages may bring into question how stable your current relationship is. Still, whether you have many divorces or only one prior divorce, the social worker will want to discuss thoroughly any previous marriages during your home study.

- **Age difference between spouses:** Although the difference between your ages isn't necessarily a deal breaker, a big age difference (a 22-year-old married to a 55-year-old, for example) will at the very least warrant more scrutiny. In some cases, the age difference will cause an agency to deny your application. See the section "Of a certain age," later in this chapter, for more information on the impact your age can have on adoptions.

What you'll be asked about your marriage

When you go through your home study interviews, you're going to be talking a lot about your marriage, and not just about whether you and your spouse agree on how you squeeze the toothpaste tube. (See Chapter 9 for more details about what to expect in the home study.) You'll be sharing things like the following:

✔ **How you met and what your courtship and dating were like:** This is the fun stuff. Who doesn't like remembering and telling the story of how they met and fell in love with their life partner?

✔ **How you handle conflict:** Believe it or not, you don't have to agree on things. You don't have to share the same religious faith, you don't have to share each other's politics, and you can even have different attitudes on parenting. You just need to be able to show that you can compromise and work through any difficult issues.

✔ **What you love about your spouse and what about your spouse irritates you:** Most people don't have too difficult a time with the "What do you love about your spouse?" question. It's the "What irritates you?" question that trips them up. For some, trying to come up with an irritation worth mentioning is the hard part. For others, the hard part is narrowing down a long list.

The social worker isn't looking for the perfect marriage; she's looking for a marriage that works and that can withstand the pressures of parenting and therefore provide stability for a child.

Unmarried couples

Vermont is the only state that has laws specifically protecting the rights of unmarried partners to adopt. In Vermont, couples joined in civil unions have the same legal status, rights, and obligations as married couples. In other words, state adoption laws apply to couples in civil unions as well as married couples, without discrimination.

No other state has laws specifically allowing unmarried couples to adopt. Here's why: If you and your partner are not legally bound together, you, as a unit, cannot be legally bound to a child. Does that mean that, if you don't live in Vermont, you're out of luck? Not necessarily, but the answer may not be the one you want to hear: If you and your partner want to adopt, only one of you can adopt the child, as a single parent. If you're willing to go this route, keep the following things in mind and see the section "Singles," later in this chapter, for information on that option:

✔ During the home study process, the person who *isn't* adopting the child will be interviewed and scrutinized just as much as the person adopting is. After all, even the one who isn't adopting will still be parenting.

✔ If you and your partner break up, the person who legally adopted the child has all the parental rights; the other person may not even have a right to visitation and would not be required to pay child support.

REMEMBER

✔ Some states (such as Alaska, California, Delaware, Pennsylvania, and a few others) have allowed second parent adoptions, in which the other adult in the home is allowed to adopt the partner's child. So one person adopts the child initially, and later, the other person may be able to adopt the child.

If you're interested in this option, keep in mind a few things:

- This rule generally applies to stepparent adoptions, in which the other adult is adopting the spouse's child. In the few instances where the other person adopting *isn't* the legal spouse, the couple is usually legally joined in either a civil union (as in Vermont) or in a domestic partnership (similar to a civil union).

- Just because some second adoptions have been allowed in particular states doesn't mean that those states have laws supporting them. Often the judge hearing your particular case is the one who makes the determination whether the second adoption is allowed.

- If you're interested in investigating this option further, contact an adoption lawyer who can explain your state's laws to you.

Singles

Every state allows single people to adopt, but you will face a few challenges:

✔ **The task of finding an agency to work with:** Not all agencies accept single applicants. Some will deny you outright. Others will consider you for special-needs children only. (Many private and state agencies welcome single applicants for their waiting children — those who, for whatever reason, they've not been able to find homes for or who have been difficult to place).

✔ **Birthmothers' preferences for two-parent families and the number of two-parent families available:** Most birthmothers want their children to be raised in a two-parent family, and they have plenty of two-parent families to choose from, especially if they're placing a healthy infant.

✔ **Your gender:** Fair or not, if you're a single man, you may have a more difficult time adopting, especially if you're adopting a female child. You're likely to be looked on with suspicion, whether you adopt domestically or internationally. A man adopting a female child in China, for example, has to be at least 40 years older than his daughter, the presumption apparently being that such an age difference guarantees that his feelings remain paternal.

Many singles decide to adopt internationally. Because an abundance of countries offers adoptions at any given time, you have an abundance of opportunities to adopt. Although not every country will place a child with a single parent, many countries do.

If you're a single parent, you may be scrutinized even more thoroughly in the home study process. Parenting is tough even when two parents are involved. The responsibility is even more difficult for single parents. So not only do you have to prove that you're prepared to be a parent, you also have to convince your social worker that you're prepared to be a parent alone. Here are some issues you're likely to discuss:

✔ **The support system you have in place to help you raise a child:** Who will provide child care? Who can you call in an emergency? If you get sick and are hospitalized, where would the child go? What if you die? If you adopt a child of a different gender, who will act as a role model as that child grows to adulthood?

✔ **Your finances:** Can you financially afford to provide adequately for this child?

✔ **Your future plans:** What happens if you decide to marry, and your potential spouse isn't keen on the child?

✔ **Your expectations of parenthood:** Are you prepared to be on call 24/7? Do you realize that you're the only one there to get up in the middle of the night with a sick child? Are you prepared to bear the entire burden of making all the parenting decisions (how to discipline, when to potty train, when to let your daughter date, and so on)?

Gay/lesbian singles or couples

In the United States, you can find one state (Vermont) that specifically guarantees the right of gays and lesbians to adopt, two states (Florida and Mississippi) that expressly forbid or restrict it, and 48 other states that deal with these adoptions on a case-by-case basis, meaning that some adoption petitions are approved and some are denied, and often the only difference is where the petition is heard.

Facing the issues you're likely to deal with

Here are some issues you're going to deal with if you're a gay or lesbian trying to build your family through adoption:

✔ **The challenge of finding an agency that accepts gay or lesbian applicants:** Many fundamental, faith-based agencies have requirements that eliminate gays and lesbians. In addition, any agency that limits its adoptions to legally married couples also doesn't accept a gay or lesbian parent.

✔ **Birth mom preferences:** Most agencies require your "gay or lesbian status" to be disclosed in the profile so that the birthmother can make an informed choice of the family situation for her child. Many birthmothers prefer straight couples over gay or lesbian couples. For some birthmothers, however, it may not matter.

✔ **International restrictions on gay adoptions:** In international adoptions, some countries restrict adoptions to exclude the gay or lesbian parent. China, for example, requires the home study to include a statement regarding the sexual preference of the applicant. Other countries don't require the question to be asked.

Although some people may suggest that you can get around these restrictions by keeping your sexual orientation under wraps, we don't recommend that you take this route. First, lying isn't necessary: Even without the agencies or countries that will deny your application, you still have plenty of opportunities to adopt. Second, as in-depth as home studies are, hiding such a fundamental part of who you are is almost impossible; not only would you have to explain significant relationships in a different context, but think of the family photos you'd have to take down. Finally, you count on your agency and the birthmother to be honest; you owe the same to them.

✔ **Your status as a couple:** If you're a gay or lesbian couple wanting to adopt, you face the same issues that unmarried heterosexual couples face. See the section "Unmarried couples," earlier in this chapter, for information on what you need to know about adopting.

Considering the opportunities you do have

Before you throw in the towel, remember that you still have many opportunities to adopt:

✔ Some agencies actually specialize in adoptions for gays and lesbians. One way to find them is to go on the Internet. Type in **Gay Lesbian Adoptions,** and you'll get a list of lots of resources, including links to agencies, facilitators, and attorneys who work with gays. Include your state name in the search, and the resources will be narrowed further.

✔ Although where you live can affect the number of opportunities available to you, this isn't necessarily a hindrance if you're open to interstate adoptions. If you live in a state that is hostile to adoptions by gays and lesbians, you can adopt from a state that is more open to that situation. For more info about interstate adoptions, go to Chapter 3.

✔ Another option for gays and lesbians are the arranged opportunities for parenting in the gay community. A female member of a couple may choose to be artificially inseminated and give birth to a child, which her partner may then adopt (if second parent adoptions are allowed in your state, see the earlier section "Unmarried couples" for information on that option). A male couple may ask a female to be a surrogate parent for them and then one male would adopt the child when it is born.

During your home study, expect to answer the same types of questions and have the same type of discussions that heterosexual parents face, as well as the following:

✔ **Issues related to being part of a nontraditional family:** These discussions focus on how you plan to prepare your child to deal with the taunting, rude comments, questions, and so on that he or she is likely to hear as a member of a nontraditional family.

✔ **Issues related to only one parent adopting the child:** In most adoptions by gay and lesbian couples, only one partner will actually adopt the child (see the earlier section "Unmarried couples" to understand why). So expect to talk about the arrangements for the child if you and your partner break up in the future. Would you both, for example, remain committed to the child?

Of a certain age

Your age may be a factor in your adoption. Some agencies have age restrictions, requiring, for example, that applicants be at least 25 and no older than 45. Other agencies may use a formula in which they average the couples' individual ages together, and this average age can't exceed a certain number of years. Other agencies may have no specific requirements, evaluating each situation case by case, or have age restrictions for healthy infants and be less restrictive for their special-needs children.

Be aware that age can also play a role if you're adopting internationally. Until recently, China, for example, preferred couples to be over the age of 35; now it accepts applicants who are 30. In addition, the U.S. Bureau of Citizenship and Immigration Services (BCIS) requires that people adopting internationally be at least 25 years old.

Age can also be a factor when a birthmother selects a family. Although many birth moms look for young couples, others may prefer someone older and more settled. Specifically, someone raised by grandparents may feel more comfortable with an older couple.

Considering Other Issues That Can Impact Your Chances to Adopt

Most, if not all, adoptive parents feel that they have to sell themselves to the agency they're working with and to the birthmothers who will be looking over their profiles. And when you sell yourself, you try to put everything in a good light. You and your spouse met at a party in college, for example, and it was love at first sight. No one has to know that it was at his frat house and you were so drunk that you proposed on the spot. Or the decision you most regret? Forget about the tongue piercing that got infected and focus on the butterfly tattoo permanently etched on your posterior.

Some things, however, aren't so easy to gloss over. These are the biggies: the health issues, the legal issues, and the financial issues that can impact your chances to adopt. You may think that the best way to deal with these topics is to just not bring them up, and if they come up, to evade the truth or downplay the seriousness of the situation. Don't.

These situations don't necessarily have to destroy your chances to adopt. In fact, they often don't. The key is to be open and honest about the challenge you face (or faced) or the mistake you made, and to thoughtfully discuss how this thing affected you as a person and how it may affect you as a potential parent.

Legal issues

A routine part of the home study process is checking your criminal history. Some agencies also check Child Protective Services (CPS) and sexual perpetrator records. If, during this check, your social worker discovers something on your record, he'll discuss these issues at length with you.

Scrutiny in attorney and facilitator adoptions

When you go through an agency to adopt, the agency is the first to screen you, which it does through the application and home study process. Once you make it past that, most agencies give your profile to birthmothers, who then decide whether you're someone they want to place their child with. You often don't encounter the same scrutiny when you adopt through an attorney or through a facilitator. Here's why:

✔ Neither attorneys nor facilitators can operate as adoption agencies; you hire attorneys to handle your legal work; you hire facilitators to locate a birthmother for you. You don't need to go through much screening to do either of those things. The biggest determinant in whether you work with a particular lawyer or facilitator is whether you can afford the retainer and fees.

✔ Reputable attorneys and facilitators require that you get a home study, but in some places, attorneys can ask a judge to waive the home study requirement for particular situations.

✔ Nowadays, in almost all agency adoptions, the birthmother chooses the family who will adopt her child. The same isn't always true of agency and facilitator adoptions. Some attorneys and facilitators, for example, offer one specific family to a birthmother. Although she has the opportunity to reject the family, she is not "selecting" them, per se, from a pile of profiles she's been given. In these cases, the match between birthmother and adoptive family is often more of a business arrangement. The birthmother discloses what expenses she needs to have paid, and the attorney or facilitator offers her a family who is able to pay the amount she needs.

Obviously, if your name appears on a sexual perpetrators list or you recently robbed the local Quick-Mart at gunpoint, you won't be approved to adopt. However, if you shoplifted a pack of gum when you were 16, you're probably safe. Other situations aren't so easy to determine.

Suppose, for example, that you were arrested for driving under the influence of alcohol six years ago. Six years is a long time, but the seriousness of the event warrants attention. So your social worker will probably want to know all the details about the incident, the charges filed, your punishment, your current drinking habits, and so on. If you were ordered to complete alcohol treatment programs, he may also require a report from the treatment facility. Your spouse may be interviewed specifically about these issues, as well.

You may be a pillar of the community now, but if your history includes a conviction of a felony (drug possession and dealing, or stealing a car, for example), adopting will be much more difficult for you. First, the BCIS won't approve anyone with a felony conviction to adopt internationally. Although some U.S. agencies may not reject your application out of hand, most agencies will turn you away primarily because of the liability issue. They don't want to risk putting a child in a situation that, because of past action, many would deem risky. What if you went back to your "old ways," the thinking goes, and your child were injured, neglected, or abused as a result? Although adopting may not be impossible for you, be aware that you face an uphill battle.

Health issues

If you have a disability or a chronic condition or illness, you may be worried that you won't be approved to adopt. But you may have nothing to fear.

Chronic conditions

Conditions such as high blood pressure, diabetes, and so on are often present in adoptive homes. Most agencies just want to be assured that the condition is being managed and that the child will be well taken care of and provided for.

Life-threatening conditions and illnesses

Although some agencies reject applicants who have life-threatening conditions, such as cancer and heart problems, other agencies evaluate these situations case by case. (Although it's controversial, some agencies consider obesity to be a life-threatening condition and have specific policies regarding significantly overweight individuals.) Even if you have a severe illness, such as multiple sclerosis or cystic fibrosis, many agencies will approve you for adoption, but they'll require that the affliction be disclosed to the birthparents and that the specialist who's treating you provide a statement as to your treatment. Obviously, if you have a condition that is potentially terminal, you'll be required to have a plan for the worst-case scenario.

Disabilities

A disability that doesn't make it impossible for you to parent a child shouldn't be a factor in finding an agency. The Americans with Disabilities Act makes discriminating against those with disabilities illegal, and this law applies to all government agencies, as well as private agencies — like adoption agencies — that provide a public service.

Mental illnesses

If you suffer from a mental illness, you may encounter some difficulties in getting approved for adoption, depending on the type of mental illness you have. Illnesses such as schizophrenia or bipolar disorder, for example, can have a significant impact on a child's life. As a result, people who suffer from those conditions may have a hard time being approved for adoption. Mild depression that you can control through medication, on the other hand, generally doesn't negatively impact your chances.

Addictions

Obviously, if you have an addiction problem now, you shouldn't be considering adoption. Past problems with alcoholism or drug addiction may or may not be a deterrent, depending on what has happened since you broke your addiction and how long you've been clean. Your social worker will definitely want to discuss your plan for sobriety, the length of your sobriety, your involvement with Alcoholics Anonymous or other alcohol or drug rehabilitation programs, and more. She'll consider all these factors when making a determination.

Financial issues

Most adoption agencies aren't seeking out wealthy adoptive parents. Instead, they're looking for parents who can adequately provide for a child. They want families to be able to provide adequate medical care, food, and clothing and a stable home environment. They check this by requiring you to submit a financial statement that discloses your monthly income, your monthly debts, the amount of savings and investments you have, and so on. Basically, they're trying to make sure that, at the end of the month, you have enough left over to provide for your child's needs.

Following are some things regarding your finances and financial history that may warrant more scrutiny or, in some cases, cause you to be denied:

Aaagh! A personality test, too?!

Some agencies require their applicants to take tests before adopting. And we're not talking about parenting skills exams. We're talking personality tests. One agency in Indiana, for example, requires applicants to take the MMPI (Minnesota Multiphasic Personality Inventory), a test devised in the 1930s to help diagnose mental illnesses in people. Overkill? Probably, but more and more agencies are beginning to use some version of a personality test or temperament analyses to gain insight into their clients.

Being approved or not usually doesn't depend on the results of these tests alone, but the agencies that require them use the information as a tool for confirming things the social worker has already observed or for uncovering red flags that had previously been missed and that can now be pursued.

So be aware that you may have to add "Pass personality test" to your list of things to do if you want to adopt. But try to keep things in perspective. At least the application and home study process doesn't require you to pee in a cup . . . yet.

✔ **A history of bankruptcy:** The bankruptcy itself isn't necessarily the problem, but the situation that led to it could be. If you have a bankruptcy in your past, the social worker will want to know how it came to pass, how it was resolved, and what you have done since then to stabilize your financial situation. Be aware that some agencies will not approve families who have filed bankruptcy recently.

✔ **Out-of-control debt:** If you can barely make ends meet because you owe so much to creditors, your social worker will question whether you're in a financial position to adequately care for a child now. Whether you make a million dollars a year or a fraction of that, your debt needs to be under control. A lower-income family who manages its money well may be approved before a higher-income family with out-of-control credit card debt.

✔ **Failure to pay back child support:** If you're not providing financially for the children you currently have, why should an agency trust that you will support the child you want to adopt? Regardless how you feel about your former spouse, how you figure what money is due your other children, or anything else that explains why you didn't (or don't) pay child support, the fact of the matter is, if you haven't provided for your children in your past, you'll probably not be approved to adopt additional children.

Getting to the Bottom Line: What Folks Look for in Adoptive Parents

After you bare your soul, dig up your past, and lay everything on the line, you're going to feel overexposed and, let's be honest, vulnerable. Sure, you'll make good parents. Sure, you have plenty of love to give a child. But you're not perfect, and now the whole world, or at least the two people in it who matter most to you right now — your social worker and any birthmother who looks at your profile — are going to know.

Guess what? Most people aren't looking for and don't expect perfection. Agencies want families who will lovingly care for a child. If you run across an agency that seems to cater to and prefer Barbie and Ken couples because they're more marketable, run the other way. Building a family is too important to let superficial things drive the process.

For their part, birthmothers want loving, kind parents. Although they may also have specific qualities in mind for the family they choose, these qualities are so particular to each birthmother that there's no way you can transform yourself into what every birth mom dreams of for her child. If you did, you'd have to be an Independent Republican Democrat who lives in the rural suburbs of a large city and goes to a Catholic Protestant church with other people of Jewish faith. In other words, what one birthmother dreams of may be another's nightmare, and you're going to run yourself ragged if you try to be all things to all people.

Trust is a huge issue in adoption: How can you make a good decision if you can't rely on the information you've been given? The same thing applies to the agencies and the birthmothers. They need to be able to trust that you're not misrepresenting things. So when you tell the stories of your life, be honest about your failings and hopeful about your future. And keep in mind that someday you'll be explaining these things — tongue piercing and all — to your kids, too.

Chapter 6

Building a Family through Adoption: Is It for You?

In This Chapter

▶ Assessing your reasons for wanting to adopt

▶ Allaying fears and concerns about parenting a child you didn't conceive

▶ Deciding whether you're ready to commit to adoption

*W*hether adoption is a good choice for you depends on what brings you to it and how you feel about it. You may be considering adoption for any number of reasons: For example, you want kids, but you don't want — or can't do — the pregnancy thing. You've heard of kids from here or there who need families and figure, why not? You've raised your first batch of kids and discovered that you want to do it again. The list goes on.

Despite the myriad reasons that bring people to adoption, one thing that successful adoptive families have in common is this: They have plenty of love to share, they want children, and they don't care — and we mean they *really* don't care — whether their child shares a genetic link with them or not.

Some people easily and naturally embrace the idea that love, and not genetics, is what makes children their own. For others, accepting this idea takes time. Whichever camp you fall into, you need to understand your motivation, be sure of your feelings, and be at peace with the issues you'll face as adoptive parents — before you get a child.

If you're one of the people who can't accept that your child doesn't spring from your loins — and thinks of adoption as the thing you do when you don't have any other choices and views the adopted child as the child you have because you couldn't get the child you want — adoption isn't for you. Children deserve to be with parents who love them unconditionally and unreservedly. Until you can do that, you aren't ready to adopt.

Motivating Factors: Examining Why You Want to Adopt

Do any of the following describe you?

- ✔ You've tried unsuccessfully again and again and again to have a baby.
- ✔ You believe it's your religious duty to help those less fortunate.
- ✔ You have very strong feelings about social awareness and responsibility, and you think, what better way to live your beliefs than to adopt a child?
- ✔ Your wife wants to adopt, and you go along with her wishes to keep her happy.

Are these good reasons to adopt a child? Not on your life. The following sections explain why.

Of course, maybe you're dealing with infertility issues. Maybe you feel a tremendous need to do good in the world or to make a statement about how lives should be lived. These things can impact your adoption (when you adopt, who you adopt, and so forth), but they shouldn't be the *reason* you adopt. If you're considering adoption, make sure that it's because you have a strong desire to be a parent and want a child of your own to care for.

Infertility and adoption

You know the saying "There's more than one way to skin a cat." Well, there's more than one way to build a family, and many couples who've experienced infertility at some point embrace adoption. Nevertheless, these people have had to work through the issues — and there are a lot of them — with their infertility.

Being able to create a child is one of life's wonders. Most people assume that, when they have children, this is how they'll do it: They'll get an egg and a sperm together, let the combo percolate for nine months, and then pop out a tiny person who shares their best characteristics and their cutely annoying tendencies.

To discover that you can't do what nearly all other normal, healthy people can do is one issue — and, as hard as it is, it's often the easiest to deal with, both physically and emotionally. Link infertility to the loss of the family you've always dreamed of creating, or the ideas you have about parenthood, and you can find yourself in an emotional abyss. Throw the word *barren* at someone, for example, and see how quickly they blanch.

Hope to tell

A few days after our first child came home, I (Tracy) had a visit from a neighbor, whose first comment was that he and his wife hadn't known I was pregnant. As I led him to the bassinet to see the baby, I told him that I hadn't been pregnant, that we adopted Adam. Then my neighbor began his tale:

He and his wife had been trying to get pregnant for over five years. They'd gone through all sorts of his and hers fertility tests before realizing that the problem was hers. Since then, she'd been on medication (from the minor stuff — Clomid — to the big guns — Pergonal) to spur ovulation, had undergone procedures to do this thing or that, and was scheduled to meet with an in vitro fertilization specialist to begin that procedure. They were going to keep going with the fertility stuff and not adopt, he told me, because they hadn't given up hope yet.

He had no idea what he had just said — or implied — about my son and our family. Most people who make stupid, presumptuous, and offensive comments don't. Still, his comment didn't stir anger in me, as I thought it would, but pity. I felt sorry for him and his wife. And as I beamed down at my newborn son, all chicken arms and legs in a too-big bunting suit and still wearing the blue knit cap from the hospital, I felt absolute joy for me. "*He* is what we hoped for," I said.

If you're dealing with fertility issues, keep these things in mind:

✔ **Know how you feel about fertility and its role in building your family.** Some people believe that the only "real" way to build a family is to conceive and bear children. The genetic link — Daddy's eyes, Mommy's hair, and so on — is an important one to them. It's so important, in fact, that they can't imagine having the same parent-child relationship with — or the same deep love for — a child who doesn't share this link. So if your goal, in your heart of hearts, is to have a child with a genetic bond to you, don't consider adoption. Children deserve to be more than substitutes for ones you can't have.

If your goal is simply to have a child — and you can separate the fertility issue (which, at its core, is about your ability to conceive) from the family issue (which, at its core, is about the love you have for your children) — adoption may be for you.

✔ **Understand your feelings about adoption.** If you think of adoption as an alternative path to the same goal — your family — you may be ready to adopt. If you think of adoption as the only path left to you because every other road was blocked, you're not ready.

Thinking of adoption as the last resort implies that children who are adopted can never be the first choice. If this is your mind-set, we recommend that you examine your motivation for adopting very closely and hold off on pursuing adoption.

✔ **Give yourself time to resolve your feeling about infertility before you adopt.** Many people facing fertility problems have feelings of anger, loss, and sadness. Work through these feelings before you consider adoption, and recognize that adoption doesn't "cure" infertility. Adopting a child may not eradicate your feelings of loss or sadness.

✔ **Don't pursue adoption as a means of getting pregnant.** We've all heard the tales — a husband and wife didn't think they'd ever conceive, so they adopted their first child only to discover shortly thereafter that she was pregnant. Yes, it happens to a lot of people. Yes, there may be something to the phenomenon. Yes, they're great stories. But if you want to adopt because you think it'll loosen a few eggs or relieve enough tension to make conceiving more likely, *stop.* This isn't some nightclub gig, and your first child isn't an opening act for the headliner to come.

The savior syndrome

Do you feel sorry for the little children you see on television who are starving, neglected, or abused? Do you believe that, because you have so much, you need to give back to someone in need? Did you grow up being taught that it's your duty to sacrifice to help others?

If so, then find a good church or charitable organization and volunteer your time and/or your money. But *don't* run to the nearest adoption agency. Wanting to help others is an honorable, wonderful thing, but it's not a reason to adopt a child.

Children deserve to be loved and welcomed as valued members of their family. They don't deserve to be treated as objects of pity, and they shouldn't have to grow up forever indebted to their adoptive parents for the sacrifices made on their behalf.

Pursue adoption if you have a strong desire to be a parent and want a child of your own to raise and love. If this motivation doesn't sound as altruistic as you think it should, keep in mind that most folks who become parents do so to meet their own needs: *They* want to be parents. Having a child would fulfill *their* dreams and make *their* lives richer. That's the way it's supposed to be. It's an admission that this child, whoever he or she may be, brings something to your life that no one else can. And a child who brings joy to your family and fills an empty spot in your life will feel cherished and valued *for herself.*

Don't pursue adoption if you think that doing so will earn you good citizenship points with whoever (or whatever) is keeping score. A child is more than a means to an end.

Doing it for your spouse

It's not uncommon for couples to disagree on the issue of adoption, just as it's not uncommon for couples to disagree on when or whether they'll add a child to their family through birth. The difference is that a woman may manage to conceive and bear a child without her husband's consent, but there's no way she can adopt a child without his agreement and participation. (You may wonder why someone would even want to. Well, believe us, some women and men are desperate enough for a child that they may consider such a thing if it were possible.)

All 50 states require that married couples either petition jointly for the adoption or, if only one spouse petitions for the adoption, the other spouse has to give his or her consent.

Some people believe that if they can just get their spouse to agree to adopt, however reluctantly, everything will work out in the end. As soon as their spouse sets eyes on that adorable little baby, they think, hearts will melt, and everyone will live happily ever after. And it can happen this way. At my agency, I (Katrina) have had couples reveal, after the fact, that one of the partners wasn't initially excited about adopting. Of course, reluctant spouses are then always quick to share how much they love their child and how happy they are that they were pushed into adoption. But how many couples whose stories didn't end happily go back and 'fess up? Probably not many.

If you loved me

If you loved me, you wouldn't deny me the chance to be a mother/father.

If you loved me, you'd give me time to work through my feelings.

If you loved me. . . . How many pleas and arguments and fights have begun with those four words? Far too many.

The fact of the matter is, the cycle that you're stuck in — one of you is ready to adopt; the other one isn't, and you keep going around and around about it — probably doesn't have much to do with how much you love each other. It probably has more to do with who you are and what you feel, not about each other, but about the situation. For some people, for example,

change is very hard. They expect things to go a certain way, for A to follow B and lead to C. For others, change is no big deal. If A skips every letter between itself and F, that's not a problem.

So don't make the discussion about how much you love each other, because the danger — and it's a real one for couples who disagree on such an important issue — is that it can destroy your marriage. The key is to make an honest effort to communicate; to understand the other person's point of view; to work together toward a solution, whatever that solution is; and to be at peace with how things finally end up.

Remember, you began the journey with your partner. You want to end it with him or her as well.

If you're tempted to press your spouse into agreeing to adopt, or if you're inclined to say, "Okay, do what you want," just because you want to stop talking about it, consider these things:

✔ You're making a life-changing, marriage-altering decision without being in full agreement. Spouses who do the pushing may end up feeling that they bear the entire burden for making things work. Spouses who allow themselves to be pushed may think what they wanted didn't matter.

✔ Children don't save marriages. In fact, children can add stress to a marriage (there is a reason, after all, why most studies show that people with fewer children are generally happier). Add a parent who was reluctantly pushed into that role, and you have a recipe for disaster.

So what do you do? Here are some ideas:

✔ Communicate your feelings *honestly*. You may need professional counseling to help you talk about this emotionally charged issue.

✔ Find out what your spouse fears or dislikes about the idea of adopting. Is it adoption or parenting that he's opposed to?

✔ Research adoption and adoption agencies and share this information with your spouse.

✔ Introduce your spouse to adoptive families in a setting where she can ask questions and have them answered.

When all is said and done, your reluctant spouse may not be reluctant anymore, and you two can look forward to planning your family together. Or maybe your spouse won't be able to overcome whatever makes him reject the idea of adoption. If that's the case, consider giving up your dream of adopting, at least for now.

Every child deserves to be welcomed, loved, and accepted by both parents. Adopted children already deal with issues of self-worth due to the fact that their birthparents didn't "keep" them. If they then encounter a lack of warmth and love from an adoptive parent, they may have nearly insurmountable difficulties with self-esteem.

Fears and Concerns You May Have

Every prospective parent has fears. Some fears fall into the every-parent-worries-about-this category: Will the baby be healthy? Will I be a good parent? Do I have the patience to read *Goodnight Moon* five times every night for the next few years? Will my pediatrician think I'm a moron because I've put him on my speed dial? Adoptive parents face these issues, as well as other issues unique to them and their children.

Bonding issues

If you have concerns about bonding with your child, welcome to parenthood. Bonding is one of those mystical phenomena that many parents fret about. New parents worry they may never bond with their child. Experienced parents worry they may not bond as deeply with additional children as they did with their first child. Adoptive parents worry that bonding may be more difficult because their child wasn't born to them. Most of these worries are needless.

My (Katrina's) experience has been that those who strongly desire to parent a child eventually bond with the child they bring home. The difficulty lies in unrealistic expectations. If you listen to some people, you begin to think that bonding has certain rules:

- It has to happen within the first few minutes of birth, certainly within the first couple of days.

- It can happen, in its deepest sense, only between a birthmother and her birth child.

- Like first impressions, it happens only once: the first time you lay your eyes on your child.

All this stuff is crap. Bonding happens this way for some people. It happens differently for others. The truth is that not all parents fall deeply and overwhelmingly in love with their children the first time they set eyes on them, regardless of whether they gave birth to them or not. Often the deepest bond develops over a period of time. To imply that only birthmothers and their birth children can share the deepest parent-child bond is an insult to birthfathers and adoptive parents everywhere.

When I (Katrina) adopted my son from Korea at the age of 6 months, I had an instantaneous, overwhelming bonding experience the first time I laid eyes on him. When I first saw my oldest birth child in the delivery room, the only thought that came to mind was, "He looks purple." Those initial reactions didn't indicate a difference in the depth of the love I would develop for my children. After bringing my children home and caring for them, I loved all of my children with the same intensity.

If you're adopting an older infant or an older child, keep these things in mind:

✔ Some people who adopt older infants (children between the ages of 6 months and 2 years, for example) feel threatened by the bond that may have existed between their child and his birthmother (if he lived with her) or foster parent. Actually, you *want* your child to have bonded — and bonded strongly — with the person who cared for him before you adopted him. First, every child needs an intimate connection with another person to be able to thrive emotionally and physically. Second, having bonded with someone else makes it easier for your child to bond to you.

✔ Bonding with an older child may take even more time than bonding with an infant. Behavioral issues and attitudes that need "adjusting" may interfere with your ability to develop those warm fuzzy feelings. The trick when you adopt an older child is to make a firm commitment to your child regardless of your "feelings" for them. As you provide and care for your child, those feelings will come.

The role of the birthmother in your life

Adoptive parents may have different levels of contact with their child's birthparents (head to Chapter 15 for information about the type of contact with the birthmother you can have). By carefully selecting an adoption agency or adoption program, you can control what this contact entails. You may, for example, meet the birthmother, exchange letters and photos with her following placement, and have visits following placement, or you may prefer a closed adoption where you don't have any contact at all.

Regardless of whether you ever meet or have any contact with your child's birthmother, she will have a role in your life and in the life of your child:

✔ No matter how long or how deeply you love your child, he will remain a child born to another woman. Although your child may acquire mannerisms, characteristics, and interests that mirror those of your family members, he will always have someone else's features on his face.

✔ You may share all the details of your child's birth family with your son or daughter and then discover that your child still wants to know more. Even if you knock yourself out trying to be the best parent in the world, you may never be able to quench your child's longings or desires to connect with his birthmother.

These things can be quite threatening for adoptive parents to consider, and they're things that people who've given birth to their children don't have to think about. Unlike the bonding issue, which is an every-parent thing, these are adoption things. The good news is that they're not bad things.

Your child's birth history is a part of who she is, so learn to embrace it. Your child's birthmother brought her into this world and then made the difficult decision to entrust her into your care. Where is the threat in that? Even if your child decides to search for her birthparents when she's older, her love for you will remain unchanged.

What you can't do is adopt a child and erase all evidence of the child's beginnings. You can't pretend away the adoption. Instead focus on the positives of adoption. Enjoy the miracle of being chosen to raise a child born to someone else.

Unknown health concerns

Many families worry about unknown health problems that might arise with their adopted children. It is true that some birthparents engage in risky behaviors that can affect the health of their children. And it is also true that the birthmother may not be honest with her agency. These risks are ones you have to accept; however, keep these things in mind:

- ✔ When you work with a reputable agency (see Chapter 7 for information on finding a good one), you can be assured that it'll share any prenatal information it knows about with you before you make a decision to adopt the child.

- ✔ Agencies make every effort to secure an accurate medical history from the birthparents. Keep in mind, however, that you can't know what medical issues a child will face just because you know the medical history of the parents. Perfectly healthy children are born to parents with serious health issues in their family, and perfectly healthy parents can have children with serious health concerns.

- ✔ The reliability of the information relies on the reliability of the birthparents. It has been my (Katrina's) experience, however, that most birthmothers disclose factors that put their child at risk.

    Why would a woman do this, you may wonder, especially if this information may make her child harder to place? The answer is that birthmothers want the best parents for their children, and they understand that the best parents are those who are prepared to deal with the issues their children may face.

- ✔ No one can predict what health issues their children will have, regardless of how they enter the family. Once you make the commitment to welcome a child into your arms and into your home, you also make the commitment to accept whatever challenges the child faces.

My pediatrician was horrified when I (Katrina) shared my plans to adopt from Korea. He went into a lengthy lecture on poor prenatal care, orphanage conditions, illnesses, and diseases. After some initial bouts with viruses, both of my Korean-born children were quite healthy. During both of my pregnancies, I did everything I knew to ensure the good health of my children. And yet, both of my birth children experienced lifelong health conditions.

Your extended family's reaction

When you share your plans to adopt with your extended family, they may embrace adoption and support you every step of the way — some even to the point of being so enthusiastically annoying that you have to tell them to lay off.

Or not.

If your family members fall into the we're-not-too-thrilled-with-the-idea group, they may do so for a variety of reasons:

- ✔ They may have concerns about the child's health, the child's looks, or the child's IQ. They may *really* object to any talk of adopting a child of another race or culture.

- ✔ They may have fears about adoption relating to things like legal problems, contested adoptions, contact with the birthmother, and so on.

- ✔ They may have a strong investment in the family "lineage." They can trace their ancestors all the way back to Jeremiah Poontangle, whose blood runs through the family vein, and how can this child be a Poontangle if he doesn't have Poontangle blood?

- ✔ They may have many "very good reasons" why this isn't the right time to adopt, why you can't afford to adopt, or why a specific child is not the right one for your family.

Do you need to listen to your family members? Yes. Do you need to follow their suggestions? No. You (and your spouse, if you're married) need to make the decision that's right for you. You do, however, need to consider how your family's reaction may affect you and your child.

Protecting your kids from toxic families

Many adoptive families have the attitude that if they proceed with their adoption, their families will "come around" when the child arrives. Indeed, families sometimes do have a change of heart. I (Katrina) have seen many instances when the cute baby wins over his new grandpa or grandma. The problem arises when grandma and grandpa (or aunt or uncle or whoever) fail to be charmed.

If your family objects to adoption, the question you need to ask is this: Am I willing to put my child's well-being first, in spite of my desire for a relationship with my family? If you want to proceed with adoption despite your family's protestations, your answer has to be "yes." You also must be prepared to protect your child:

✔ Never place your child in a family situation where he feels "less than." He should receive the same gifts and affection that he sees his cousins receive. If the gifts, attention, and affection aren't doled out equally, then he shouldn't be there to see it.

✔ Adopt a policy of zero tolerance when it comes to unkind comments, racial or inappropriate jokes, or unequal treatment that may be detrimental to your child. You can't shelter your children from those things in the outside world, but with careful planning and steely resolve, you can protect them in the family setting.

Bringing your family around

You can take steps to encourage family members to get on board the adoption train:

✔ Choose the right moment and setting to discuss your plans with your family.

✔ Do your research and be prepared with good answers for any question that may come up.

✔ Have your statistics handy to debunk any adoption myths that surface.

✔ Show your family that you've thought through this decision and that it's not just some spur-of-the-moment thing.

✔ Give family members a list of famous adoptees. Don't know any? Head to the sidebar "Famous adoptees" in this chapter.

✔ Provide your family with adoption books and other literature. Buy *Adoption For Dummies* for them, or give them your copy.

✔ Share written information about your agency.

✔ Invite them to an adoption support group meeting, where they can meet adoptive families.

✔ Ask your family members for their support.

Famous adoptees

Lots of people have been adopted. Here are just a few of the more famous ones:

- **Actors:** Gary Coleman, Halle Berry, Ingrid Bergman, James MacArthur, Marilyn Monroe, Melissa Gilbert, Ray Liotta, Priscilla Presley, Richard Burton, Ted Danson

- **Athletes:** Dan O'Brien (decathlete), Eric Dickerson (running back), Greg Louganis (diver), Jim Palmer (pitcher), Peter and Kitty Carruthers (figure skaters), Scott Hamilton (figure skater)

- **Authors and poets:** Charles Dickens, Edgar Allen Poe, Edward Albee, Harold Robbins, James Michener, Langston Hughes, Leo Tolstoy

- **Beauty queens:** Charlotte Anne Lopez (Miss Teen USA), Lynnette Cole (Miss USA 2000)

- **Biblical figures:** Jesus and Moses

- **Classical heroes and military leaders:** Alexander the Great, Aristotle

- **Comedians:** Art Linkletter, Tommy Davidson

- **Entrepreneurs:** Dave Thomas (Wendy's), Larry Ellison (Oracle), Steve Jobs (Apple Computer)

- **Musicians:** Bo Diddley, Debbi Harry, Faith Hill, John Lennon, Nat King Cole, Sarah McLachlan

- **U.S. Presidents and First Ladies:** Gerald Ford, Bill Clinton, Eleanor Roosevelt, Nancy Reagan

- **Other notables:** George Washington Carver (inventor), Jean Jacques Rousseau (philosopher), Jesse Jackson (minister), John J. Audubon (naturalist), Malcolm X (civil rights leader), Nelson Mandela (human rights activist and president of South Africa)

How old you'll be when your child finally arrives

Most adoptive parents are older than other first-time parents. Here's why:

Round 1: Many married couples delay thoughts of childbearing until they have had time to adjust to marriage and each other. They usually want to get their careers established and perhaps purchase a home before they even entertain the idea of children.

Round 2: Once they begin "trying" in earnest, a year or two may go by before they realize that they're having enough difficulties to warrant a trip to the fertility specialist. Then they begin all the appointments, make trips to numerous specialists, and undergo various tests to discover the source of their fertility problems.

Round 3: Next, they may start treatments or have surgeries to correct those problems, or they may begin a series of in vitro fertilizations or other procedures.

Round 4: If these procedures are unsuccessful, the couple needs time to grieve the loss of the birth child they'll never have before moving forward to consider adoption.

Round 5: *Then,* once they decide to pursue adoption, depending on the route they go (agency or attorney), they could wait another two or three years (or more).

Our decision to adopt

Like most little girls, I, too, pretended that I was a mommy to my doll babies while playing house. Then I grew up and fell in love, got married, and dreamed of starting my own family. Then my dream became a reality: I went to my doctor; he confirmed I was indeed pregnant. I rushed home to tell my husband, and my heart was about ready to burst because I was so happy. Then several weeks later, I started having complications. My doctor was away on vacation, and another doctor had to tell me, "I am sorry, but you are not going to be able to carry the baby." This doctor gave me the statistics: Twenty-five percent of all women miscarry, and usually it is with the first pregnancy (not a very comforting thought at the time).

Then I became pregnant a second time. I was more cautious and yet still very excited. I had an ultrasound. I saw my baby. I heard the heart beat. And I thought to myself, "Everything is going great. I have only two more weeks to go, and then I'll be out of danger of losing this baby." Unfortunately, I was not blessed with being able to carry my baby two more weeks. My husband, Bill, and I were heartbroken.

My doctor is a very compassionate man. Knowing that I had a strong faith and belief in God, he gave me this verse from the Bible: "The Lord stays close to the broken hearted and saves those whose spirits are crushed" (Psalms 34:18). That verse perfectly summed up how I felt.

My doctor stayed in very close contact with my husband and me, and he referred us to two different specialists. I became pregnant a third time under the care of a specialist in Indianapolis, but we lost our baby. I became pregnant a fourth time, this time with twins, under a specialist in Cincinnati. And we lost our babies again. I fell into a state of depression and underwent grief counseling.

I knew deep in my heart that I was meant to be a mommy. A friend of ours, whose son and wife were also having difficulties, told us that her son and daughter-in-law decided to adopt. They now have a beautiful little girl and feel that their family is complete. Our friend gave us the name of the Coleman Adoption Agency (an agency in Indiana), and we didn't hesitate to call. We are currently number one on the waiting list and have waited a total of 15 months thus far. I do not have any doubt in my mind or heart that I will love this baby just as much as I would have loved my other babies, had they lived. This baby has grown in my heart instead of my tummy.

Sherry Frazer

If this is you, the question you may be asking is, Are we too old? You're the only one who can answer that. How you answer depends on how you answer *these* questions:

- What's your energy level?
- How's your health?
- Are you overwhelmed with caring for aging parents?
- Have you made provisions for others to step in to parent if you're unable to continue?

Satisfied with the answers? If you are, then go for it!

Some people believe that older parents are preferable to younger ones because they're often more stable, mature, and financially secure than younger parents. So don't let the idea of how old you are now or how long adoption can take deter you. Besides, the time is going to pass anyway, regardless of whether or not you adopt.

Part II
Getting Started and Moving Forward, One Milestone at a Time

The 5th Wave   By Rich Tennant

"It's just until we hear from the adoption agency about finding a match for us."

In this part . . .

Once you make the decision to adopt, you're going to find yourself doing a lot of stuff, and most of it publicly. You have to find the agency or attorney you want to work with. You need to fill out applications, go through interviews, and submit to a home study (the social service equivalent of a proctology exam). You're going to await your child eagerly (and impatiently). And then you're going to have to make it through the supervision period in order to get to the finalization hearing so that you can finally heave a huge sigh of relief. Of course, all the work is worth it, and knowing what to expect can help you gear up for some of the more mind-numbing, patience-testing tasks you're going to encounter. This part helps guide you through those tasks.

Chapter 7

Getting the Ball Rolling: Finding an Agency or Lawyer

In This Chapter

▶ Making phone calls to obtain preliminary information

▶ Knowing what to look for in agencies and attorneys

▶ Using the services of an adoption facilitator

▶ Watching out for unscrupulous people

We can't stress enough the importance of the agency or attorney you work with in adopting a child. Good agencies and attorneys play it straight: They conduct their business in an ethical way. They're honest about what you can expect. They're experts on adoption laws and can help you avoid situations that may endanger the adoption. They inform you of any risks related to the adoption — and usually there are some And they keep the *child's* best interest at heart. But unless you've worked with a particular agency or attorney before — or know someone who has — you may be starting from scratch and wondering how in the world to find a good one.

This chapter helps you determine whether the agency or attorney you're interested in is reputable, explains the types of services you can expect from trustworthy agencies, gives you questions to ask — and the answers you should hear — and offers you tips on how to protect yourself from those who would take advantage of you. For information on pursuing adoption through an agency or an attorney and deciding which option is better for you, refer to Chapter 2.

Step One: Get on the Horn

The first step in an agency or attorney search is to take an afternoon, pick up the phone, and call the listings in the phone book that catch your eye. Keep a notebook handy with the name and number of each agency you call and jot down notes to yourself: "Left message." "Will send information packet." "5- to 7-year wait." "Presbyterians only." You'll get information, which is good, but you'll also get a feel for the agency or attorney. Are the people friendly and helpful? Are they willing to answer your questions? Do they *sound* like people you'd be comfortable working with?

While you have an attorney or agency on the phone, ask about the following:

✔ **Information packets:** These packets include general information about the agency or attorney (process, fees, application requirements, contact information, and so on), as well as encouraging stories and photos of families they've brought together.

✔ **Informational meetings offered:** These meetings, scheduled on a regular basis, give you an opportunity to meet the agency staff, hear about the process, and meet an adoptive couple.

Don't hesitate to ask for packets from every agency you contact. Receiving a packet doesn't obligate you to work with a particular agency. The same applies to the informational meetings. These aren't sales conferences, after all, and nobody will hound you to make a commitment or a decision.

The Internet may be a good place to start your initial agency/attorney search, but we strongly recommend that you make personal contact, if you can, with the organizations or people who run the sites. So much happens in an adoption that having an actual person to talk to or ask questions of can be both a help and a comfort.

When you're done making your initial phone calls, you'll discover that your initial list (which may have included everyone and her brother) is quite a bit smaller and includes those who sounded really nice and those who gave you the answers you wanted to hear. Now the *real* investigation begins.

Finding a Reputable Agency

Plenty of reputable agencies are out there, but not all of them are the right ones for you. Some may have application requirements you don't meet. Some may have philosophies you're not comfortable with. Some may have waiting periods that are too long or fees that are too steep. In the end, the agency you end up working with must be two things:

✔ **Reputable:** Reputable agencies don't fall into a single category, so, for example, you can't just look up nonprofit agencies and be assured that you've found a good agency. You have to do a little more homework than that.

✔ **One you like and are comfortable with:** Some people say that every woman falls in love with the obstetrician who delivers her baby. True or not, that adage illustrates the importance of the people who help you build your family. For you, that "person" is the agency. You have the right to feel good about the services you're getting and the people you're working with.

We can't help you with the latter. Only you know whether an agency feels "right" to you. But we can help you with the former. Reputable agencies do certain things, as the following sections explain.

What to look for

What you really want to find is an honest, ethical, licensed adoption agency that has several years of experience and that places many children each year. You want the staff to be competent, compassionate, patient, helpful, efficient, and available to you when you need them. If all this sounds too good to be true, don't despair. Many agencies that fit this description are out there.

The agency license

The very first thing you should find out is whether the agency is licensed or not. Licensed agencies must meet both state and federal regulations, and a licensing board regularly evaluates them. Agencies also have strict guidelines regarding the kinds of fees they can charge.

In doing the license investigation, call the office in your state that licenses agencies. Although the names of these offices differ in the different states (for example: Alabama, Department of Human Resources; California, Department of Social Services; Indiana, Division of Family and Children; Kentucky, Cabinet for Families and Children), you can call your local welfare office and ask specifically for the licensing office's number. When you reach the licensing agency, ask the following questions:

✔ **Is the license of the agency you're interested in current?** You want the answer to be yes. If the license isn't current, there's a reason why — and it probably isn't a good one.

Small problems don't cause the agency to lose its license. The agency is told about any minor issues, and it develops a plan to correct those within a certain amount of time. But stay away from agencies whose licenses have been revoked. Reasons for having a license taken away include big transgressions like

- Not following state adoption regulations or laws

- Not letting state personnel on the premises for an inspection or investigation of the facility

- Employing someone who's been convicted of a crime that could put children at risk

- Not submitting required reports or documents

- Practicing in an unethical or fraudulent way

✔ **When did the licensing board last visit the agency?** Depending on the laws in your state, the last review should be within the standard review period. Most states, for example, require an annual review.

✔ **Are there are any current or unresolved complaints against the agency?** These complaints can come from clients — both birthparents and adoptive parents — who've used the agency and include things like fraud; misleading statements and false promises; accepting money but not placing a child; increasing fees and tagging on additional, undisclosed fees; and making threats (pay this now or lose this child, for example).

Unlicensed agencies and facilitators (individuals who locate birthmothers for you; see Chapter 2 for details) aren't evaluated by licensing boards, and they aren't required to follow any specific regulations or guidelines. In fact, in many states, it's illegal for an agency or facilitator to operate *without* a license. If you're absolutely set on using an agency or facilitator who doesn't have a license (and we strongly recommend that you don't), make sure that you know your state laws regarding licensing and be extra vigilant as you move forward with your adoption plans.

Services to adoptive parents

Reputable adoption agencies provide numerous services to adoptive families. Following is a list of the ones you should expect:

✔ The agency should provide you with a completed home study. (If you don't know what the home study is or entails, head to Chapter 9.)

✔ The agency should provide education, training, and preparation in the area of adoption and the issues you'll face as an adoptive family.

✔ The agency or the assigned social worker should be accessible to you to discuss any questions or concerns you may have.

✔ The agency should closely communicate with you about your status while you wait for a placement.

✔ The agency should offer consistent support and encouragement.

✔ The agency should honestly communicate any areas of concern or any barriers to you as you try to build your family through adoption.

✔ The agency should maintain its commitment to you following placement of your child and offer all the necessary supervision visits and court reports for the court finalization.

✔ If you need help finding an attorney to do the legal work associated with all adoptions, the agency will either have one on staff or be able to give you some leads.

✔ The agency should be the mediator between you and the birthmother of your child if a mediator is desired. In this capacity, a social worker from the agency is present to help you and the birthmother decide the amount of openness you want in the adoption or how much contact you have during the pregnancy. The social worker also can help resolve conflicts, like when the birthmother drives the adoptive family nuts with continual phone calls or when the family hasn't sent the promised letter or picture to the birthmother.

Services to birthmothers

The services that agencies provide to birthmothers are a key component of a successful adoption. Following is a list of the services that reputable agencies commonly offer the women who come to them wanting to make adoption plans:

✔ **Ongoing counseling and support:** Reputable agencies offer counseling and support to the birthmother that lasts from the time she initially contacts the agency, through delivery and placement of the child, and as long as she needs help after placement. Most agencies offer home visits or transportation for these appointments if the birthmothers can't arrange transportation themselves. Some agencies also offer support groups for birthmothers.

✔ **Information about her options:** Not every woman who contacts an agency makes an adoption plan. Many decide to parent their children themselves. In counseling birthmothers, reputable agencies never try to coerce a birthmother into making a decision to place her child. They include a discussion about options other than adoption.

✔ **Help with doctor visits and referrals for other necessary services:** Some agencies offer referrals for prenatal care, transportation to doctor visits, and even baby-sitting for other children while the birthmother is being examined. Some agencies facilitate the birthmother's application for Medicaid or other public services.

✔ **Other stuff:** If the birthmother needs maternity clothes, housing, or food, most agencies assist in some way, often by offering referrals to shelters, transportation to food pantries, gift certificates to grocery or clothing stores, and so on. Some agencies ask the adoptive family for financial help to meet the birthmother's housing or other needs.

Birthmothers should always seek the services of the agency voluntarily, and they should always be treated with respect and understanding.

Miscellaneous signs of good agencies

Following are some other characteristics of reputable agencies:

✔ They know and follow adoption laws in their states.

✔ They keep the best interests of children in mind and work with state legislatures to enact adoption laws that are child-friendly.

✔ They often place information ads in the phone book and in local papers, but they don't go "shopping" for birthmothers.

✔ They allow the birthmother to secure the amount of openness she's comfortable with in the adoption and make sure that she understands she has the right to change her mind about the adoption before she signs the legal documents relinquishing her parental rights.

Questions to ask — and the answers you should get

Don't be afraid to ask questions. Agencies are asked questions several times a day. The folks at the agency will respect you for doing your homework and see it as a sign of thoroughness and responsible research. And believe us, the agency will not hesitate to ask *you* questions.

Here are some you can start with:

✔ **Is the agency licensed in your state?** If the answer isn't yes, thank whomever you're talking to for his time, hang up, and go to the next agency on your list.

✔ **What are the agency fees, what are they for, and when do you pay them?** Agency fees can range from a couple to several thousand dollars. What's important to you is whether you can afford the fee you're quoted. For more information on the costs of agency adoptions, head to Chapter 4.

✔ **What are the agency's specific requirements for families?** These requirements vary by agency, but you want to know two things: Do you qualify as an applicant, and are you comfortable with the agency's biases?

✔ **What type of adoptions (open, semi-open, infants, special needs, and so on) does the agency facilitate?** Again, the answer will differ by agency, but you want to make sure that the agency offers the type of adoption you're interested in pursuing.

✔ **What type of preparation or education is offered to the families?** In addition to the counseling you'll receive as part of the home study process, the agency should also offer — or be able to refer you to — additional educational opportunities like seminars, informational meetings, and so on. Many agencies can also suggest support groups that may help you prepare for the adoption.

✔ **What does the home study process entail?** The agency should inform you how many visits you'll have with the social worker, what information he'll peruse in making a recommendation, how long the process takes before approval, and so on.

What you *don't* want to hear is that a home study isn't necessary or that it's a formality. If an agency isn't interested in making sure that you can provide a suitable home, how interested do you think it is in making sure that other safeguards are followed?

✔ **What is the estimated length of time for the process — that is, from application to placement?** This is a hard question because the answer usually isn't what you want to hear. For many domestic adoptions, the answer can be anywhere from one year to several years. Sometimes things can happen much faster than that, of course. Sometimes, unfortunately, they can happen much slower.

✔ **What kind of post-placement supervision will be required?** The post-placement supervision refers to the visits the social worker arranges with you after your child comes home. The number and timing of the visits depend on your state's laws (if applicable), the country's requirements (if you're adopting internationally), or agency requirements. Most adoptions — international and domestic — require so many visits over a certain period of time.

✔ **What services does the agency offer birthmothers?** Head to the earlier section "Services to birthmothers" for the type of answers you should get to this question.

✔ **What happens when a birthmother we have connected with changes her mind about the adoption?** This question speaks to the fear that every adoptive family has at one time or another. And the answer is never a good one because, if people are honest, it can never be "Oh, don't worry about that. It won't happen" because it *does* happen, and no one can say with certainty that it won't happen to you.

The results of a contested adoption depend on the stage of the adoption (before the child is born, after the child is born, after the child is placed in your home, and so on) and the particular circumstances in your case. But before you panic, remember two things: First, a reputable agency doesn't involve adoptive families with placements that are likely to fall through. Second, every adoption carries some risk, and your agency should make sure that you understand the risks associated with your situation. For more information on how to deal with birthparents who change their minds, head to Chapter 18.

✔ **How many adoptions did the agency complete last year?** "None," obviously, is not a good answer. But what's a good answer? Basically you want to compare the number of placements to the number of waiting families. An agency that placed 50 kids sounds great — until you find out that it has 500 waiting families. Ask what the ratio is between placements and waiting families and then ask how this translates into the amount of waiting time.

Most agencies have a significant number of birthmothers who don't place, but actually, that can be a good thing. It means the birthmother isn't pressured and that she feels comfortable making the decision that's right for her — which means that she's more likely to be at peace after the child is placed in your home.

✔ **Can the agency provide a list of references of former clients you can contact?** The answer should be yes. If you're told that references are impossible because of confidentiality issues, be skeptical. The confidentiality that people want to protect is that between themselves and their child's birthparents. Most families who've built their families through adoption would love to help others do the same.

Finding a Reputable Adoption Lawyer — No Joke

Some adoption attorneys like working in the area of adoption because they enjoy the sense of satisfaction that comes when they help bring families together. Other adoption attorneys enjoy the warm feeling that comes from making lots of money. Your job is to discover which is which.

You can find attorneys in a lot of ways. You can check the Yellow Pages or search the attorney yellow pages on the Internet, for example. The trick is finding qualified attorneys who are competent and experienced in handling adoptions.

Many states offer a lawyer referral service through the state or city bar association. This service can provide you with names of qualified attorneys. The court that handles adoption in your state can usually provide you with a list of adoption attorneys practicing in your area. To find out what court handles adoptions in your area, call your local child welfare office — or, if you prefer, call any court number in the phone book — and ask.

What you want to see

Once you find a qualified attorney who has experience in or specializes in adoption, you're ready to dig a bit further. Look for an attorney who displays the following characteristics:

- ✔ **Sensitivity to the issues that adoptive parents face and compassion toward birthparents:** Listen for respectful language when describing birthmothers.

- ✔ **Honesty and an upfront attitude about the difficulties encountered in adoption:** If the attorney you're talking to paints a perfect picture, you can be sure that he isn't being totally honest.

- ✔ **An ethical approach, meaning that he doesn't believe in selling babies:** If the entire initial conversation with your attorney is about money, run the other way.

You should expect your attorney to answer phone calls promptly, speak to you in a language you can understand (not legalese), and allow time for all of your questions and concerns.

Services to adoptive parents

The major service an attorney offers to adoptive families is a legal one. As such, the adoption attorney should be an expert on the adoption laws in your state and fully aware of all laws that apply to your case. You should be able to count on your attorney to do the following:

- ✔ Prepare and provide all the legal documents necessary for an adoption
- ✔ Prepare and, in some cases, administer the adoption consent documents

- ✔ Prepare and file the petition for the adoption in court
- ✔ Accompany and represent you (the adoptive family) at the adoption hearing
- ✔ Negotiate the agreement for payment of birthmother expenses. Some attorneys may even handle the exchange of money.

Many people assume that, if you go through an attorney adoption, the attorney hooks you up with a birthmother. This may or may not be the case. Some attorneys have programs in place for locating birthmothers. Others rely on the adoptive family to find a birthmother.

Services to birthmothers (not many)

The attorney who represents you can't legally represent the birthmother, too. Although your attorney can offer information to the birthmother (for example, general points about the process or what to expect during the proceedings), she should get her legal guidance from her *own* attorney. In some states, separate legal representation for the birthmother isn't optional. State laws mandate that the birthmother have her own lawyer, and the adoptive families often provide that service for her.

Consider providing separate legal representation for the birthmother. Even if your state doesn't require it, it's still the ethical thing to do. It can also protect you. If the birthmother ever changes her mind and tries to claim she was misled or coerced, the fact that she wasn't represented could work in her favor. If your attorney suggests that separate legal counsel isn't necessary, you may want to find a different attorney.

Your attorney (unless he's also a licensed social worker with the necessary credentials) also isn't qualified to offer counseling to the birthmother; and he shouldn't even try to. Remember, your attorney works for *you,* and you don't want him to engage in any practice that could be seen as a conflict of interest.

Other things to look for

A reputable attorney will also do the following:

- ✔ Take any needed action to address the rights of the birthfather. Head to Chapter 14 for information on what rights birthfathers have.
- ✔ If the attorney facilitates adoptions across state lines, be familiar with the Interstate Compact on the Placement of Children (ICPC), the laws governing adoptions across state lines. (Refer to Chapter 3 for details on what the ICPC is and when it applies.)

✔ Insist that you undergo a complete home study and refer you to qualified agencies for this purpose.

✔ Encourage you to provide an opportunity for the birthmother to receive adoption counseling.

Questions to ask

When you speak to an attorney, you want to find out about her competence and area of expertise, her track record for adoptions, and other things regarding how she conducts business. To get you started, here are some questions to ask attorneys:

✔ **How long have you practiced law?** The answer to this question can give you an idea about the experience your lawyer has, but if she's spent most of her years working in real estate law, it's not going to be of much help to you. So whether the answer is 5 years or 25 years, make sure that you follow up with the next question.

✔ **What is your legal specialty?** If the answer is personal injury, find someone else. If the lawyer doesn't specialize in any particular area, probe some more, specifically about the adoptions, if any, she has helped facilitate. If you choose to adopt through an attorney, you want one who has experience — and a lot of it — specifically in adoption.

✔ **Do you belong to any professional organizations that relate to adoption?** Remember, however, that being listed as a member does not indicate the quality of the service she provides.

✔ **What is your familiarity with adoption laws in your state?** The attorney who represents you must know — forward and back — the adoption laws in your state. And remember, if you adopt from another state, your attorney needs to be intimately familiar with the legal aspects of that state as well.

✔ **What types of adoption (domestic, international, interstate) do you handle?** Make sure the lawyer has experience in the type of adoption you want to pursue.

✔ **How many adoptions do you facilitate each year?** You want adoptions to make up a significant part of the attorney's practice. Be wary if she doesn't do many. Think of it this way: How many brain surgeries would you want your doctor to perform before you're comfortable with him doing yours?

- ✔ **Have you ever had a complaint filed against you with the bar association and, if so, what action was taken?** Complaints include things like misleading advertising, exorbitant fees, failure to disclose known information (regarding the birthmother's or the child's medical, health, or family history), and misrepresentation. The complaints that should concern you more are the ones that indicate the attorney was dishonest or plotted to deceive the families she worked with.

  You can verify the information you get from the attorney by calling your state bar association and asking.

- ✔ **What is your experience with contested adoptions?** Although adoptions are contested, it doesn't happen often, so don't be surprised if the lawyer says that none of her adoptions have been contested. If this is the case, just make sure you're comfortable working with someone, who, in the event that your adoption *does* get contested, doesn't have any experience in those situations. On the other hand, having a lot of experience with contested adoptions doesn't necessarily bode well, either. The question then becomes, why have so many of her adoptions been contested?

- ✔ **What are your fees and when are they paid? Do you charge a flat fee or charge by the hour?** You also want to find out whether expenses such as photocopying and telephone calls are charged separately. For more information on the costs of attorney adoptions, head to Chapter 4.

- ✔ **If a birthmother changes her mind, do you expect me to pay the retainer fee again if I want to pursue another adoption?** Attorney adoptions can be expensive, and the *retainer* (the amount you give the attorney upfront to represent you) may be a significant portion of the total cost. If you're wealthy and have money coming out the wazoo, this may not be a big deal for you. For most people, however, it is a big deal, so make sure that you understand the attorney's policy.

- ✔ **Can you give me the names of references?** There's no reason not to get a yes answer here.

- ✔ **What services do you offer birthmothers?** Basically, your attorney can't ethically offer any services to the birthmother. After all, she represents *you*. But she can indicate the types of services she wants the birthmother to get (counseling, independent counsel, and so on) and how this can be arranged. See the earlier section "Services to birthmothers (not many)" for more information.

- ✔ **Who's responsible for securing background and medical information from the birthmother?** Some lawyers get the information for you as a routine part of the service they provide. Other lawyers don't. If the lawyer you hire is one who doesn't gather this information, you need to meet with the birthmother and get the information yourself.

Finding an Adoption Facilitator

Essentially, facilitators are baby finders: For a fee (most of which goes for advertising and profit), they locate a birthmother and hook the two of you up, and you make arrangements from there. If you use the services of a facilitator, you *still* need an attorney for the legal work and an agency for the home study, if a home study is required.

Most states don't license facilitators (California and Pennsylvania are the only two that do), which means that they work independently of any oversight or review board. In addition, their services are illegal in many states. If you decide to pursue adoption through a facilitator, become familiar with the laws in your state, know what you're getting into, and thoroughly investigate the facilitator you want to use.

Beginning the investigation

Adoption facilitators find birthmothers. That's about it. So when you talk with facilitators, you're basically trying to figure out whether they behave ethically in their search for birthmothers and how they screen the women who respond to their ads. Here are some questions you'll want to ask the facilitator:

- **What credentials do you have for doing this job?** Ask about education (degrees in social work or counseling, for example) and experience with adoption.

- **Why did you decide to become a facilitator?** This answer will differ from facilitator to facilitator, but what you'll probably hear is some version of the following:

  - I just love bringing families together.

  - My personal adoption experience (often as an adoptive parent) puts me in a unique position to help other families adopt.

  - I wanted to be a resource that wasn't available to me but that would have helped me when I was adopting.

  What you won't hear is "I'm in it for the money," but be advised that some adoption facilitators are.

- **What is your fee, when is it due, and what happens if the adoption plan falls through?** Most facilitators charge the majority of their fee upfront, just to put you in contact with a birthmother. Most don't guarantee a placement (how can they? No one can force a woman to follow through with an adoption plan). For more information on what fees to expect in a facilitator-assisted adoption, head to Chapter 4.

✔ **If we're working through a separate agency and get a placement through it, will you refund the fee (or any part of it) that we've already paid?** Although you'd like to get a yes answer on this one, you're more likely to hear no. Most facilitators make it pretty clear upfront that any fee paid is nonrefundable. As a result, many families who find themselves in this situation (having paid a fee to a facilitator but receiving a placement from somewhere else) just accept their losses.

✔ **How do you go about locating birthmothers?** Unlike agencies, whose birthmothers seek them out, facilitators actually go looking for birthmothers, and they can attract women in various ways — some ethical, some not. Advertising in newspapers, on bulletin boards, through obstetrical clinics, and so on is common. If you can, ask to see copies of the materials she circulates and then evaluate her tactics against your own sense of what is and isn't appropriate. Do the ads focus on the birthmother's options, for example, or do they focus on the financial aspects of placing a child?

✔ **How are birthmothers screened?** Do the facilitators verify, for example, that the woman is actually pregnant? Most reputable facilitators, as well as agencies, require a statement of pregnancy from the birthmother. Other things that the facilitator should pay attention to during the screening include whether the birthmother appears to be of sound mind and tells the same story (about the birthfather, her situation, and so on) each time she tells her story or changes the story during retelling. She should also note whether the birthmother denies using drugs but appears to be high, asks for lots of money or is overly concerned with the money aspect, sees a doctor regularly, and so on.

✔ **How do you handle potential problems or "red flags," such as drug or alcohol exposure, in a birthmother?** If the person you're talking to tells you that she's never encountered a problem with the birthmothers, probe a little deeper. Why hasn't she encountered red flags? Perhaps she hasn't been in business long, or maybe she doesn't work with birthmothers whose histories may present a challenge. More likely, though, she has dealt with these issues before, and you want to make sure that her policy is to inform you of any situation that may impact the adoption.

✔ **How many successful adoptions have you facilitated?** If you work with a facilitator, you want this number to be high. It may be a good indicator that the facilitator has had significant experience in locating and screening birthmothers and that she works through potential problems and risks in a responsible way.

✔ **How many of your adoptions have been challenged in court?** Obviously, you want this number to be low. But, unfortunately, there are few ways to independently verify the information you receive, other than talking with families who have used her services.

If you live in a state that licenses facilitators, call the licensing board and ask for information about any complaints filed.

✔ **Can you give me names of references?** Ask for lots and lots of references and question those references fully. The next section tells you how.

In many facilitator-assisted adoptions, you're in one state, and your facilitator is in another. (Many families hook up with facilitators through the Internet.) If this is the case, try to arrange to meet the facilitator in person. Given the relative newness of adoption facilitators and the fact that most states don't license them, you don't really have much to go on in your investigation. So your gut instinct may end up playing a bigger role, helping you answer any questions you may have. Is she trustworthy? Is she someone you'd feel comfortable working with? Do you agree with her philosophy on adoption? Are you satisfied that she can even get the information you need to make a good decision for your family?

Getting in touch with a doctor

I (Tracy) told my doctor that my husband and I were planning to adopt when I asked him to fill out our agency's physical exam form. He assumed I was telling him we were adopting because he was an Ob/Gyn and had access to a bunch of pregnant ladies and could perhaps hook me up with one who was considering adoption. Some people, it seems, get referrals for birthmothers from their family doctors. If you're one of them, keep these things in mind:

✔ If a doctor gives you a name and phone number of a woman who may be considering adoption, you have to arrange a private adoption, through an attorney.

✔ You can pretty much forget about any anonymity. Unless a special arrangement is made in which a representative acts as a go-between, you'll be the ones getting in touch with the birthmother, making the arrangements, and so on. And don't forget, you and she share the same doctor, so you'll be connected in that way, too.

✔ Two major concerns in any adoption in which the primary agent helping you is not a qualified social worker or agency are "Who is counseling the birthmother?" and "What is her understanding of the adoption process?"

✔ Laws about who can and can't facilitate an adoption vary by state. Some states, for example, stipulate that only licensed adoption agencies can match a birthparent with adoptive parents. So when a doctor hooks you up with a person considering adoption, he's essentially performing a function that, in those states, only licensed adoption agencies can perform. In other states, where adoption facilitators are illegal, using a doctor in that role is illegal, too. So know the laws in your state before you pursue this option.

Checking on the references

With your list of references in hand, you can gather quite a bit of information about how the facilitator works, whether her clients have been happy with the service she provides, and so on. Here are some questions you'll want to pursue with the folks you call:

- ✔ What was your experience with this facilitator like? Was she competent? Was she honest?
- ✔ Did things occur as she led you to believe they would?
- ✔ Was she helpful, supportive, available, fair, kind, and so on?
- ✔ What did she charge you? Did you encounter any unexpected expenses?
- ✔ How long did you wait for a match? How many matches did you get before you received a placement?
- ✔ What did you dislike about her?
- ✔ Would you use her services again or recommend her to your friends?

The reference list is only as good as it is complete. If clients who experienced problems aren't included, the impression you'll get will be skewed.

Protecting Yourself

You can do several things to protect yourself from the vagaries of adoption. First, be realistically hopeful: You will have a child, but no one can guarantee when that'll happen. Second, work with reputable people. The preceding sections explain how to figure that out.

The following sections outline a couple other things you can do to protect your interests, increase your chances for a quick placement, and help you recognize when you should bid farewell to the agency or attorney you're working with.

Scouting around

As you proceed with your adoption plans and share your excitement with others, you're going to hear all kinds of stories from people who've been through it or who know someone who knows someone who's been through it. You'll hear things like "We decided to use an attorney instead of XYZ agency, and *we* got a baby in two months," or the always popular "I've heard of that attorney. I know a couple who used him, and their adoption fell through."

You want to feel comfortable enough with the agency or attorney you're working with so that, when you hear stories like these, you don't begin to question whether you made the right decision. One of the most important things you can do to protect yourself and your interests is to take the time to investigate as many options as possible that are available to you. If you're looking for an agency, look at a lot of agencies. If you're hunting for an attorney, call several. Yes, much of the information will be the same, but that's not the point. The point is finding a fit that's good for you. What makes *you* comfortable? That's what's important.

The other thing you can do is to try to independently verify the information you get. Contact the following organizations for information on the people and agencies you're investigating:

- ✔ **Better Business Bureau:** You can get the number for a local office from the phone book. Alternatively, you can use the Internet: Go to `www.betterbusinessbureau.com`, click the About the BBB option, and then click Locate a BBB.

- ✔ **State attorney general's office:** To contact your state's attorney general, simply look the number up in the government section of your phone book. If you're online, you can go to the Web site of the National Association of Attorneys General at `www.naag.org` and select your state from the list in the Find Your Attorney General box.

- ✔ **National Council for Adoption:** NCFA is a national organization of non-profit adoption agencies. Based in Washington, D.C., it provides information and education on adoption and monitors public policy relating to adoption. You can contact the NCFA through this address: 225 N. Washington Street, Alexandria, VA 22314-2561. The number is 703-299-6633. Or go online to `www.ncfa-usa.org`.

Working with more than one agency

If you're anxious to adopt as quickly as possible, you can try to speed the process by getting your name on the lists of more than one agency. Doing so increases your opportunities to be selected by a birthmother. Although some agencies won't agree to work with a family that is already working with another agency, other agencies welcome it.

If you want to work with more than one agency, you work through one agency to get your home study completed. With the completed home study in hand, contact other agencies and ask whether they'll add you to their waiting list. If they will, you usually have to pay their application fee (and possible other fees) and provide them with copies of your current home study. When you receive a child, you pay the fee that the agency placing the child charges.

If you do work with multiple agencies, keep these things in mind:

✔ Working with multiple agencies may cause some confusion. Each agency may have different policies, fees, and so on.

✔ You may be simultaneously matched with birthmothers from more than one agency. If this is the case, you'll be asked to select just one. No matter how you look at it, that decision will be hard.

Knowing when you should move on

Sometimes, despite the positive beginnings, it becomes apparent that an agency and a family are no longer a good fit. If the agency's practices and/or personnel aren't compatible with the adoptive family, it may be time to look elsewhere. You may have reason to be concerned if

✔ The agency promises big things that don't come to pass, such as "a baby in six months or less," and you've already waited a year.

✔ The agency staff isn't consistently available and willing to respond to your questions or concerns.

✔ You notice the lack of agency organization during the initial intake process (when you get your initial info from the agency, submit your application, and so on). Examples of lack of organization include failing to mail promised documents, not knowing the answers to your questions, not being able to find the necessary paperwork, forgetting who you are and what you wanted, missing scheduled appointments or arriving late, and so on.

✔ The agency doesn't return your phone calls.

✔ The agency charges extra fees that it hasn't discussed with you.

✔ The agency pressures you into situations you're not comfortable with (for example, pressuring you to accept more openness than you're comfortable with, more expenses than you can afford to pay, or a child with more medical challenges than you think you're emotionally and financially prepared to handle, and so on).

✔ The agency isn't open and honest with you or operates in an unethical way. Examples of dishonest behavior include things like the following:

- Failing to mention the birthmother's regular cocaine use or failing to disclose her negative mental health status

- Promising you things it can't deliver and offering excuses when you ask what happened

- Suggesting that you do something illegal or unethical, like slipping some extra money to the birthmother when the agency worker isn't looking

- Pressuring you to pay more if you "don't want to lose this placement"

- Talking about birthmothers in a disparaging way or suggesting that you misrepresent yourself to the birthmother

Chapter 8

Thinking about Your Future Child

*W*henever I (Tracy) thought about my future children, they were always in overalls and, for some reason, standing in a spotlessly clean kitchen and holding tomatoes they had picked from the garden. Now, I don't garden. And my kitchen could be accurately described as spotlessly clean only one time in my memory — and that was after our house was built but before we moved in. The point? Most people have idealized images of their future children and never have to think much beyond that backlit, soft-focused picture. But *you* do. The people who are going to help you build your family are going to ask you to describe the child you want, and they need more information than "wonderful." They need specifics.

The questions you're going to be asked are hard to answer because you may discover that you don't like — or you feel guilty about — your answers. But as hard as it is and as much as you may want to say, "*Any* child would be a welcome addition to our family," you must be honest. And maybe you honestly don't know. That's okay, too.

This chapter lists the things you're going to be asked about the child you want to adopt and explains some of the things you need to think about. You can also find advice on what you can do to prepare yourself to parent the child you've described.

Describing Your Child

When you approach your agency with the intent to adopt a child, one of the first things you'll be asked is, "What type of child are you interested in?" Specifically, the agency wants to know the following:

- ✔ What age child do you want to adopt?
- ✔ Do you have a preference for a boy or a girl?
- ✔ Would you consider adopting a child outside your race?
- ✔ Are you interested in parenting a child who may have special needs?

The more requirements you have regarding age, gender, race, and health status, the fewer the opportunities to adopt will be. Be honest about what you think you can handle, but at the same time, remain as flexible as possible.

Baby, toddler, adolescent, teen: Specifying age

One of the first considerations you have to make in describing the child you want to adopt is the child's age. Whether you're most interested in parenting an infant or an older child is, of course, a very personal decision. The following sections give you things to consider about your options.

In the United States, most infant adoptions are arranged through a private agency or an attorney. Older children and sibling groups are most often placed through public agencies. Keep this idea in mind as you choose who you want to help you build your family.

Infants and toddlers

Although each agency seems to have a different definition of what constitutes an infant, infant placements generally include newborns to children up to 2 years old. To understand what ages your agency specifically considers to fall into the infant category, simply ask. If you're adopting internationally, you don't usually request an "infant" or "toddler" per se. Instead, you indicate the ages you're interested in: 0–2 years or 2–4 years, for example.

Most first-time parents prefer to start off with a newborn infant. Benefits of adopting an infant include the early bonding, the opportunity to significantly mold that developing little character, and the chance to have the experience that most closely resembles that of having a child by birth.

When you adopt an infant, you need to be prepared to deal with the following issues and situations:

- **Prenatal "hangovers":** Prenatal care, or the lack of it, as well as prenatal exposure to medications, drugs, and alcohol can have both short- and long-term effects on the baby. You need to be willing to accept some degree of uncertainty regarding what exactly the effects are, how long they will last, and how serious they are. Remember, however, that you may never know everything that your child was exposed to. When you adopt, you take the risk that the baby was exposed to something you aren't aware of.

  Reputable agencies and attorneys inform you of any information they have that could impact a child's health and development, and they don't sugar-coat things, either. But that doesn't mean they can guarantee that you will or won't have to deal with certain issues. To find out more about the ramifications of certain types of medical conditions or prenatal exposure, talk to a pediatrician, a neonatal specialist, or any other expert who can give you the information you need.

- **Unknown or undisclosed health issues and genetic histories:** Agencies and attorneys gather the medical information from the birthmothers — and birthfathers if they're involved in the adoption plan. They ask for all sorts of information about the birth mom *and* about her family so that they can give you as complete a picture as possible. But even if the birthmother tells everything she knows (and most of them do), you still don't know everything. And even if you *did* know everything, you still wouldn't necessarily know what that information means specifically for your child.

- **Telling your child he's adopted:** If you adopt an older child, you'll have all sorts of issues to deal with, but introducing the idea of adoption isn't one of them. They already know. An infant won't — and you get to be the one to tell her. Chapter 16 explains how and when to share this information.

- **Life histories of older infants:** If you adopt an older infant, you need to be aware of that child's life history — as brief as it may be. Of course, knowing whether your child was abused or neglected is important, even if she's just a couple months old. Similarly, you may want to find out whether your child has bonded to her previous caregiver. But keep in mind, even with this information, no one can know what that specifically means for your child.

Older kids

Although most first-time parents prefer to start off with a newborn infant, many other parents prefer the challenge of older children. Benefits to adopting older children include the satisfaction of making a huge difference in a child's life and the rewards of seeing a child learn to trust and possibly return your love. When you consider adopting older children, keep in mind that it helps if you have certain, specific qualities. You should

- Be tolerant of difficult or disruptive behaviors and consistent in your approach to them.
- Be willing to take the classes or training necessary to help you better parent your child.
- Be confident enough that you don't need the "warm fuzzies" and can tolerate a child's negative or ambivalent feelings toward you.
- Be flexible in your expectations but structured in your routine.
- Have a good sense of humor.
- Have lots of support from your spouse, family, and friends.
- Know how to seek out professional help and resources and be willing to become an advocate for your child.
- Know how to take care of yourself so that you remain strong and emotionally healthy.
- Be prepared to commit to a child for "better or worse."

When considering a specific older child for adoption, knowing that child's history is important. Pay special attention to these issues:

- **The child's history of emotional bonding:** Has the child bonded with anyone, and if so, who? What is the status of that relationship now?
- **Whether he has ever been physically or sexually abused:** If your child has suffered any kind of abuse, you're going to be the one who helps him deal with the aftereffects. Consequently, you need to know everything you can about the situation so that you can anticipate and respond to the behaviors that commonly spring from abuse.
- **What he thinks about being adopted:** You may be on cloud nine, but your child may have very different feelings. You need to be able to accept those feelings without being hurt or interpreting them as rejection.
- **How long it's been since he was in contact with his birth family:** Depending on the situation, your child very well may know his birth family. If he does, he *will* feel connected to them, even if he's been horribly abused. In fact, he will most likely wish he could still live with his birthparents again.

Chapter 16 discusses in detail these and other issues you're likely to face when you adopt older children, and it offers suggestions and advice on how to deal with them.

On your mark, get set, go! Specifying race

You're white or black or Asian, and you want to adopt. In America, you can adopt a child of any race. No one presumes anymore that you want the child you adopt to be the same race that you are. So the question comes to you: What race(s) are you open to? Before you answer this question, you need to decide whether it's important to you that your children share your race. For most people, the answer is either yes or it depends on the race. For others, the answer is no.

Some white couples are willing to adopt lighter-skinned minority children or kids who have few, if any, characteristics of another race, and then kid themselves that they're open to transracial adoption. If you're open to minority children who "look white," you ain't open to transracial adoption. And if you claim that you want a lighter-skinned child so that you won't have to deal with racism, you're fooling yourself.

Sometimes, minority children are more readily available for adoption than white children. This is wonderful if you're also of a minority race or are open to transracial adoption. Obviously, if you're white and you want a white child, the situation can be frustrating. But don't adopt transracially just for the convenience. Deciding to become an interracial family changes your life forever, and you're going to have to deal with many things that same-race families don't:

- ✔ **You'll be a family that other people notice.** Not only will you receive stares, but some people will be bold enough to ask questions: Is she adopted? Are you baby-sitting? Is this your foster child? Is this your child from another relationship? When you adopt transracially, this part of the adoption experience never goes away.

    You're a grown-up. You can handle the questions without letting other people's curiosity or stupidity or presumptuousness affect your sense of worth and belonging. But when you have a little one at your elbow wondering why people are asking about her, you need to help her come out of the experience whole, too. Head to Chapter 17 for guidance and suggestions.

- ✔ **You're making the decision to become a minority family, and people will treat you differently because of it.** Don't kid yourself. People are still race-conscious, no matter what they say, and you'll get unpleasant reminders of this throughout your child's life.

✔ **To protect your child from hurtful situations, you may end up having to sever relationships that mean a lot to you.** Your family, for various reasons, may not support your decision to adopt transracially. If your family's lack of support turns into hostility or if your family treats your child different from other kids in the family, you have to put your child first, and if that means no longer visiting Grandma, that's what you have to do.

Here are some things you may want to consider if you're thinking about adopting transracially:

✔ Do you live in an integrated neighborhood? Are the school systems in your area integrated? If not, are you willing to move?

✔ Are you prepared to face the discrimination that will come?

✔ Are you comfortable with interracial relationships and marriages?

✔ Are the people close to you supportive of your decision to adopt interracially?

✔ Are you willing to learn about your child's racial and cultural heritage and to make the effort to share your knowledge with your child?

✔ Can you make the commitment to seek out same-race positive role models for your child?

If you can answer yes to all of these questions — or if you're willing to make the necessary changes — transracial adoption may be for you.

Native American children and adoption

A federal law called The Indian Child Welfare Act (ICWA) establishes a policy for the adoption of Native American children. ICWA rules apply if the child or the child's birthparents are registered members of a tribe, or if the child is eligible to become a member of a tribe.

Basically, this law gives the tribe a legal interest in a child, similar to the legal rights of a biological parent. Basically you have to get tribal permission for the adoption. Many tribes cooperate in an adoption when they know the biological parent (also of Indian descent) wants the adoption and if the adoptive parents agree to honor the child's heritage. (If you have a Native American background or heritage, bring this to the attention of your social worker. Tribes may be more favorably inclined to a placement if they know that the adoptive parents have Indian ancestors.)

Many people erroneously interpret this law to mean that non-Native Americans can never adopt a child of Native American heritage. You can; you just need to follow the rules when you do. So if you adopt a child of Native American heritage, make sure that your attorney is knowledgeable about the ICWA and plans to follow the proper procedures. If the procedures aren't followed, the adoption could be challenged at a later time.

Considering special needs and disabilities

The category of special needs can include a wide variety of situations, illnesses, or conditions. The title *special needs* may include the following:

- ✔ Children with surgically correctable conditions
- ✔ Children exposed to drugs or alcohol prenatally
- ✔ Children with worrisome family health histories
- ✔ Children with serious disabilities or challenges
- ✔ Children with a physical, mental, or emotional disability that may range from mild to severe
- ✔ Children who are older or who are part of a sibling group

So before you quickly say no to a special-needs child, ask the agency what type of special-needs children it places.

If you're drawn to adopting a special-needs child and ask for one specifically, your agency will probably ask you to fill out a questionnaire regarding the types of special needs you would consider. Take the time to thoughtfully consider and discuss each category. When you do, be sure to figure in the following:

- ✔ **Think about the ages of the children you have (if you have any) and the needs of the child you want to adopt.** If you have young children who take up a lot of your time, you may not be the best fit for a child who needs a lot of one-on-one attention.

- ✔ **Think about your interests and pastimes and how you would incorporate a child with specific needs into your lifestyle.** If you take regular hiking and rock climbing vacations, a child confined to a wheelchair may not be a good fit. A child with emotional challenges or a child with a hearing loss, however, may fit right in.

- ✔ **Think about the resources available in your community.** If a child requires regular therapy and the closest therapy center is a two-hour drive away, you may want to rethink that specific scenario. Check out the specialists in your area and the availability of pertinent support groups. Also think about day-care and child-care availability in your location.

Most agencies let you consider each situation on a case-by-case basis. They'll tell you about the specifics of each case and allow you to decide whether you want to be considered.

Bats in the genetic belfry and other family history issues

If a birthmother suffers from schizophrenia or her grandmother suffers from schizophrenia, what does that mean for her child?

If a child is born from an incest situation, does that mean that child will be mentally retarded or impaired?

If a birthmother comes from a family full of addicts, will her child suffer from addictions as well?

These questions are ones that families commonly ask when offered children with scary family histories. But because the answers to these and other questions might surprise you, follow this advice:

✔ **Don't automatically rule out specific situations before you investigate them.** You may think that you know the correct answers, but you may not be aware of what current research is saying.

✔ **Think about your own family history.** Do you have a relative who suffers from a mental illness or who is prone to depression? Does your family history include any incidents of alcoholism or addictions? If so, then your birth child would have had a questionable family history, and yet you may have tried desperately to conceive that child.

✔ **Use the information to help your child.** Information is power. Say that you know that your daughter's birth grandmother and aunt both had breast cancer. Yes, you may worry that your daughter will get it too, but you can use this knowledge to protect her.

You certainly have the option of saying that you don't want to be considered for any child whose genetic tree has skeletons hanging from a few limbs. But know that you're significantly reducing your chances of being offered a placement. A better solution — if you want a child, anyway — is to be open to different scenarios and then investigate them as they arise.

One, two, or more? Sibling groups or singles

Obviously, two or more children may require more work than one; raising them will definitely be more expensive than raising just one; and people are likely to think you're crazy to consider more than one. However, adopting a sibling group or twins has its advantages:

- ✔ Older children who are placed with siblings are comforted by the presence of the others and may make a smoother adjustment.

- ✔ As your children grow older, they'll appreciate having that genetic connection to someone.

- ✔ Most domestic agencies place twins for one placement fee, and sibling groups are most often placed through state public agencies, which generally have no adoption fee. In international adoptions, many agencies increase (but don't double) their fees for twins or siblings. Here, you reap the savings because you may be able to build your entire family in one trip, instead of making multiple trips.

When you adopt older children, you usually have some significant issues to deal with, and those issues are multiplied by the number of children. For information on the situations you can expect to face with older kids, head to Chapter 16.

Honesty Is the Best Policy — Honest

When you tell your agency what situations you're interested in and what you think you can handle, be honest and straightforward. Keep these things in mind:

- ✔ **No one is judging you or being critical of you.** Your social worker knows that it's in the child's best interest to be placed in a family that's prepared to parent that child.

- ✔ **All children deserve to be valued and loved for who they are.** There's a family out there for every child — a family who would welcome that child as a blessing in their life. Don't take that opportunity away from a child by grudgingly accepting him into your home when another family would welcome him with more-open arms.

Before you can be honest with someone else, you need to be honest with yourself. But maybe you don't know what you can handle as a parent. If that's the case, now's the time for contemplation — even if it means putting off your adoption plans for a while. You owe it to yourself and your future child.

Making the Info Work for You

When you adopt, you actually get quite a bit of information upfront — information that you can use to get a running start on parenting. You usually have info on medical histories, prenatal conditions, and so on. In many cases, especially when you adopt a healthy infant, this is information you keep in the back of your mind, to draw on when needed. If you adopt an older child or a child who has special medical or emotional needs, you can use this information now, not only to help you understand what you're going to be facing as a parent but also to amass the resources and help you need for your child. The following sections explain how.

Finding out what you need to know

Take every opportunity to get all the information you can on your child. Ask your agency for thorough medical and social histories. Peruse them, talk to your social worker about things you don't understand, or ask your pediatrician or family doctor about medical issues you're uncertain about.

If your child has special medical needs, also ask for copies of all medical testing and reports, and get a list of all doctors who've treated your child. If you think that talking to the doctors yourself would be helpful, schedule appointments with them.

If you adopt an older child, you'll also want to do the following:

✔ **Ask your social worker about your child's *life book*.** This book is like a scrapbook of your child's life. It contains photos, info about each placement, mementos, and birth family info. If he doesn't have one, ask the worker to assist you in making one. For more information, see the sidebar "A child's life book" in this chapter.

✔ **Ask to speak with any foster mothers, teachers, or child-care workers who have been involved with the child.** Here are some things you may want to know and can find out from these people:

- The child's personality, as well as her likes and dislikes

- The discipline techniques that are successful

- The child's usual schedule

- The specific challenges the child has and how those are being addressed

- What medical problems the child's had, what treatment she received, and what medications she's on

- The child's strengths and positive qualities

✔ **If available to you, ask for copies of birth certificates, Social Security cards, Medicaid cards, and so on, for your child.** These may have sentimental value to your child. (*Note:* If someone has a concern about maintaining confidentiality, you may not get these records, because they have the child's last name on them.)

Seeking resources to help you parent your child

Depending on the child you adopt, you may need to seek out therapies, counseling, or other programs to help you parent your child and to help your child adjust. Your agency should be able to assist you in the following ways:

✔ Guide you to appropriate counseling or parenting resources in your community

✔ Recommend any adoptive parent support groups available

✔ Provide you with preliminary information on any subsidies or reimbursement programs you qualify for (for more on these, refer to Chapter 4)

You can also ask your doctor for referrals for any medical or therapy needs your child may have. Some communities offer special clinics to address the specific needs of internationally adopted children. You can find information about these in the phone book and on the Internet.

A child's life book

Years ago, kids who grew up in foster care often, as adults, didn't know who in the world they lived with, for how long, or where they were located. Life books are designed to keep that from happening. The idea is to keep the book with the child so he always has access to his own personal history with the hope this will help him to make some sense out of what he has been through.

The life book contains as much factual information as possible and includes every placement (foster and adoptive), along with names, dates, addresses, photos, souvenirs (like ticket stubs), and so on. When photos and other information aren't available, the child and worker can use drawings to illustrate the events. The life book is an ongoing project. With each placement the child goes into, information gets added to the book.

A risk worth taking

When we told the agency we were interested in adopting, we received a questionnaire. After some soul searching, we checked the "will consider" box to indicate that we would consider adopting babies affected by drugs, alcohol, rape, and other areas that some people would consider too risky. When the agency called us with a possible placement, our worker told us that the birthmother drank heavily, smoked marijuana, and admitted to cocaine use through her pregnancy.

I called my husband at work and filled him in on all the details and then spent the rest of the day researching fetal alcohol syndrome (FAS), fetal alcohol effects (FAE), drug exposure on children in utero, and what we might expect in the future based on the information we had. The research was pretty scary. Fetal alcohol syndrome is permanent. No matter how much you love a child, nurture a child, pray, whatever, you cannot reverse the effects of FAS. We learned that FAE is a more subtle form of FAS, and that it's harder to detect in a newborn. We also learned that cocaine and marijuana exposure is actually less harmful than alcohol.

My husband and I spent the entire evening reading over the information, asking ourselves important questions like, "What if he's mentally handicapped?" "How much of a disability can we actually deal with?" and "What about our other son?" As we pondered these questions and tried to make a reasonable and logical decision, our hearts were telling us that this was our son.

We decided to trust our intuition.

About a week and a half later, the baby was born. In addition to other information, our social worker told us that he tested positive for marijuana and that some of the hospital personnel believed that he had a few initial characteristics of FAS. When we arrived at the hospital and saw him, he was so tiny and fragile looking. I picked him up and immediately felt a bond with him. I handed him to my husband, and we both fell in love. I spent the rest of that day and night by his bed. As a nurse who happened to have a lot of experience with drug-exposed children was talking with me, the baby began to cry. When I picked him up to comfort, he immediately stopped crying. She told me my being able to comfort him was an excellent sign. Nothing anyone said could have made me any happier. Problems or not, I was his mother, and I could comfort him and stop his crying.

On the day that we were to check out of the hospital, the doctor informed us that he had found a Grade II brain hemorrhage. After hearing this news, the director of the agency asked if we were changing our minds. How could we? In our minds, this baby was our son, and no matter what, we would stand by him and take care of him. I am happy to say that our son is now a happy, healthy 23-month-old who is a never-ending source of joy for our family. He is a smart, affectionate, rambunctious, and energetic little boy who lights up the lives of all who come to know him. I would not go back and change one thing. My husband and I thank God every day for our son. No one knows what the future will bring, but good or bad, our son can count on us to help him through. After all, that what's families are for.

Identifying information withheld

Chapter 9

Applications, Home Studies, and Other Really Fun Stuff

In This Chapter

▶ Completing the application

▶ Preparing for and making it through the home study

▶ Creating your profile for the birthmother

*R*emember seventh-grade science class and the teacher who exposed you to animal dissection with the class frog? Well, now you get to be the frog. After you commit yourself to building a family through adoption, the dissection — make that investigation — begins.

People you don't know (yet) will want information about you: your views on adoption and parenting, your finances, your health (mental and physical), your relationship with your spouse (and any marriages you may have had in the past), the house you live in, and the family you come from, ad nauseum. They want to know what brought you to the decision to adopt (and how you feel about that) and what you plan to do after you get your child. They'll do a criminal background check, and they'll check with your references to make sure you're as wonderful as you claim to be. And then, when you're done convincing the agency that you'll be a good parent, chances are, with the openness of adoptions today, you're going to have to convince the birthmother, too, and you do that by creating a profile of your family.

The information in this chapter can help you survive the intensive investigation with as little stress — and hair pulling — as possible. You also can find information on what to put in your profile so that you can help the birthmother see all that you have to offer a child.

This process may feel intrusive, but it's necessary. It's also an indication that the agency or attorney/facilitator you're dealing with is a reputable one. No person or agency should be in such a hurry to place a child — nor should you be in such a hurry to adopt — that the well-being of the child isn't the first and most important consideration.

Filling Out the Application

When you work with an adoption agency, the application is the first thing you fill out. In addition to a questionnaire, you may also be required to submit other paperwork — things like doctors' reports, financial statements, and so on. Most agencies, however, consider the supporting documentation to be part of the home study (see the section "Show and Tell Time: The Home Study" later in this chapter for details on that).

The application is really the first step in the screening process. The agency reviews the application to make sure that you meet its criteria before the home study begins.

If you work with an attorney or facilitator who requires a home study, you still need to fill out the application and pay an application fee to the agency that does the home study. Even though you're not working with the agency for a placement, the agency application serves as the initial information for the home study, and the application fee goes toward the background checks and other stuff that the agency will be performing.

Providing the required info

When you ask an agency for an application, don't be surprised if the application is several pages long (and this is just the beginning of the paperwork you fill out; see the later section "The orientation: Welcome to paperwork heaven" for details on the supporting documentation you need to provide).

Although applications vary by agency, you can expect to see the following categories in most of the applications you receive:

- ✔ **Contact information:** This includes info like your name, your address, and the phone numbers that agency personnel can use to reach you.

- ✔ **Personal information:** This info includes your Social Security number, your birth date and place of birth, your height and weight, your hair and eye color, your race, your education, and your religion and what church you attend.

✔ **Health information:** Your health info includes your health history, your doctor's name, and your health insurance info.

✔ **Information about your marriage:** If you're married, you need to provide info regarding the date of your marriage and how long you've been married, as well as info about previous marriages and the dates of your divorces.

✔ **Work history:** Here, you include your current occupation and employer and how long you've been employed there. You also need to list previous employment, including the length of time employed and names of your former bosses.

✔ **Criminal history:** Include in this category things like arrests, convictions, and so on.

You may be tempted to lie or gloss over the criminal history section, but don't — for a couple reasons. First, the agency will run a criminal background check and find whatever you're trying to hide anyway. Second, having been in trouble with the law won't necessarily disqualify you, but *lying* will. Head to Chapter 5 for tips on how to deal with events in your past you'd rather forget.

✔ **Financial information:** This info includes how much you make, as well as how much debt you have.

✔ **Information about where you live:** Most agencies want to know what type of home (apartment, mobile home, and so on) you live in and whether you're renting or buying.

✔ **The type of child you're interested in:** Often a series of check boxes that you mark to indicate whether you're open to certain things or not, the categories include things like age, gender, race, and so on. See Chapter 8 for information on describing your future child.

✔ **Names and addresses of references:** Usually, the agency has rules regarding whom you can list as references. It may, for example, want only non-relatives whom you've know for a certain number of years.

✔ **Previous home study info:** This applies if you've had another home study done either in the past (for another placement, for example) or recently, which may be the case if you were working with another agency that didn't approve you for a child. See the upcoming section "Dealing with the news if you don't 'pass'" for an explanation of why this situation may occur.

✔ **Info on your family:** If you already have children in your home, you have to give their names and their birth dates and specify whether they are birth children or adopted children. You may also be asked to give info on your parents, including their name, address, age, occupation, employment, health, education, and religion. Similar information may be requested for each of your siblings.

✔ **How-you-heard-about-us info:** You'll probably be asked to state how you heard about this particular agency. To mess with their minds, write "It came to me in a dream" here.

Show me the money! — application fees

Application fees, which are usually not refundable, are required to cover the agency's cost in processing your application. (Processing includes things like creating a file for you and adding your information to agency databases. It can also include things like submitting requests for criminal history reports and contacting references.)

Paying the fee shows the agency that you're serious about adopting a child from it. Once the agency receives your application and the fee, it considers you one of its clients and gets busy helping you build your family.

For more information about application fees and all the other fees and expenses associated with adoption, head (trepidatiously) to Chapter 4.

Show and Tell Time: The Home Study

After you complete your application (as described in the preceding section), the agency schedules your home study.

Although the name of this step in the process may lead you to believe that the most important part of the home study is the actual examination of where you live, that is only one facet. The home study actually includes these elements:

✔ **Interviews with you and your spouse (if you're married):** These interviews take the questions from the application to a whole new level. Expect to go into more detail about the answers you gave on the application form, as well as discuss other issues.

✔ **Forms, forms, and more forms, as well as supporting documentation:** This documentation, which includes things like your medical report, your personal references, and so on, is used to verify the information you provide.

✔ **A visit to your home:** The social worker who works for or is appointed by the adoption agency will schedule a time to visit (she won't surprise you).

✔ **Education on adoption issues:** In addition to checking you out, the social worker takes this time to discuss issues that you're likely to encounter as an adoptive parent and to offer information about any special resources you may want to tap into.

Depending on the time of year, how busy your social worker is, and how long it takes to run the necessary checks and amass the necessary documents, a home study can take anywhere from a few weeks to a few months.

Although you can't impact when holidays fall throughout the year or how much vacation time your social worker has to use up, you still have a big impact on how long the home study takes. Before your social worker can complete the home study report (discussed later in this section), she has to have all your completed paperwork (your financial statements, your medical reports, any extra questionnaires the agency requires, and so on). The more quickly you get that material turned in, the sooner your home study report can be completed.

The home study is a cross between a celebrity interview and a parole hearing. You may be the star, but the social worker runs the show. Fortunately, most social workers are very helpful. They understand how nervous you are and do their best to make you feel at ease.

The orientation: Welcome to paperwork heaven

Once your application is accepted and you become a client of the agency, you get a packet of paperwork to fill out (if you haven't received it already). If you're lucky, the packet will come with a social worker or agency representative attached. This person's role is to initiate you, as gently as possible, into the world of adoption paperwork and to keep the smelling salts close at hand. She can also answer any of your questions.

Packet basics: For all adoptive families

The packet may be intimidating, but you should already be fairly familiar with the type of info you have to provide. You're essentially answering the same questions and providing the same information that you did in the application, but in more detail and, sometimes, in a different format. So, for example, whereas on the application, you may have been able to check the "Good" box to describe your health, on the medial report form, you give all sorts of specifics (see the section "Let's get physical: The doctor's exam," later in this chapter, for the gory details).

In addition to the modified forms, you may have to amass legal documents (marriage certificate, birth certificates, and so on). You'll get a list of the documents your agency needs and forms that others (like your employer or your minister) have to fill out. In addition to these documents, your social worker will also do some sleuthing on his own. See the next section, "Making a list and checking it twice: Supporting documents and background checks," for details on these items.

Finally, most agencies have a few tasks for you to complete, so you can expect to get a list of assignments, too. These assignments include putting together a profile (see the later section "Profiling your family" for details), writing your autobiography, and performing an interpretive dance of your feelings about adoption.

You're going to be filling out and getting together quite a bit of paperwork. So that you can keep track of all this material, create a folder just for this information. On the outside of the folder, make a list of the items you need. As you complete each item, drop it into the folder and cross the item off the list. That way, you'll be able to see, at a glance, what you've done and what you have left to do. When everything's marked off, you're ready to send the stuff to the agency.

A note on dossiers: It's an international adoption thing

When you adopt internationally, you get to do all the paperwork associated with a domestic adoption, in addition to all the paperwork required to complete your *dossier,* the packet of information containing all the paperwork and documentation you need to adopt a child from another country. The dossier is made up of the following:

- ✔ Immigration documentation and fingerprint clearance and approval from the U.S. government

- ✔ Supporting legal documentation you've collected on your own (like notarized copies of birth certificates, marriage license, health reports, financial statements, and so on)

- ✔ Your home study report (described later in this section) and any other required paperwork from your adoption agency

In short, the dossier is a behemoth of a file that will cost you a small fortune to assemble and another fortune in postage to mail to your agency, which will then make any necessary translations and mail it on to the agency in your child's birth country. Head to Chapter 3 for complete details regarding the information you need to provide and what you need to do.

Making a list and checking it twice: Supporting documents and background checks

You can be the nicest, most responsible person in the world, and you can talk about how upstanding you are until you're blue in the face, but the social worker wants independent verification on certain items. So be prepared to provide proof of the following:

- ✔ **Your marriage:** The matching rings and wedding pictures with you and the priest aren't enough. You're probably going to have to show marriage certificates (and divorce decrees, if you have any) to prove your marriage history.

- ✔ **Your credit:** Social workers want more than your word about what you owe and how responsible you are about making your mortgage, car, and credit card payments. You have to prepare a fairly detailed financial statement (complete with documents from your bank), and you may have to give permission to have your credit checked.

- ✔ **Your age:** If you don't have a copy of your birth certificate handy, better make a trip to the appropriate office in your state for a birth certificate to prove you are how old you say you are. (To find out where to write for vital records in your state, head to the National Center for Health Statistics Web site at www.cdc.gov/nchs/howto/w2w/w2welcom.htm.)

- ✔ **Your employment:** Your employer may have to verify your employment, your job title, and job stability. He may also be asked to verify your salary.

- ✔ **Your health:** This is what the medical report is for (see the later section "Let's get physical: The doctor's exam"). In this report, your doctor verifies the state of your health, identifies any concerns about your health, and explains any treatment you're receiving. He may also need to verify any infertility issues.

- ✔ **Your character and lifestyle:** How do you verify that? you wonder. Through your personal references, so make sure you pick good ones.

- ✔ **Your criminal background (or lack thereof):** The social worker is going to check with quite a few people: state police, to verify your criminal history; the state's child welfare office, to verify that you haven't been charged with child abuse or neglect; and a sexual perpetrator list, to be sure that your name isn't on it.

If your agency isn't verifying all these things, it may also fail to verify matters like the pregnancy of the birthmother that it asks you to pay expenses for.

Let's get physical: The doctor's exam

Another part of the home study is the medical report that your doctor fills out. In order to fill in the report completely, you must undergo a complete exam — and we mean complete. You're going to be poked, prodded, x-rayed, leached, and kneaded. So be prepared to spend an intimate morning or afternoon with your doctor and other medical professionals.

The doctor's exam is designed to determine the state of your health and to see how you're coping with it. It isn't intended to rule you out as an adoptive parent if you have a specific medical condition.

Your doctor fills out the health report, which includes this information:

- Your height, weight, and age.
- The date of the visit (it usually must be within the last year).
- Specific results of the exam (including your blood pressure; your pulse rate; an assessment of your eyes, nose, and throat; and the condition of your heart, lungs, and abdomen). The medical report may also require that you undergo a urinalysis and have a tuberculosis test.
- Your medical history, including past surgeries and conditions.
- A statement regarding any infertility issues you've dealt with.

In addition to the strictly medical information, the form usually asks the doctor to indicate whether he considers you physically and emotionally qualified to adopt. So smile and be nice.

The medical report is one of the things that generally takes the longest amount of time to complete simply because of how far in advance you must schedule an appointment. Add to that the time your doctor takes to fill out the form. If you aren't lucky enough to have a doctor who can see you within a week or two of the time you call, go ahead and send the rest of your information to the agency and include a note that you'll send the medical report when it's done. If you've had the exam, and it's still taking an inordinate about of time to get the completed medical form, call the agency and ask your social worker to give the doctor a nudge. She may have more luck than you in getting the doc in gear.

Telling your life story: The autobiography

By the time you get to the autobiography, you'd think that the agency had all the info on you that it could possibly want. But, alas, it doesn't.

In the autobiography, you get to tell your life story from birth to the present. Although some agencies don't have specific requirements for what goes in your bio, most agencies (thankfully) give you an outline to work from. This outline tells you what to include, such as where and when you were born, where you grew up, the types of activities you shared with your family, the discipline you received, your religious upbringing, and so on.

Don't worry. You don't need a journalism degree or any special writing ability to write your autobiography. Your social worker isn't grading you on punctuation, grammar, or plot points. The purpose of the autobiography is simply for you to tell about your life in your own words. And don't worry about how long it has to be. My (Tracy's) husband's autobiography was a mere two pages (with wide margins and big fonts); mine topped five before I was done. Go figure.

Profiling your family

A profile is basically just a notebook of information that you compile to introduce yourselves to a birthmother. The profile can include a letter to the birthmother, with specific information about you and photos of your family, your home, and the activities you enjoy.

Some profiles are quite plain; others are prepared by scrapbooking party graduates. Your agency may be very specific about the appearance of your profile, or it may turn you loose to "do your own thing."

Whatever you create, you usually have to provide identical copies to your agency or lawyer (who'll tell you specifically how many you need) for a couple of reasons:

- ✔ Your profile may be mailed to several birthmothers at the same time.

- ✔ Even if the social worker meets with the birthmother individually to show her the profile in person, the birthmother may want to take the profile home so that she can consider it. If that's the case, the agency will want another profile in the office.

Writing a Dear Birthmother letter

The purpose of the birthmother letter is to allow the birthmother to get a feeling for the type of people you are. Remember, she's trying to decide where her baby will live and who he'll live with. She wants to know what kind of life her child will have with you. If your agency allows, make the letter personal and let your personality shine through. Here are some other tips:

- ✔ Show some concern and empathy for the birthmother. Let her see that you understand her situation and respect her for the decision she's making. Don't lay it on too thick, and be sincere.

- ✔ Put yourself in the birthmother's shoes and think about what you'd like to know if you were selecting parents for your child. Then provide the birthmother with all that information about you.

- ✔ Speak to the birthmother as though you were having a conversation with her. Don't try to impress her with a lot of flowery language.

Your agency may show you examples of birthmother letters, and you can find many examples on the Internet. Just enter **Birthmother letters** in your search field, and a whole slew of Web sites appears. Most of these sites contain actual letters from adoptive parents looking for birthmothers who want to place their children for adoption.

Beware of an agency coaxing you to give false or misleading statements in your letter, like saying you work in the health field when you really work in the hospital cafeteria. If they're fudging on *your* information, they may also be fudging on the info they give you about the birthmother.

Describing yourself and your spouse

Don't worry about trying to impress the birthmother with your good looks and major achievements. She's going to be more interested in discovering your feelings about becoming a parent, what having a child will mean to you, and how you plan to interact with that child. Your agency may ask that you provide certain information in a particular format, but if not, make sure you include basic information about your age, education, occupation, hobbies and interests, and religion. You can also include the reason you want to adopt, how you plan to raise your child, and how you feel about building your family through adoption.

If you're married, the birthmother will also want to know that you have a strong and stable marriage, and she'll be interested in how you feel about your spouse. You may also want to explain how you met and how long you've been together.

Say cheese! Including pictures and albums

In your letter, you try to tell the birthmother what your life is like so that she can imagine what her child's life will be like with you. With pictures and albums, you're trying to show her.

A picture really is worth a thousand words, so don't be stingy with them. You want to include photos of each member of your family (don't forget your pets!), as well as activities you enjoy. Also include a picture of your home, and if you have the baby's room prepared, you may want to include a photo of that, too.

Here are some other suggestions for selecting these photos:

- **Pick photos that illustrate what you tell the birthmother in your letter.** If you mention that you like vacationing at the beach, include some snapshots from one of those vacations.

> ✔ **A few professional photos may be okay, but most birthmothers want to see the casual snapshots.** The ones with the wonderfully goofy smiles or the dog sleeping in your lap are always better than studio shots, so be sure that most of the pictures in your album fall into this category.

> ✔ **Select pictures that reveal personality or emotion.** A photo of your father pushing a grandchild in a swing is much more appealing then the photo of him standing stiffly in front of the fireplace.

> ✔ **Include captions under the photos, identifying the people and events.** For example, "This is all of my family at my mother's house last Christmas."

Considering other profile issues

No such thing as the perfect profile that would be selected first by every birthmother exists. All birthmothers are individuals with different preferences and dreams for their child, and you have no way of knowing the personal preferences of each birthmother. So just be real and try to paint an accurate picture of your family, home, and lifestyle.

As you do that, keep these things in mind:

> ✔ The agency may intend to mail the profiles to birthmothers, so don't make them too bulky.

> ✔ Different birthmothers have different educational levels. Use language that all birth moms can understand.

> ✔ Although you want to share a lot of info about your family, don't ramble on and on. If your letter's too long, the birthmother reading it may lose interest.

Opening your home for the white-glove inspection

At some point during the home study, the social worker will schedule a time to go through your house. She'll want to walk through and view every room in your home. She'll make notes as to how many rooms there are and how they're currently used. She'll probably want to look out into your backyard and view that space as well.

The cleanliness factor

The purpose of the home visit is to actually see the living environment you'll provide for your child. Most social workers don't inspect for dust balls under your bed or check to see how orderly you store the items in your closet, but they do have expectations of certain housekeeping standards. Children's toys on the floor of the playroom won't be an issue, for example, but last week's garbage strewn across the kitchen floor may be.

The absolute minimum standard includes a home that is reasonably free of rodents and insects; has heat, electricity, and running water; and meets basic standards of cleanliness. If the health department has issues with your home, you can bet that an adoption agency will, too.

If you're not a neat freak and are concerned about passing inspection, check with your agency about its specific standards.

The size factor

Many people erroneously assume that agencies have all sorts of rules about the size of house you live in. Here are some of the myths you may have heard or worried about yourself:

- ✔ **Myth 1: You have to have separate bedrooms for each child.** Wrong. Most agencies don't require a separate bedroom for each child. Kids can share bedrooms, and brothers and sisters can share the same rooms while they're still young.

- ✔ **Myth 2: One-bedroom homes are out because the baby needs her own space.** Wrong again. If you live in a one-bedroom apartment or house, it's usually acceptable to start out with the baby in your bedroom as long as you have plans to provide a separate room in the future.

The truth is, your home doesn't have to be big to pass inspection. In fact, most agencies only require that you have enough space in your house to accommodate another person. If you have a large family and a small home, the worker just needs to determine that you can fit in the new family member.

The interview: Topics (about a million or so) you'll talk about

You have the coffee brewing, the muffins made, the house clean. You've checked the bathrooms and set out the nice soap. You're ready. Or so you think. The home study is about more than what a good housekeeper and muffin maker you are. Be prepared to spend most of your time talking; the examination of the house itself takes only about ten minutes; see the section "Opening your home for the white-glove inspection," earlier in this chapter. Following are the talking points:

✔ Info about your infertility (if applicable), treatments you've tried, and how you came to decide it was time to adopt

✔ Your feelings about adoption, your personal connections to adoption, and how you've prepared for adoption

✔ How and when you plan to talk to your child about adoption

✔ Your experience with children, and your views on discipline and child raising

✔ How your family and friends feel about your adoption plans

✔ What other adoption agencies, if any, you're working with

✔ Your occupation, where you work, your work hours, and so on

✔ Who the child's doctor will be and what insurance company will provide the child's medical insurance

✔ Your income and your monthly expenses

✔ What property you own, your credit card balances, and how much you have in savings or investments

✔ Who handles the finances and whether you and your spouse or partner agree on the use of your money

✔ Your religious beliefs, and, if you attend religious services, where and how often

✔ Your other children (ages, names, and so on)

✔ Your home and neighborhood

✔ Your pets

✔ Your child-care plans

✔ The school system your neighborhood is in or information about the private school where you plan to send your children

✔ The type of child you're interested in and what special needs you're willing to consider

✔ How much openness you're comfortable with in your relationship with the birthmother

Because you've already written your autobiography (see the earlier section "Telling your life story: The autobiography") and the social worker has already read it, expect her to ask questions about what you wrote, pinpointing things that may be red flags or need clarification. If, for example, in your autobiography, you wrote, "My dad wasn't around much," your social worker will probe that point in more depth. She may say, "Tell me about your father; what did he do?" or "Describe the relationship between your parents."

In addition to these topics, the social worker will discuss other issues. If you're married, you and your spouse will have to answer these questions individually. (The social worker may want to discuss these things with each of you separately; if so, she'll schedule separate interviews.) You'll each talk about the following:

✔ Your childhood, including things like your parents, your siblings, and the discipline you received

✔ Your education, work history, and relationships (other than your marriage) that you've been in

✔ Your hobbies, interests, and types of activities you participate in as a family

✔ Your relationship with your spouse, including topics like

- How you met

- Your courtship

- When and where you married

- The existence of any prenuptial agreements

- Your feelings about your spouse (and how you would describe him or her)

- What you would change about your spouse if you could

- What you disagree about

- How you handle your disagreements

Putting it all together: Your home study report

The home study report is basically a summary of the social worker's experience and interviews with you. It contains all the information the social worker has gathered about you, including the following:

✔ A description of you

✔ A description of your home and neighborhood

✔ Information about the type of child you hope to adopt

✔ Your financial situation, health info, and criminal history reports

The home study report also includes the social worker's assessment of your ability to love and parent an adopted child, and it ends with the statement saying that you've been approved to adopt. (Occasionally, a family may not be approved. To understand what things can prompt a denial and what your options are if that happens to you, head to the later section "Dealing with the news if you don't 'pass.'")

Understanding what the report's used for

The home study report is important documentation for both you and the agency. It's important for you because, if you're working with an agency (or a reputable attorney or facilitator), you need the home study report before you can proceed in your adoption.

The report is necessary for the agency for licensing purposes. The home study proves that the agency has investigated you in all relevant areas and that you've received education and preparation for your adoption. It may never be used beyond that. In other words, the report may never leave the agency and may just take up room in your file.

If you're adopting internationally and you have an agency other than your international agency doing the home study (which usually happens if the international agency doesn't have an office in your state), the home study has to be copied and authenticated and sent to the international agency. From there, it's sent on to the other country.

If you're working with more than one agency, this report will be required by any agency considering you. If you're working with an attorney or facilitator, he should also request a copy of this report.

You can see your home study report, too. Either ask your social worker for a copy or ask to see the report the next time you're visiting the agency office.

Knowing where you go from here

When you receive the agency's approval to adopt, you deserve to celebrate. A completed home study is a beautiful thing. Not only does it mean that you're approved to adopt (they liked you — they really, *really* liked you!), but it also means that the agency is going to start giving your profile (see the section "Profiling your family," earlier in this chapter) out to birthmothers. And that means that you can get a call at any time to pick up your child.

So now you're facing the "wait" — that seemingly endless expanse of time you spend twiddling your thumbs and pestering the agency while you wait for your child. Hop to Chapter 10 for ideas on what you can do to pass the time.

Dealing with the news if you don't "pass"

Before it even begins the home study, the agency should have prescreened you to be certain that you meet its requirements for age, length of marriage, and so on. Once you enter the home study stage, the agency's social worker considers deeper issues. And if she has serious concerns about your family, you may not be approved to adopt. Reasons for denial may include the following:

- ✔ Criminal history
- ✔ History of addictions
- ✔ Mental health issues
- ✔ Low income
- ✔ Unpaid past child support obligations
- ✔ Lack of stability

Note that these issues *may* be reasons for denial. Denial isn't automatic if you fall into one of these categories. Most agencies examine these issues on a case-by-case basis and make a decision after having taken an in-depth look at the particular circumstances. If you're worried that certain factors may impede your chances to adopt, head to Chapter 5 for more information on how some of these issues can impact you. Also talk to your social worker, the best resource you have.

In most cases, if you've been denied, the worker will sit down with you in person and explain the reasons for the denial. This meeting is your opportunity to understand fully the reasons you weren't approved and to have your questions answered. If your agency doesn't offer such a meeting, ask for it.

After you know the reason behind the denial, you may be able to figure out whether another agency might consider you. Maybe the first agency you used has a bias or prejudice affecting its decision. Maybe not.

Different agencies have different standards. So contact other agencies. Tell them right upfront what's hindering you from adopting and ask whether they would be as stringent.

There's no use hiding the negative info from the other agencies you contact in the future. If a proper home study is done, the same issues will be discovered again. And never lie or fail to disclose info. You don't want to jeopardize your relationship with the agency or your future adoption.

If you continue to hit a brick wall, you may need to consider the possibility that the agencies have a point. Rethink your desire to adopt. Maybe you aren't in the right position to be a parent right now. Remember, the well-being of the child is always first and foremost.

PERSONAL STORY

Extra! Extra! Read all about it!
Agency paperwork forms solid foundation

When my husband and I received the paperwork we were supposed to complete from our adoption agency, we were amazed. We joked with each other about the number of trees that had to die so we could answer questions. After a few days of looking at the folder, we got serious. There was a checklist, and I began gathering necessary documents. In addition, we both had a list of questions to answer. There were more than 30 questions each! We worked independently over several weeks to complete our answers.

What surprised me was that the questions pushed us to talk to each other about what we thought about the questions. These conversations led us to talk about our views about parenting. We moved from the abstract — *we want to have a child* — to the concrete — *how exactly will we raise a child?* We were able to discuss *before* we were parents how we wanted to parent. I'd like to say that we're always in complete agreement now (more than four years and three children since we began the adoption process), but that's not true. What is true is that we have a strong foundation from which to begin discussions about how we want to raise our children. Without the questions from our agency, we might not have this foundation.

Christine and Maurice Rembert

But I'm a Good Person! The Reasons for the Scrutiny

REMEMBER

At some point — like when the social worker sits in your recently sanitized home, eating your fresh-baked muffin and asks you, "So *why* do you want children?" or "Do you plan to stay home full-time after you receive a placement?" — you're going to think, "People who bear their children don't have to go through this crap." And you're right. They don't. But before you let this idea fester too long, keep a few things in mind:

✔ **There's a good reason for all the questions and probing.** And it's this: As much as people want to help you build your family, their main goal is to protect the children in their care. And they're trying to find out whether you will be (or are, if you have other children) a fit parent and whether the child they entrust to you will be safe, loved, and well cared for.

✔ **This period gives you an opportunity to think about — and plan for — things that many other parents don't give a second thought to.** By the time you have your home study report in your hands, you'll have had the opportunity to examine yourself, your history, and your motivation. Such introspection won't make dirty diapers any more pleasant to change, but it can help you become the parent you want to be.

✔ **This is your labor story.** Someday your child will ask you to tell him about what you did to bring him home. And now you have an adventure story and a love story all rolled into one — and he gets to be the hero of the tale. What kid wouldn't like that?

Chapter 10

Doing Hard Time: The Wait

Americans are, by and large, an impatient bunch. We want instant gratification: short lines, green lights, and clear passing lanes. After we check off A and B, we expect C to follow pretty darn closely — and if it doesn't, we want to know why and we want to know *now*. We even have a phrase to denote how quickly things should happen: *lickety-split,* two words that no self-respecting grown-up should be able to utter without at least a little blush of embarrassment.

But the truth is, most adoptions don't happen lickety-split. You may get all your paperwork, interviews, and reports done in record time, but you're still going to face a wait. And the wait is, arguably, the most difficult time of the adoption process.

For domestic adoptions, the wait refers to the time between the time you're approved and the time a child is placed with you. For international adoptions, the wait refers to the time between the time a child is assigned to you (essentially placement) and the time when you can actually bring the child home. No matter how you define it, however, the wait seems to last forever.

So what's a lickety-split person to do in a wait-and-see world? Pass the time. This chapter gives you suggestions and ideas for how to spend your time waiting productively, if not happily. And remember, patience is a virtue — or so they say.

Facing the Wait and Staying Sane at the Same Time

After you complete the paperwork and the home study process, as we describe in Chapter 9, the task that faces you now is to wait without going crazy and without driving your partner, your friends, and your social worker up a wall while you do it.

One reason waiting is so hard for most adoptive parents is because most don't know how long the wait will be. It may be a few months or a few years. Like a kid who has no idea how long the drive to Grandma's house is and begins asking, "Are we there yet?" precisely a half block from home, you're not going to know whether your happy news (that you've been selected, for a domestic placement, or that a child has been assigned to you, in an international placement) is just around the corner or still miles away.

Another reason the wait is difficult, especially for people who adopt domestically, is that, until their child is *literally* in their arms, they're often afraid to be expectant parents. In the United States, birth moms generally can't relinquish their parental rights until a certain amount of time after their child is born, and many change their minds during that period. Expecting a particular child and then learning that that child will not be yours is losing a child. (This situation isn't usually an issue in international adoptions, in which the parental rights already have to be relinquished and the child declared an orphan before she can be assigned to an adoptive family.)

If you're adopting from another country, the real wait for you begins after you've been assigned a child, and this period is difficult for a different reason. The child assigned to you is, for all intents and purposes, your child, but she's not home yet. You may have pictures and letters from the foster mother who's caring for her or the orphanage staff where she lives, but she's not in your arms yet, and you still have a lot of work to do to bring her home (see Chapter 3 to understand the process).

The following sections can help you make it through the waiting period.

Staying in contact with your agency

Agencies expect that you'll call and check up on how things are going. So don't hesitate to use your social worker as an information resource. She can tell you the status of your adoption: Has your profile been given out, and if so, to whom? Has this person made a selection yet, or is the agency still waiting? Would your family be a good fit for other birthmothers working with the agency? If you're adopting internationally, your social worker can keep you apprised of how things (the paperwork, essentially) are progressing.

In the initial stages of the wait, give your social worker a call about every month. This schedule is frequent enough to enable you to stay informed without being a pest. If a birthmother has already selected you, calling more frequently (like weekly) is okay, especially if the baby's due soon. But remember, your social worker isn't going to leave you hanging. She'll keep you informed as things happen that impact your adoption.

If you feel that your social worker isn't keeping you informed or that your concerns aren't being addressed, discuss the issue with her. Just tell her you'd like to hear from her more frequently. And keep in mind that the reason she may not be keeping you up-to-date on all the latest developments is that she's so busy working with the birthmothers (that's a good thing for you). Just take the initiative and make a habit of calling her instead.

Still, if you have a serious concern about your social worker and she isn't responding to your concerns, ask to speak to her supervisor. But take that step as a last resort and only if your concerns are serious ones. Your social worker is the one advocating for you, and you don't want to ruin that relationship over petty complaints.

Giving yourself — and others — a break

Everyone handles the wait differently. Some people decorate the child's room, buy all sorts of cute clothes, and talk incessantly about their coming child to anyone who'll listen. Some prepare more guardedly. They may paint the child's room, but in a color that won't scream "There should have been a baby here!" if the child doesn't come, and they share their hopes only with family and close friends. Others decide not to do anything at all until they get the call and usually find themselves at toy and baby supply stores at midnight on the eve of their child's arrival.

Whichever of these groups you fall into, fine. Handle the wait however you need to in order to be okay during it. And if you know someone who is adopting and handles the wait differently than you do, don't assume that her outward behavior means anything about how excited she is or how much she's looking forward to her child's arrival.

Preparing for the Arrival of Your Child

Like any prospective parent, your to-do list is probably pretty long, and at a certain point, you're going to begin to nest. Depending on how guarded you are in your approach, your nesting may last from the moment you turn in your paperwork (see Chapter 9) to the time you get the call (see Chapter 11), or it may be remarkably shorter — like however much time you have from the time you get the call to the time (usually later that same day or the next day) that your new addition comes home. If you're adopting internationally, your nesting period will probably span the time between when your child is assigned to you and when he arrives home.

The following sections outline the things you can do while you wait and explain what you should keep in mind while you stock your house from baseboards to crown molding with kid paraphernalia.

No kid is going to be disadvantaged by sleeping in a crib that doesn't have a matching sheet-and-comforter set. Nor is a library full of books necessary to keep your little (or not-so-little) one happy. Some things can wait. Other things, however, are better done beforehand so that, when you get the call, you can hit the ground running, whether that's to the agency or to the baby superstore. Here are some tasks that you want to do early:

✔ Select a doctor or pediatrician.

✔ Notify your insurance company that you'll have an addition to the family.

✔ Inform your boss of your plans for taking time off.

Because of their importance, these are the first of the following sections.

Finding a doctor

Finding the right doctor to treat your child can take a while, but it's an excellent way to pass some of those endless hours you spend waiting during your adoption process. In fact, selecting your doctor even before you have been matched to a particular birthmother or assigned to a specific child overseas may be a good idea. That way, if the birthmother or child has any specific medical concerns or conditions, you'll have a physician in place to turn to for a medical opinion or advice.

One of the best ways to find a doctor is personal references. Just ask your friends and family about their experiences with the local doctors.

Deciding between a pediatrician and a family doctor

One decision you'll make is whether you want your child's doctor to be a general practitioner or a pediatrician. The answer to that question really depends on what you're comfortable with and the circumstances that affect your child. General practitioners are well versed in general infant and child-care. And one possible advantage of going with your family doctor is that she knows all of you pretty well.

On the other hand, if you're adopting children internationally or adopting an at-risk infant, you may want to start with a pediatrician who is well versed in the issues your child may deal with. Some cities offer clinics designed specifically for the treatment of the internationally adopted child. If this is the route you want to take, you can call physician referral services in your area and request the names of the doctors specializing in those conditions.

Interviewing the doc

Whether you go with a doctor recommended to you or one you find listed in the phone book, you may decide to ask for a personal appointment to meet the doctor face to face. Such a meeting is a great time to ask important questions. Many doctors will agree to this (be aware that many doctors often charge for an office visit). If you're not interested in a personal interview, you can request a phone interview with another member of the doctor's staff. You may want to ask the following questions:

- What is your after-hours policy?

- Do you allow new parents to e-mail questions from home?

- How available are you for new parents' questions or concerns?

- How much time do you spend in the examining room with the parent of the patient?

- Will you be seeing the children, or will it be a nurse practitioner?

- What is your attitude about adoption?

- What is your experience in treating children from China (or Russia or wherever your child is from)?

- What is your experience with treating children with (insert any special medical condition that applies)?

Before you make an appointment with a local doctor, check with your insurance company for a list of doctors covered by your plan. If your insurance covers only certain health care providers, make sure that the one you hook up with is one it accepts.

Talking to your insurance company

Like any expectant parent, you need to inform your insurance company of the pending arrival. Although you usually can't add the child to your insurance policy until the child has been placed with you, you do need to find out the following:

- ✔ **Whether your policy allows you to add people on:** If it doesn't, find one that does. Most agencies require that your child be covered by health insurance.

- ✔ **Whether a child born with preexisting conditions will be covered by the policy:** Again, find out early so that you can make any necessary insurance changes.

- ✔ **What the company's procedure is to have your child added to the policy:** Insurance companies are required to cover your adopted children just as they would cover children born to you. Most companies just need to see a copy of the signed placement agreement to start the insurance coverage.

If you come across an insurance company that tells you your child will be covered at finalization, call your social worker. In many counties across the United States, there's a big difference between placement and finalization. Your child's insurance coverage must begin at placement. Any reputable insurance company will comply with this requirement; it's the law.

Arranging to take time off from work

Here are a couple reasons why you may want to schedule some time off from work: First, spending some good quality time together is important, especially if the child isn't a newborn. Those first few days, weeks, or months together help the child adjust, encourage the child's bonding, and allow the two of you to develop a schedule and get to know each other. Second, most agencies expect at least one parent to have extended time with the child immediately after bringing the child home. Some agencies even require it.

Fortunately, most families have options regarding whether they can take time off from work and how much time they have.

The Family and Medical Leave Act

The Family and Medical Leave Act (FMLA) is a federal law that requires businesses who employ 50 or more people to give families the equivalent of 12 weeks of unpaid leave for certain family situations. And adding a child to your family — whether through birth or adoption — is one of the family situations that apply.

Be sure you know the laws in your own state. Some states have enacted laws that broaden the FMLA to apply to employers with fewer than 50 employees. In Louisiana, for example, it applies to anyone employing 20 or more employees; in Maine, it affects businesses with 15 or more employees.

Employer leave plans

Most employers have some policies stipulating how much leave an employee can have for the birth or adoption of a child (ask your employer early on so you can make your plans in advance):

- ✔ Some employers allow adoptive parents to take more than the 12 weeks leave (stipulated in the FMLA; see the preceding section), and sometimes, the amount of leave can stretch to 6 months or a year.

- ✔ Some employers allow families to use accumulated vacation days or sick time as paid time off after their adoption.

- ✔ Some employers even offer their own version of paid family leave for adoptive parents.

Talk to your boss or to your company's human resources department to find out what your company's policies are and what you need to do to qualify.

Getting the child's room ready

The upside of getting your child's room ready is that planning, painting, papering, and decorating a room can be a really good time filler. These tasks are also a good way to prepare emotionally for your child.

The downside of preparing the child's room in advance is the chance that you may end up with a decorated room and no child, at least for a while. Many people aren't up to seeing an empty child's room day after day. The empty room may be that much harder to face if the specific adoption you're involved with falls through and you have to come home without a child.

Unlike fertility treatments, adoption itself is a pretty sure thing once you've been accepted by an agency. So your room won't stay empty forever. If you decide to prepare the room in advance, keep in mind that eventually a child will fill that room, even if you have some disappointments in the interim.

If you're adopting an older child, you may want to save some of the decorating until after your child comes home. That way, she can have some say in what her room looks like. After all, you don't want to spend a lot of time and money on a bunch of Hello Kitty posters when your daughter prefers motorcross bikes instead.

Attending showers

If you're adopting domestically, you may want to hold off the friends and family who want to give you a shower, at least until after the birthmother signs the consent forms (see Chapter 11 for information about those) and you bring your child home.

Although showers are fun — and who doesn't like seeing all of those pretty baby clothes? — it may just be more than you can handle to have to put all the stuff away if your adoption doesn't take place. Or picture this: You're matched with a birthmother who's expecting a girl, but that adoption falls through, and you find out you're getting a boy instead. What would you do with all that pink stuff?

Remember, however, that the call is yours. You will eventually get a child, so if you want to have showers while you're waiting, go for it! (Just remember to ask for non-gender-specific stuff.)

If you're adopting internationally, you'll probably get your referral well before you travel for your child. In most cases, you'll be bringing home the child referred to you. So if you find yourself the guest of honor at a shower, you may want to remind the hostess of a few things to pass along to the other guests: You won't know for certain the exact age or size your child will be when you bring him home. Your adoption could possibly experience an unexpected delay, which would make your child older than you planned. So maybe the hostess could suggest that, instead of buying clothes that may not fit the child, guests shop for other things a child needs, like toys, books, room accessories, photo albums, picture frames, and so on.

Taking classes

If you aren't feeling confident in your parenting skills, now is the time to get prepared. Believe us, you won't have much time to attend classes or sit around reading *after* your child arrives. For general parenting tips and suggestions, head to your local library or bookstore. You can find wonderful child-care and parenting videos and books at either of these places. You can also contact area hospitals. Many of them offer classes on newborn infant care, and some even offer classes specifically for adoptive parents.

If you know that your child will have special needs, you can take some other steps to prepare yourself for the issues and challenges you're probably going to face. Head to the later section "Making Special Preparations for Special-Needs Adoptions."

Doing some fun stuff

In addition to tackling the big chores, you can take care of some smaller and perhaps more-pleasant tasks to prepare for your new child. Many parents send announcements to let family and friends know of the new arrival and buy memory books to mark their children's milestones. If you're an adoptive parent, finding the right announcement or book is about more than just picking a design you like. You also want to get one that celebrates your child's unique experiences.

Deciding on an adoption announcement

You can find plenty of really nice adoption announcements just by going to your local card shop, bookstores, and the Internet (enter **adoption announcements** in your search engine). A couple of Web sites that have nice selections are

- **Baby's Here.com** (www.babyshere.com): Just click on the Adoption link to see a vast selection of adoption announcements.

- **Adopt Shoppe.com** (www.adoptshoppe.com): This site offers all sorts of things — lifebooks, cards, announcements, and a bunch of other things — especially with adoption in mind.

Or, if you're crafty and have the time, you can even create your own announcement, complete with a special poem or photo.

Although you don't have your child yet, you can add the information you do have to the announcement, address the envelopes, and add the postage. Then, when you return home with your child, just add the few remaining pieces of information, such as "date of arrival," and you're good to go.

Picking an adoption memory book

Another fun thing you can spend hours doing is selecting the perfect adoption memory book for your child. You can find many traditional baby books available that have been adapted for the adopted child. These books have special sections, such as "The airport" and "Finalization day," that allow you to record and celebrate these milestones in your child's life. Like the announcements, you can find these books in your local bookshops (usually) and on the Internet.

An adoption memory book is a helpful tool when talking with your child about her adoption, so find the right one. What's the right one? The one that speaks to your child's experience and that you'll feel good sharing with her as she grows.

Taking Care of Special Prep Work for International Adoptions

When you adopt internationally, you don't have a lot of empty hours to fill — at least not initially. Trying to locate all the forms and documents necessary for the dossier is akin to going on a scavenger hunt from hell. Not only do you need a zillion things, but you need about all of them in triplicate. Once you have everything certified, notarized, and authenticated, you'll be ready to rest up a bit. But after you receive your referral and you're waiting on a travel date, you may start to get a little antsy. Fortunately, you can choose from many productive things to do. (Head to Chapter 3 for a list of the types of documents you need for international adoptions.)

Hitting the books

Educate yourself about the country of your child's birth. Learn about the customs, the government, and the lay of the land. Study maps, download Internet info, and buy a simple language phrase book and learn some practical phrases. You need to know this info for a few reasons:

✔ **You're probably going to be traveling there.** Who wants to be an ugly American — especially on such an important trip? Surely not you, so bone up on the customs and expectations of the culture you're visiting.

✔ **This is the environment your child is from.** Not only can the info help you anticipate some issues you may encounter, but someday you're going to be sharing this information with your child.

✔ **Your child won't be a newborn when he comes home, and he'll probably know or respond to some basic native words.** Being able to say "potty" in Chinese may be very important. For you and your child.

Joining an adoption support group

If you haven't done so already, join an adoption support group. Your agency can give you the names of support groups in your area. These groups are helpful for a number of reasons, not the least of which is that they're full of people who've been in your shoes.

After you make some connections at the support group, ask some families who have already traveled to your child's country over for a barbecue or out to dinner. Then pump them for information. Ask them about the hotels, the transportation, the food, the shopping, the tipping, the agency greeters/guides, and so on. The more you know in advance, the less stressed you'll be when it's your turn to travel.

Even if your agency has provided you with written information regarding these topics, you can still talk to the folks in the group to discover whether the agency info is current and accurate.

Doing good deeds

Your agency may encourage or allow you to do some philanthropic work for your child's orphanage. If so, consider doing what other families have done.

Many families plan to take extra (and empty) luggage on their trip to accommodate all the purchases and souvenirs they plan to bring home. They fill that empty space with items for the orphanage. For example, these families collect toothpaste and toothbrushes from local dentists, medical supplies from local physicians, baby items from local department stores, and so on. Making all of these contacts and collecting these items can help you fill some time *and,* more importantly, benefit the children who remain in the orphanage.

Buying gifts

Your agency may recommend that you provide gifts for the people you interact with during your adoption. In South or Central American countries, for example, you may be expected to provide gifts for the lawyer, the social worker, the foster mother or "nanny," and your escort or driver.

If giving such gifts is the local custom, your agency will inform you and give suggestions for the type of items to buy. Now's the time to shop for those items and to pack them safely.

Making Special Preparations for Special-Needs Adoptions

If you're adopting a child with special needs, you can take certain steps to prepare yourself for the parenting challenges you're going to face. The following sections explain how.

Educating yourself

Information is power, and the best way you can help your child is to know as much as you can about the condition or issue that she faces. Head to the library, the Internet, the pediatrician (if you don't have one already, now's the time to get one; see the earlier section "Finding a doctor"), and any other resource you can find and scour the pages for information or pump the people for whatever they know.

Find a support group for parents of children with special needs and join now. The other experienced parents can help you prepare in advance for issues that may arise, guide you to important resources you may need, and, more important, offer you their friendship and support during the wait and the years ahead.

Taking the special-needs adoption parenting classes

When you adopt older children or children who've experienced abuse or neglect, most public agencies expect you to attend the special-needs adoption parenting classes, which they offer at no cost to you.

These classes usually include group discussion, role-playing, and problem solving for specific scenarios. In addition to general parenting information, they offer the following:

- ✔ **Specific help and information about how to parent behaviorally challenged children and children with attachment disorders:** (See Chapter 18 for more information about attachment disorders.) This discussion also includes ideas for creative discipline.

- ✔ **Education for the parents regarding the issues these children deal with:** The issues of grief and loss, abuse, neglect, and multiple placements are discussed and explored.

Along with the education and preparation that parenting classes offer, don't overlook the connection you can make with the other participants. Because you're all dealing with the same issues, these classes give you an opportunity to form supportive relationships that can last through the placement of your children.

Chapter 11

A Child's Available! Now What? Placement and Follow-up Visits

*A*s you already know if you've been working on adopting for a while, or as you've probably figured out if you've read the preceding chapters in this book, a lot of stuff has to happen before you finally get a child. Some of the stuff — the interviews, the profile writing, the filling out of forms, and the waiting — is stuff that you do. In adoption, though, what *you* do isn't the only thing that impacts how your family gets built. Not only do you have to be ready, but a child must also be available — and that doesn't happen until the birthparents' rights are terminated, sometimes by court action and sometimes voluntarily.

So in the end, you spend months or years preparing for the call, but when the social worker actually does phone to say that a child's available, your first thought may very well be, "The room's not ready!" or "I'm woefully short of onesies!" But believe us: Despite your momentary lapse of composure, you're probably really, *really* ready — unfinished room and all — to bring your child home.

So that you'll know what to expect during this emotionally charged time, this chapter explains how children become available, what information you'll get when you receive the call, and what you can anticipate during the supervision period.

Looking at How a Child Becomes Available

Before you can adopt a child, the birthmother's (and sometimes birthfather's) parental rights have to be ended. In some cases, the state terminates parental rights. In other cases, the birthmother relinquishes her rights voluntarily. The following sections explain what you need to know about these scenarios. (Head to Chapter 14 for information about birthfathers, their rights, and the role they can play in your adoption.)

In nearly all instances of newborn adoptions, the birthmother voluntarily gives up her parental rights. In adoptions of older children, chances are that the state has stepped in and terminated the parents' rights.

Voluntarily relinquishing parental rights: The birthmother and the consent form

The birthmother's signing of the consent forms is one of the most important things in the adoptive parents' lives, and unfortunately for them, they have no control in this area. The birthmother must first make her own decision that she *wants* to sign the papers. Then she decides how quickly she will sign them. Although most states have laws governing how early birthmothers can sign the consent forms, no state has laws concerning how long she can wait before signing them. (See the later section "Timing is everything: When the birth mom can sign" for details.)

Someone from the agency or the attorney makes the arrangements with the birthmother for the consent signing. You should not be involved at all in the signing. Even if you've developed a close relationship with the birthmother, now's the time to butt out. You must give the birthmother the space and freedom she needs to make a thoughtful decision. Here's why: Your presence, however well-meaning and loving it may be, may be felt as a form of pressure or be misconstrued as coercion. She knows that you want her baby. She knows she has told you that she'll place her baby with you. If you're standing there, looking over her shoulder, she may feel that she has no other choice.

If a birthmother changes her mind and contests the adoption, the court scrutinizes everything that happened during the adoption and the consent signing. Although a birthmother probably wouldn't win based solely on the fact that she felt obligated because you were present, the situation wouldn't look good. Why risk it?

Looking at the consent form

The consent form is the voluntary consent to the termination of parental rights. After a woman signs these papers, she has no other legal rights or responsibilities to her child. The consent papers also can be called the "Relinquishment" or the "Voluntary Termination of Parental Rights."

Agencies and lawyers have their own consent form, based on the laws in the states where they practice and their professional judgment regarding what information must be attached to ensure a safe adoption. The consent form may require birthmothers to sign the following:

- Statements that she

  - Is signing of her own free will

  - Isn't under the influence of any drugs or medication that would impair her capacity to make this decision

  - Hasn't been threatened or coerced

  - Has read the consent form and understands what it says (some, but not all, agencies even read these forms aloud and explain to the birthmother as they go along, to make sure that she understands what she's signing)

- Information reiterating information the birthmother has provided about the birthfather: whether she named him as the father or not, what his connection has been to her and this pregnancy, and so on

- An affidavit that transfers custody of the baby to the agency and the family, allows both to seek emergency medical attention for the child, and releases all the medical records

- An agreement of understanding that says that, even though the family may have promised to send letters and pictures, if the family doesn't follow through on this promise, the adoption still stands

- If the adoption is transracial, perhaps a separate affidavit stating that the birthmother is aware that her child will be placed with a family of another race

The laws governing the consents vary from state to state. Some states require that the papers be signed in court or in front of a judge. Some states allow the papers to be signed with a notary public or just an agency representative.

Timing is everything: When the birth mom can sign

Most states don't allow birthmothers to sign the consent papers before the birth of the child. Alabama and Hawaii are two exceptions. Most states also designate how soon after the delivery the mother can sign. In some states, the birthmother can sign immediately after the birth; other states require several days of waiting. Many hospitals also get into the act, stipulating how much time must pass after the delivery before the birthmother can sign the consents in their facility. Twenty-four hours is pretty common.

A birthmother can take as long as she wants to sign the form. If her child is 3 months old and she decides to do an adoption then, she can still sign the papers at that point.

When final means final

Most states also have laws regarding when these consent forms are truly final (that is, the birthmother can't simply change her mind and demand her child back). In many states, consents are final immediately after the birthmother signs them. In other states, the birthmother may have a period of days, weeks, or even months during which she can change her mind and cancel or revoke her consents.

Although most adoptions have some legal risk, the legal risk associated with adoptions that have grace periods are generally considered more significant. So if you live in (or adopt a child from) a state that allows grace periods, be sure that you work with a reputable agency or a reputable attorney. They will do what they can to minimize the risk, help you deal with the uncertainty, and make sure that the birthmother gets the counseling and support she needs to feel at peace with her decision. Head to Chapter 7 for information on finding reputable adoption agencies and adoption attorneys.

When the state terminates parental rights

Contrary to what you may believe about the power of the state, state welfare agencies can't just pick a family at random, step in, and terminate the parents' parental rights. The state has to have reason to believe that a problem significant enough to pose a danger to the children in the home exists, and officials have to follow an entire, lengthy process that can sometimes take years to complete. (The exception to this is in the rare cases of children who have been orphaned with no one to care for them or children whose parents have become incapacitated.)

The process begins when someone (a relative, neighbor, doctor, or teacher, for example) calls Child Protective Services (CPS) to say that he suspects a child in the home is being abused or neglected.

CPS workers investigate the reported abuse. If the abuse or neglect is substantiated (the investigator believes it happened based on what she sees and what the folks involved say), the judge rules that the child is a CHINS (child in need of services) and determines an appropriate placement for the child, often with another family member or with a foster family.

The initial goal of CPS is to reunify the family, so steps are taken to that effect: The judge may order the parents to go to parenting classes, participate in counseling, undergo drug treatment, submit to random drug screens, take anger management classes, find appropriate housing and employment, and so on. The judge also orders the type of access the parents are allowed to have with their children during this period. In addition, the family attends regular court hearings (usually every six months) to monitor the progress of the parents and the child.

When enough time passes that the case manager or the judge decides that the parent has failed to make the necessary changes or progress, the goal changes from trying to reunify the family to terminating the parent's rights so that the child can be placed for adoption. At that point, a termination trial takes place.

During the termination trial, the state has to prove that enough evidence exists to involuntarily terminate the parental rights. After hearing all the testimony, the judge makes a ruling to terminate or not. This ruling, which is final when the judge signs it, may not come until days or even months after the trial ends.

This whole process has traditionally taken years (from that first report of abuse to the ruling from the termination trial). In the meantime, these kids languish in foster care or institutions. For this reason, many states have tried to speed up the process. Still, the entire process, from beginning to end, can take at least two years — and that's often in the fast states.

Getting the Most Important Call in Your Life

Without a doubt, the call you get telling you that your child has been born or is ready to come home ranks right up there in the annals of Great Telephone Interruptions. It doesn't matter what you're doing, what you were planning to do, or how far you are through your dessert or business meeting or sex. That call changes your life. But before you slam down the receiver and begin your victory dance, you'll want to pay attention to what the person on the other end of the line is saying. She's got important info to share, not the least of which is "You're now a parent."

When the call comes

If you're adopting domestically, when you get the call depends on the arrangements you've made with the birthmother. In many agency adoptions, you're notified after the birthmother (and sometimes birthfather) signs the consent form. In open and semi-open adoptions, you may receive the call when the birthmother goes into labor so that you can attend the delivery. (See Chapter 2 for more information about adoption arrangements.)

If you're not involved in labor and delivery

If you have no plans to participate in the delivery, chances are that you'll receive this all-important call from the social worker soon after the baby is born and after the adoption papers have already been signed. The benefit to this arrangement is that, when you hear the news, you'll know immediately that you're a new parent. You'll probably be asked to go to the hospital to collect your child. Be sure to bring a going-home outfit, blankets, a car seat, and your camera. Once there, expect the following:

- The nurse may want to spend some time with you to give you instructions on caring for a newborn. She'll cover things like how to take care of the umbilical cord and the circumcision (if it's a boy, obviously).

- The doctor may be available to answer your questions regarding any blood tests or treatments your child has received.

- You'll be given the newborn pack of supplies, including samples of enough formula, bottles, wipes, and diapers to last you a couple days.

- The wristband that comes home with the baby says "BUFA" in place of the name. The initials stand for "baby up for adoption."

PERSONAL STORY

The best-laid plans

Here was the plan that my husband and I (Tracy) made when we were waiting for the call on our first child: After hearing from the agency, my husband would call me; we'd leave work immediately, meet at home, make calls to our families, and then head to the agency or the hospital. So much for planning.

When I got the call for my first child, I was at work and couldn't reach my husband, so the first people to find out were two close friends; my husband, therefore, was the third person to learn that he had become a father. When we got the call for our second child, we had out-of-town guests who had just arrived. We dragged their luggage in, kissed all the kids hello, and then hit the road ourselves. I was at home when the call came for our third child, but because we couldn't fit three baby seats in the backseat of a sedan (which we had been planning to replace for that very reason anyway), my husband and I and Child 1 and Child 2 spent that evening at a local car dealership buying a van. Two days after Child 3 came home, we realized that Child 4 was on his way.

They say that kids can take a lot out of you. Organizational skill, it seems, is one of the first things to go.

Birthmothers, delivery, and you

If you meet with the birthmother during her pregnancy, you'll have an opportunity to make plans concerning her labor and delivery experience. The birth mom may invite you to the hospital while she's in labor. If that's the case, she may want you to remain in the waiting room, or she may ask one or both of you to accompany her in the delivery room. Or she may prefer that you not be included in the labor and delivery. Remember: She has the right to invite you to participate in any way she desires, and you have the right to accept or decline her invitation.

Some families complain that the birthmother gets to make all the decisions. If you're inclined to whine about this too, slap yourself upside the head and remember this: It's *her* body feeling the labor pains, going through delivery, and experiencing all that giving birth entails. And at this point, it is *her* baby — not your baby — about to be delivered. And, if everything goes as planned, you're going to be leaving the hospital with the wonderful gift of a child. She'll be leaving with empty arms.

It would be nice if you graciously agree to whatever arrangements make her most comfortable. Having said that, you need to consider something else. If you agree to participate in the delivery, you must keep in mind that the adoption isn't final. You may watch a baby being born, hear the words "It's a boy," cut the cord, hear that first cry, be the first to hold the little miracle — and then discover the following day that she has decided not to sign the adoption papers. If that's a risk you just can't take, explain your fears and concerns to the birthmother. She'll probably understand and be happy to change her plans.

If you are involved in the labor and delivery

If you're involved in an open adoption, you'll probably exchange phone numbers with the birthmother so that she can call you when she goes into labor. Additionally, you may have been participating in some of her prenatal appointments or, at the very least, kept in touch with her and been informed of her progress. If that's the case, then the phone call telling you that she's going into labor shouldn't come as too much of a surprise. If you're planning a semi-open adoption, you may still give the birthmother a cell phone number or perhaps a pager number so that you can hear from her directly when she goes into labor.

If you have plans to participate in the delivery, you need to rush to the hospital when you receive the call. We recommend that you have your own "going to the hospital bag" packed. Include reading material (for lengthy labors), a camera, change for vending machines, your cell phone, toothbrush, and even a change of clothing. And don't forget to have cash on hand. You'll need it for the parking garage.

Purchasing some flowers or a small gift for the birthmother following the delivery is always thoughtful. If this gesture is in your plans, make sure that you have a credit card or cash with you.

Getting the call for international adoptions

When you adopt internationally, you actually receive two very important calls: The first important call is the one when you receive your referral, meaning that a specific child has been selected for you. Someone from the agency will call you to tell you the child's gender, birth date, and specific history. Along with information regarding the child's height and weight, current development, and medical situation, you'll receive photos or a video. You can make arrangements to either go to the agency to view the materials or have them mailed to you.

The second important call is when you receive your travel date. This call signals a flurry of activity. You need to make travel arrangements, shop for last-minute necessities, pack, make plant watering and pet feeding arrangements, go to the bank, and figure out who will take you to the airport. As you get ready, review your agency literature very carefully. The agency knows best what items you need for your trip. And, of course, don't forget your camera.

Supplying you with information on your child

When you receive the call, you get a lot of information relating to the child's health, background, birth family information, and so on. The following sections offer the highlights.

The vital statistics on newborns

If you're not involved in the delivery and you get the call after the baby's born and the consent forms are signed, your social worker will give you the following info:

- **The baby's weight, height, and head circumference:** This info is always good to know because when you tell people that you have a new son or daughter, the first thing they're probably going to ask is, "How much does she weigh?" and "How long is she?" Of course, these numbers are also handy info for your child's pediatrician, who will want to know.

- **The baby's Apgar score:** All newborns have an Apgar score, which is a quick test that doctors perform at one minute after birth and then again at five minutes after birth. This test helps doctors rate the physical condition of a newborn in five areas: activity (muscle tone), pulse, grimace (reflex irritability), appearance, and respiration. The child's Apgar score can rate from 1 to 10, with 10 being the best score. A baby with an average score of 7 to 10 is considered normal. A baby with a lower score than that may have needed some resuscitative measures.

If you're present for your child's delivery, you'll be privy to all of the child's birth information from the very beginning. You should be allowed to watch the weighing, the measuring, and the bathing. You may be given the opportunity to give the first feeding. (The birthmother usually needs to sign a hospital form that allows you this contact with the baby. In addition, many hospitals will put wristbands on you for the purpose of identification. These bracelets give you access to the child and the nursery.) Also remember that, although you're very involved with and probably already attached to the baby, the birthmother still hasn't signed the adoption consents at this point. Before you put yourself in this position, make sure that you understand the emotional risk you're taking if this child doesn't become yours.

Other health info that's known

The hospital runs all the routine newborn tests. If specific risk factors are present (such as past known drug use, lack of prenatal care, and obvious behavioral indications of drug use), the doctors may do some extra tests to check for the presence of drugs.

If you're at the hospital when the baby is born and afterwards, all these test results should be available to you. If you aren't present at the hospital, the test results are given to the agency, which then passes the information on to you.

The agency worker will also have the complete medical history of the birthmother and her family members and the medical history for the birthfather if it's available. If these histories reveal any areas of concern (mental health history, genetic conditions, and so on), your social worker should have discussed these with you before offering your profile to the birthmother.

After your child is placed in your home, you'll receive a typed summary of all of the child's health information, along with an extra copy for your child's doctor.

Additional info about older children

When you adopt older kids, you get the following information:

- ✔ Why the child was removed initially from her birthparents
- ✔ The length and type of all the child's placements
- ✔ Any test results, psychological and otherwise
- ✔ Types of medications that have been prescribed, currently and in the past
- ✔ Types of counseling the child has had and the results of that counseling
- ✔ The original medical history of the birth family
- ✔ School records
- ✔ Anything else the agency has in the child's records

The agency may give you a copy of the file, which includes all this information, or offer you the opportunity to come in and view the file.

This information is confidential and won't be given to someone who is only casually interested in the child. If you're just beginning to think about adopting a particular child, the agency will give you a broad overview of the child's information and share the specifics at the point when you seriously consider adopting the child.

Finally, Signing the Placement Agreement

The word *placement* usually refers to the time when the adoptive parents sign the placement agreement, agreeing to accept the child into their home for the purpose of adoption. Like consent forms (explained in the earlier section "Voluntarily relinquishing parental rights: The birthmother and the consent form"), these forms differ from agency to agency. Despite the differences, you can expect the agreement to contain the child's name and a statement to the fact that he or she is being placed in your home for the purpose of adoption. You (and your spouse, if you're married) sign the placement agreement when your child is placed with you.

When you sign the placement agreement, some agencies and attorneys also require that you sign legal risks forms. These forms outline all the legal risks involved in your particular adoption, as well as all the legal risks of every adoption. A legal risk form may say, for example, that the agency was unable to locate or contact the birthfather and that he has the right to come forward to challenge the petition to adopt.

Seeing all the risks in print can be pretty scary, but remember two things: First, this list is the agency's or attorney's way to make sure that you're aware of any situation that *could* impact your adoption; it isn't a list of things the agency or attorney thinks *will* happen. Second, most adoptions go off without a hitch.

Your Child Is Home! Welcome to the Supervision Period

Bringing your child home is one of the most exciting and exhausting things adoptive parents do. You're so happy to have your child at last, all your friends and family are happy for you and begin showering you with gifts, people you don't even know are stopping by to take a peek at the child, and the little angel sleeps all day and stays awake all night.

Obviously, you're going to be doing during this period what every parent who has a new child does: lamenting the loss of personal time, personal space, and locked bathroom doors; calling the pediatrician or your mother at every whipstitch; and reveling in all the changes your child has brought to your life. The supervision period is also an important time for bonding with your child and spending a few more quality afternoons with your social worker.

 You may want to begin setting some limits on visitors and reminding others that this is your special time with your child, especially if you've brought home a young child internationally or an older infant. Explain that you and your son or daughter need to get to know one another and that lots of visitors can interfere and confuse a young child.

How long the supervision period lasts

Individual agencies and attorneys have their own requirements regarding how long the supervision period lasts, often based on what the judge at the local adoption court requires. On average, the supervision period lasts between two and six months.

If you're adopting older children or children from other countries, your supervision period will probably be longer. The reason is the expectation that these kids and their families may have a more difficult adjustment due to the child's past experiences and any cultural differences that need to be worked through. Some international agencies, for example, require regular supervision reports (performed by the agency) for two or three years.

Your agency or attorney can tell you how long your supervision period will last and can answer any questions you have regarding the specific requirements in your case.

Bonding with your child

The most important thing that happens during the first few days and weeks of an adoptive placement is the bonding between you and your new child, and it may be one of the things that you're most worried about. Well, here's a news flash: Almost all parents worry about bonding: What if their child doesn't like them? What if they don't love the second child as much as the first? What if they never develop that deep connection? What if, what if, what if? This question can drive you crazy and actually impede what would otherwise come naturally.

No scientist or psychologist has been able to adequately explain the parent-child bond, when it has to happen, and under what circumstances it is strongest. It's a mystery that has little or nothing to do with whether your child shares your DNA.

Having said that, it's also true that some people completely believe that having a genetic connection or being the one from whose womb the child sprang is an integral part of bonding. If you're one of the people who feel this way, don't adopt. Children deserve to be with those who love them without reservation and feel connected to them without barriers.

Bonding with baby

Bonding with a newborn adopted baby is just like bonding with a newborn birth child: You're strangers to each other until you get to know one another. As you develop a relationship with your child, you'll also develop an attachment for him or her. You can do certain things to encourage this bonding:

- **In the beginning, try to be the ones who primarily take care of the baby.** Shove your mother-in-law out of the way, decline your sister's well-meaning offers, and *you* give your baby his bottle or soothe him while he cries. Spending time with your infant and being the one to consistently meet his needs teaches him to look to you for comfort. Later, when the bond between you is strong, you can share the pleasures of feeding, diapering, bathing, and dressing with the folks waiting in line.

- **When you care for your baby, talk to him, sing to him, and make lots of eye contact. Lots of physical contact is good, too.** (Using any of the myriad types of infant snuggly carriers or infant slings is a good way to maintain physical contact.) Holding, caressing, and patting reassure the infant and the parent. With all this contact, the baby will learn the sound of your voice, your smell, and your loving touch. In return, you'll learn to distinguish your baby's cries and expressions and know how and when to meet his needs.

- **Develop a schedule that works for you and your child.** Babies love — and need — routines. (So do parents, for that matter.) Knowing what's going to happen next makes babies feel safe and helps them put their world into context. Being the one to create this safe and predictable world makes parents feel good — and lets them look forward to the rest *they'll* get when the kid goes down for nap times and bedtimes (a biggie whether you have one child or several).

As you care for your child the way you think is best, on the schedule you created, you feel a sense of pride and develop a deeper understanding that this really is your very own child. And as you learn to successfully interpret your child's cries and satisfy him, you'll feel a deep satisfaction. Few things in life are sweeter than having a distressed someone hand you your crying child and watch as he immediately calms down when you put him on your hip, just so.

Bonding is an ongoing process that deepens over time. You can tell your child is bonding when you see her respond to your voice, when she prefers you to a stranger, when she looks to you for comfort, and when she enjoys your interactions. You'll know you have started bonding the first time you have an evening out and find yourself talking constantly about the baby and calling home frequently to check on her.

Bonding with older children and kids from other countries

When you adopt older children domestically or internationally, your child may experience a sense of grief and loss over leaving her other life behind. Even if your child's other life wasn't all that great, it was all she knew, and it was familiar. Your child will need time to heal from these issues and to open her heart to you. As these first weeks and months unfold, remember this: As happy as you are to have your child home, she may not want to be there.

Here are a few suggestions to help your child feel comfortable and safe in her new home:

- **Go slowly and tread softly as you and your child develop a new schedule.** When she arrives, your child is already accustomed to a particular schedule, and you may have no way of knowing what that schedule is. So develop a new schedule and a rhythm that you're both comfortable with.

- **Look to your child for cues.** If your child is too young to talk or if she doesn't know your language, watch her reactions to your specific behaviors and to situations she's exposed to. Through trial and error, you can discover whether she likes to gad about or prefers to stay home, whether she likes vegetables or French fries, whether she's quiet or outgoing, whether roughhousing or reading books is her thing, and so on.

    As you learn about your child and respond accordingly, your child learns to trust you. And as she learns to trust you, you'll feel closer to her.

- **Make eye contact with your child and touch her lovingly.** Using eye contact and physical touch is beneficial with the older children. Even if your kid rejects these bonding attempts at first, modify your tactics but keep trying. If your child rebels at being snuggled, for example, try holding her hand or stroking her hair.

- **Develop daily rituals — reading before bedtime, napping after lunch, and so on — and follow them consistently.** Your child can relax more easily if she knows the routine and doesn't need to fear any surprises.

- **Limit the number of visitors and caregivers, at least initially.** Doing so is especially important for an older child, particularly if she doesn't understand the language. She needs to figure out who her parents are and who belongs in her family before you broaden her connections.

✔ **Remember that your child may act younger than her chronological age.** She may regress and need more care and holding than other children her age. If so, give her the attention she needs. You can't spoil a child in this situation with too much love and attention.

Bonding with children with a history of abuse or neglect

When you adopt children with a history of abuse or neglect, you may not see them respond to you as quickly as you hoped. A big reason for this is that many of these children erect huge walls to guard their hearts from future hurt and rejection. Tearing down that wall may take years. The key is to keep trying and measure success in small steps. Here are some pointers:

✔ **Be patient and try to remain optimistic.** Your child may not feel affectionate toward you and may even resent you. Or, he may behave extremely well during the honeymoon phase and only start misbehaving when he wants to test your commitment.

✔ **Be creative in finding ways to make extended eye contact and spend one-on-one time together.** Your child has an entire history that doesn't include you, and he has thoughts and feelings that you haven't helped to shape and that you may have a hard time understanding. You have to show him that you're there for him. And if he feels resentment or insecurity, he may make it difficult for you.

✔ **Find ways to encourage casual physical touch, like an arm around the shoulder, a pat on the back, and so on.** Keep in mind that a child who's been abused may fear physical contact and may have to develop trust before he's comfortable with it. Don't force the issue, but don't give up either.

You may not have warm and fuzzy feelings for your child, especially if he has severe behavior problems (skip to Chapter 16 for information about behavior problems that are common to children who've been abused or neglected). After all, it's hard warming up to a child who is cursing and spitting in your face. Your job is to remember the commitment you made to this child, seek outside help when you need it, and keep on keeping on.

Expecting more visits from the social worker

Yes, the adoption agency social worker is still in your life. And she will be until your adoption is finalized. So expect a few more visits. How many visits you'll have depends on whether you're adopting domestically or internationally and the requirements of your agency.

(Although international adoptions are usually finalized in the country before the children even leave, many agencies require a certain number of post-placement supervision visits for the families when they return to the United States. For example, one Russian agency requires two post-placement visits a year for three years.)

Typically, domestic adoptions require two supervision visits. These visits take place during the first few months after your child arrives in your home and before the adoption is finalized in court. Your social worker will probably come to your home for at least one of the supervision visits. Occasionally, the visits occur at the agency.

What the social worker looks for

During the supervision visit, the social worker wants to observe you interacting with your child. She'll also interview you. She wants to know things like the following:

- **Whether you're beginning to bond with the child:** Bonding, that feeling of unquestionable attachment between a parent and a child, is different for everyone. For some people, it happens immediately; for others, it takes a while. So don't fret if you're in the it-takes-a-while category. Your social worker just wants to make sure that no impediments are preventing you from bonding with your child. She can also be a resource if you have questions or concerns about your own bonding experience.

- **How you and the child are adjusting:** Your social worker expects that you may be tired, sleep deprived, and even stressed. So you can be honest with the worker about how you feel. Remember, she understands that adding a new child to a family can be a difficult adjustment, and she wants to help you through this time.

- **Whether your extended family has welcomed the child:** Some social workers ask outright how your family has accepted the child; others get the info by chatting it out of you. Expect to talk about who's been to visit and how they responded to your child.

- **Whether your child is receiving regular medical care:** Expect to talk about the child's doctor appointments and how much the child has grown. Your social worker may even ask for the baby's current length, weight, head circumference, and so on from the latest doctor visit. (If you're adopting a newborn or an infant, regular visits to the doctor, known as *well-child visits,* are the norm; this info is just part of what the doctor's exam includes.) If your child has special medical needs, you'll talk with the social worker about any developments in that area, too.

You don't have to worry about trying to look like the perfect family. In most cases, the worker comes expecting to see a healthy family situation, and for most of us, that means love and happiness mixed with various amounts of clutter, noise, weariness, and stress. She's not looking for a utopian version of the perfect family. So put the pearls away.

If the supervision report is really, really bad

Most supervision periods go well. Some go very badly. If you're adopting domestically, the agency has the right to remove a child from your home if the social worker has concerns about the child's well-being. Typically, concerns are raised over serious issues, like any sort of abuse or neglect, mental or emotional instability of the adoptive parents (such as attempted suicide), or criminal activity that puts the child at risk. If the agency removes a child from your home, the child is usually put in temporary foster care and eventually placed with another adoptive family.

In international adoptions in which you legally adopt the child in the other country before returning to the United States, the child can't be removed from your home simply based on the social worker's concerns about the child's well-being. In that case, the worker calls Child Protective Services (CPS) and reports her suspicions. CPS then investigates the report in the same way that it investigates any other report of abuse or neglect. See the section "When the state terminates parental rights," earlier in this chapter, for details.

The details of the report

After the social worker gets all the info she needs, she writes a report to document her visit. She may also ask for family photos to accompany the report. In a domestic adoption, this report remains in your file. For an international adoption, the report is sent to the international agency and then forwarded to the child's birth country.

Sharing info with the birthmother

If you're adopting domestically, you've probably made some sort of arrangements with the birthmother regarding future contact. Perhaps you agreed to send letters and pictures; maybe you agreed to other types of contact (see Chapter 15 for a detailed discussion about keeping in touch with birthmothers). Following through with whatever you agreed to do is important, and the supervision period is an especially good time to begin. Here's why:

- ✔ Birthmothers worry that the people who adopt their children won't follow through with what they've promised. If you promise to keep her updated and then don't, she's probably going to worry that you have something to hide. She could very well think that you're not who you represented yourselves to be, and she may begin to think that the whole adoption was a mistake. If you send something shortly after your child is placed with you, on the other hand, she'll be reassured that you're trustworthy.

Some adoptive parents say whatever they have to say to the birthmother to convince her to place her child with them, without any intention of following through with their promises. Despite all the things they may tell themselves to justify this behavior — they'd be good parents, the baby would be better off with them, yadda yadda yadda — the fact of the matter is that they lied to a woman to get her baby. This ruse is not only unethical but also cruel. And it could jeopardize your acceptance by the agency to adopt additional children in the future.

✔ The birthmother is going through a time of grief and loss. Hearing from you may help alleviate her suffering. Some birthmothers worry that they've made the wrong decision; others worry that their child is being abused or has become ill. Seeing photos of the child and hearing from you in a letter can really reassure the birthmother that her decision was a good one and that her child is happy and healthy.

✔ Although you may worry that sending pictures to the birthmother will make her want to contest the adoption, the correspondence actually does just the opposite. A birthmother who hears from the family is reassured and content she made the right choice.

Helping the birthmother feel comfortable with her decision is in *your* best interest. If you understand she needs reassurance that she made the right decision and if you help her work through her grief, your family is more secure.

Lizzie

We got a call about Elizabeth on Friday, April 26, 2002. Having been foster parents for over three years, we had grown accustomed to having children enter and leave our family, sometimes at a moment's notice. We knew very little about Elizabeth, except that she needed a place to stay on an emergency temporary basis and that the placement was likely to happen that evening. We were told that Elizabeth was 12 years old and that she had some behavior problems (which are typical with all foster children due to the abuse, neglect, and separation they have suffered). We had no specifics on what those behavior problems were, and we knew nothing about the original circumstances with her birth family that resulted in her being in the foster care system.

After numerous telephone calls, it was decided that Elizabeth would come to our home that evening. As we do when any child comes to live with us, we spell their name with die cuts on their door. So on the closet door of the room that would be Elizabeth's, I put up the letters to spell "Lizzie's Room." When Elizabeth arrived at about 8:30 p.m., we learned that she was not 12, but 9 years old and in third grade. What a beautiful little girl she was. We did not see many smiles from her, but you could tell that the smile was heartwarming. The goodbye between her

(continued)

(continued)

and her former foster mother was tear filled and heartbreaking; it was apparent that both Elizabeth and her foster mother loved one another very much.

After her former foster mother left, we tried to get Elizabeth somewhat settled in her new home. We didn't have much to unpack. She came with only a small suitcase and a few special stuffed animals. Elizabeth was quiet and didn't say much. I believe for the first few weeks she was just trying to comprehend the changes that had happened in her life. As we got to know Elizabeth, we developed a special bond with her. We had no idea how long she would be with us because her caseworker was looking for an adoptive family for her. I hoped that her caseworker would allow her to stay with us long enough to finish the school year. During that time, my husband and I discussed the possibility of our becoming Elizabeth's adoptive family. As the school year ended, we let Elizabeth's caseworker know that we were considering the possibility of adopting Elizabeth.

When we decided we wanted to adopt Elizabeth and make her a permanent member of our family, we felt it was important to ask Elizabeth's permission to make sure that she also wanted that same thing. On a Sunday afternoon, we sat Elizabeth down in the living room and told her of our desires to adopt her. We told her that we felt she was an important member of our family and that she had touched so many people's lives in our family — grandparents, aunts, uncles, and cousins. All of those people also wanted her to become a permanent member of our family. We explained that we understood she has a birthmother and birth sisters and that the importance of them will never be discounted in our home. We explained to her that we still wanted her to feel comfortable having a picture of her birth family displayed in her bedroom. We told her it was okay if she did not call us Mom and Dad, but if she wanted to, that was okay, too. We explained to Elizabeth that much like she misses her birth family, we feel sad that we didn't get to experience her early years with her. Thankfully, through the process of making a life book and talking with previous foster care providers and teachers, we have managed to piece together a small bit of Elizabeth's history. We even obtained a picture of Elizabeth as a toddler.

To help give Elizabeth a sense of control during the adoptive process, we told her that she can change her first or her middle name if she would like. Although she is allowed to choose a new name, we told her that she had to keep Elizabeth as a part of her name since that is something that her birthmother gave her. We also told her that she has to continue to use the name Lizzie because that is the only way we have ever known her. She is thinking she will change her name to Erynne Elizabeth Allen. (Mom influenced that decision a little by telling Lizzie that she really likes the name Erynne for a girl.)

Elizabeth is a bright, attractive, creative, and resilient fourth grader. With all the adversity she has experienced in her short life, it is amazing to us that she handles herself so well. We are blessed to be able to provide a permanent home for her through adoption.

Laura and Brian Allen

Chapter 12

Here Comes the Judge: The Court Appearance

*I*n nearly every single adoption, the finalization hearing is pretty much a formality. If you've been working with a reputable agency or attorney, you already will have done everything that needs to be done to convince a judge to put his or her stamp of official approval on the adoption. The court proceeding itself, in fact, usually takes only about 10 or 15 minutes.

But what a nerve-wracking 10 or 15 minutes that can be — especially if you've never been a participant in a court hearing before. Just remember that everything, for the most part, is scripted, and your attorney will tell you whatever you need to know. To give you a heads up on what to expect, this chapter explains who you'll find at the hearing, what each person — including you — is responsible for, and what happens in the courtroom (or the judge's chambers).

REMEMBER

Forget the histrionics of *The Practice* or the surprise confessions in *Perry Mason*. Your biggest challenge will be keeping your little one quiet so that the court reporter can hear the testimony.

Where and When and How to Dress

Although in your heart, you considered the adoption a done deal as soon as your child came home (placement in domestic adoptions) or was assigned to you (for international adoptions), the government takes a little more time to catch up. So when you adopt domestically, your finalization date *follows* the supervision period of your adoption, which can last anywhere from just a couple of weeks to a few (usually three) months for infant adoptions and up to a year for adoptions of older children (to allow enough time to see how the child adjusts and how the family deals with everything). (See Chapter 11 for information on what you can expect during the supervision period.) When you adopt internationally, the finalization usually happens when you pick your child up. See the later section "When finalization isn't finalization" for the exceptions to this rule.

For domestic adoptions, the finalization hearing takes place in a county within your state. What county you finalize in depends on your state laws (if your state has laws governing this), the policies of your agency (many agencies finalize in the county where the agency is located), or the preferences of your attorney. Once at the courthouse, you go to either a courtroom or the judge's chambers, where you meet your lawyer and wait until the judge is ready for you.

Following are a few tips and suggestions to keep in mind:

- ✓ **Give yourself extra time and arrive early.** Finding a parking spot near a courthouse is usually a feat all its own, and it's that much harder if you're not used to driving around downtown, where one-way streets abound.

- ✓ **Stand when the judge enters and leaves the room.** A safe rule to follow is to stand whenever the judge stands.

- ✓ **Dress up.** First, proper attire shows respect for the court (and judges like it). Second, this is a big day, and chances are that you'll end up with photos to commemorate it.

  If you don't own a suit, don't worry. You don't have to dress fancy, just neatly.

- ✓ **Don't take pictures during the hearing.** Most judges don't object to cameras or video recorders in the courtroom, as long as you wait until after the hearing before you get them out and start shooting. Before you take any pictures, though, ask the judge for permission.

If you adopt internationally, you may get to do the finalization twice: once in your child's birth country when you pick him up and one more time when you get back home. (See the later section "Making Your Court Appearance in International Adoptions" for specific details on what you can expect.)

Your agency or lawyer will tell you, well in advance, exactly when your court date is, where you need to be, and what you can expect during the hearing (questions, procedures, and so on, which the following sections cover in detail). Nothing about this day should surprise you.

The Cast and Crew and Their Roles

You have a whole cast of characters (literally and figuratively) to help you adopt, so why would you expect the finalization to be any different? When you head to the courthouse for your finalization hearing, you can expect the following people to be there to cheer you on.

Your lawyer

Your attorney has to be at the hearing to represent you. Your attorney will guide you every step of the way. He'll show you where to sit, tell you what to do, and do most of the talking (go figure). He is your friend (okay, so you pay him to be there, but the point's the same: He's on your side). His job is to convince the judge that you're good parents and should be allowed to continue parenting the child.

Most attorneys take time, either in a separate meeting before the hearing date or in the few spare minutes you have before you go before the judge, to go through exactly what will happen once you're inside. He'll prep you by telling you the order of appearance, what questions he's going to ask (some lawyers send you a typed list well in advance of the hearing), what questions the judge may ask, and so on. He won't ask any surprise questions that you're not prepared to answer.

No other attorney is present, and no one cross-examines you.

You

You (and your spouse if you're married) must attend the finalization hearing. Your job is to answer the questions your lawyer (and possibly the judge) asks in a voice loud enough that the court reporter can hear.

All those present in the courtroom understand that this is a special day for you; they also understand it can be a nerve-wracking experience. They expect you to have the jitters and to be emotional, and they won't be surprised or suspicious if you forget your birth date or spell your name wrong.

I, Tracy, got so flustered by the dates that I ended up testifying that our son Adam came home to us one day before he was actually born. Fortunately, they're very forgiving of these mistakes.

Your child

If you're adopting an infant, you're welcome to bring your child with you for the court hearing, but the child's presence isn't required. If you're adopting an older child through a public agency, your child's presence may be required. If your kid is 12 years old or older, she may even be asked to testify. (Again, your attorney will prep anyone who has to speak.)

If you have a little one, bring a grandparent or another adult who can step out into the hall with the child if the baby begins to make too much noise. The judge will stop the hearing if the court reporter can't hear the testimony.

The judge

The judge may be male or female, old or young, and friendly or all business. It doesn't matter who or what the judge is, though; she is still the one in charge. She can conduct the hearing any way she wants.

The judge's job is to make sure that the adoption is handled appropriately and according to the laws of that state. She can stop the attorney at any time to ask her own questions. If she feels everything is satisfactory, she'll grant the adoption. She may even be happy to pose for photos with you and your child after the hearing.

The social worker

If you've been working with a social worker, she may or may not come to the finalization hearing. Her presence depends on the laws in your state and the agency's policies. (Some agencies don't routinely send the social worker to the hearings.)

When the social worker's presence is required, the judge may want her to testify that she recommends the adoption be finalized. When her presence isn't required, she may come just as a courtesy to you. She may want to give you encouragement, calm your nerves, and share in your joy.

Other people

Here are a few other people you're likely to see at your finalization hearing:

- ✔ **A court reporter:** This person records everything that transpires during the court hearing.

- ✔ **The court clerk:** This person operates like a secretary to the judge. She handles paperwork, gets copies made and distributed, handles the application of the birth certificate, and so on.

- ✔ **Family and friends:** Many people invite their parents or close friends to the hearing. Before you invite too many people, check with your attorney to see what size the courtroom is. Some of them are pretty small.

Taking the Stand: What Happens

After the introduction of the judge — you know, the "All rise. The honorable so-and-so presiding" speech (although some courts dispense with this formality) — and everyone is assembled in the courtroom, the fun begins.

First, someone (sometimes the bailiff, sometimes the judge) announces the purpose of the hearing ("We are here on the matter of Court Case <Whatever>. . .). This announcement is necessary to give those folks who may have entered the wrong courtroom the chance to gather their belongings and hie themselves thither.

Then, before any of the testimony begins, you and all the other witnesses may be instructed to stand, raise your right hands, and swear to tell the truth, the whole truth, and . . . well . . . you know the rest. (If this doesn't happen at the beginning of the hearing, each individual will be sworn in right before testifying.)

Now you get down to business. Your attorney calls you to the stand to testify, or you may be instructed to give your testimony from your seat. You'll probably be speaking into a microphone, so talk slowly and distinctly.

The order of appearance

You and your spouse may be the only witnesses, or the social worker may also testify. You generally are the first up. If you're married, both of you will testify. Which of the two of you goes first usually depends on who you *want* to go first. If you have a preference, tell your attorney, and he can probably accommodate you.

Choose wisely when deciding who will testify first: The first one to testify gets to answer the bulk of the questions (explained in the next section), so pick the one who did better in Public Speaking 101 or who is less inclined to pass out in front of an audience.

Questions you'll be asked and how to respond

The questions you're going to answer are very straightforward. No tricks. No surprises. No conundrums you have to puzzle over. (In fact, your lawyer has probably already informed you of the questions you can expect.)

The first thing you're asked to do (at least after you take the oath that you'll be truthful) is to identify yourself. So state your full name and spell it. (All witnesses have to do this at the beginning of their testimony.)

Then you have to give your complete address.

The first one to testify is asked about the following:

- ✔ The date of your marriage
- ✔ The date of your child's birth
- ✔ The date the child was placed with you

Of course, these don't sound like hard questions, but you'd be surprised how easy it is to actually forget these important dates. Some attorneys make this easier and say things like, "Were you married on October 16, 1979?" and all you have to do is say yes. Ask your lawyer if you need to have the dates memorized.

Usually only one parent has to answer all of these types of questions. The other parent is just asked whether he or she heard the spouse's testimony and agrees with the answers that were given.

You'll both be asked the following:

- ✔ Whether you understand that your child will have all the legal rights of any child born to you and will inherit from you equally
- ✔ Whether you understand that you will have child support obligations if the marriage ends in divorce or if one parent dies
- ✔ Whether it's your desire to legally adopt the child

The judge can interject any questions she wants to ask, but in routine adoptions, she usually doesn't. Remember, your judge probably has a full docket of adoption cases to listen to on the day your hearing is scheduled, and she probably wants to get through them as quickly as possible.

After all the questions have been asked and answered satisfactorily, the judge grants the adoption. Head to the following section to find out what paperwork you get and what your next steps will probably be.

What you'll get at the end of the day

When the judge grants the adoption, he signs the *adoption decree* (an example is shown in Figure 12-1). You get a copy.

In addition to the adoption decree, your child's new birth certificate is ordered. Called the "Delayed Certificate of Birth," this birth certificate uses the child's new legal name and lists you as the child's parents. Except for the heading using the word "delayed," the birth certificate looks like any other birth certificate and doesn't indicate in any way that the child is adopted. It may take anywhere from two weeks to two months to receive the certificate in the mail.

You'll be given the opportunity to order as many copies of the birth certificate as you like, but you need to pay for them upfront. Bring your checkbook and plan on spending $5 to $10 for each copy.

Making Your Court Appearance in International Adoptions

One of the highlights of adopting internationally is traveling to your child's birth country and finalizing your adoption. Of course, the rules and procedures vary from country to country. (In some cases, you won't be finalizing; see the later section "When finalization isn't finalization" to see details on that.) Here are some issues you'll want to ask your agency about:

✔ **Does anyone escort you to the courthouse?** Reputable agencies have someone — guides or staff members, for example — in the country to meet you at the airport when you arrive and basically shepherd you through all the things you need to do — including going to the finalization hearing or any interviews you need to attend. Often this person acts as your translator as well, if you need one.

Follow this person around like a lamb. He knows the customs. He knows the procedure. He knows the way to the courthouse. By relying on this person, you can focus your time and attention on your little one.

- ✔ **Will you be alone or attending the finalization hearing with a bunch of other adoptive families?** The answer usually depends on the country you're adopting from and the travel policy of your agency. When you adopt from some countries, your agency may schedule you to travel with a group of parents who are adopting from the same place you are. Even if you travel with a group and go, en masse, to your hearing or interviews or whatever else, you generally can expect to have individual meetings with the officials.

- ✔ **Whom can you expect to attend the hearing?** Your legal counsel in the country and a translator (who may be one and the same person) will be present, and so may an agency representative. Typically, the birth-mother doesn't attend, but ask to know for sure.

- ✔ **How many court appearances will you have?** The procedures in some countries require, in addition to a finalization hearing, preliminary hearings that you may or may not have to attend. If you don't have to attend, an attorney who has power of attorney will represent you. Keep in mind that, in addition to a hearing, you may have other meetings with officials.

- ✔ **What do you receive at the end?** Often you get an adoption decree, written in the language of the country you're adopting from. If this is the case, your agency may require that you register the foreign decree with your state when you get back home. Doing so essentially puts the adoption in your state's record books and automatically means that you get another adoption decree, this one in English. You will also receive a birth certificate issued in your child's birth country. When you return home, you can request that a state birth certificate be issued. Each state has its own procedure (some, for example, require that you re-adopt; others simply want to see the proper documentation from the finalization in the other country), so ask a local agency or attorney for guidance.

The adoption laws in foreign countries vary greatly and can differ from similar laws in the United States. And, like U.S. laws and procedures, the laws and procedures in other countries can change at any time. So if you're adopting internationally, your best resources are your agency and other people who've recently adopted from the same country you're planning to adopt from. (If you're not a member of an adoption support group, this is a good reason to join. Your agency should also be able to give you names of folks who've adopted recently.)

STATE OF INDIANA   IN THE MARION COUNTY SUPERIOR COURT

SS:

COUNTY OF MARION   CAUSE NO.

FILED

Judge of the
Marion Superior Court
Probate Division

IN RE THE ADOPTION OF

ADOPTION DECREE

    COME NOW the Petitioners, _____ and _____ , husband and wife, having filed their Verified Petition for Adoption of the above-named child, a minor, as their child and heir-at-law, which Petition is as follows:

(H.I.)

and the written consent of the biological mother to the adoption of said child to be adopted having been filed with the Court as Exhibit A to the Verified Petition for Adoption, which written consent is as follows:

(H.I)

and the Court, having heard the evidence in the matter involved herein and being duly advised in the premises, now finds:

1. This Court has jurisdiction over the parties to and the subject matter of this proceeding;
2. The allegation of the Petition have been proven and are true;
3. The child was placed in the home of the Petitioners on_____ and has resided there for more than sixty (60) days;
4. The proper consents have been obtained, are in the proper form, and have been filed;
5. The biological mother refused to name a putative father of the child. The unnamed putative father was given notice via publication pursuant to Ind. Code § 31-19-4-1, et seq.;
6. All of the requirements of Ind Code § 31-19 with respect to putative fathers have been satisfied;
7. The child cannot or should not be returned to the biological parents' home;
8. _____a duly licensed child placing agency, has filed its final report recommending approval of this adoption;
9. Petitioners are not prohibited from adopting the child as a result of inappropriate criminal history under Ind. Code § 31-19-11-1(c);
10. Petitioners are of sufficient ability to rear said child and furnish suitable support and education;
11. It is in the best interest of the child to be adopted by Petitioners.

IT IS, THEREFORE, ORDERED, ADJUDGED, AND DECREED that said child be, and hereby is, adopted as the child and heir-at-law of_____ husband and wife, and that said child's name shall be changed to that of _____ .

So Ordered on_____ .

_____
JUDGE, MARION COUNTY SUPERIOR
COURT, PROBATE DIVISION

Figure 12-1:
A typical adoption decree.

When finalization isn't finalization

In some international adoptions, you don't have a finalization hearing in your child's birth country:

- ✔ **If you're *not* traveling to your child's birth country (in other words, your child will be escorted to the United States alone):** In many cases, you must actually meet your child face to face before the birth country allows you to finalize. If this is the case in your adoption and you can't travel to the country, you don't meet this requirement. Keep in mind, however, that not all foreign governments have this rule; some countries, like Guatemala, let you adopt "by proxy." Your agency will let you know the rules for your particular situation.

- ✔ **If you're adopting from a country that grants you *guardianship* of the child:** In this situation, the child can leave the country with you with the expectation that you'll adopt back home. Some countries won't allow you (as foreigners) to actually adopt a child; instead they'll let you become the child's legal guardian.

For these adoptions, you're granted guardianship of your child in the child's birth country, and you finalize back home in the good ol' U.S. of A.

When you need to finalize more than once

Even if you finalize in your child's birth country, that doesn't necessarily mean that you're done with your finalization hearings. In the following cases, you have to finalize again back in the United States:

- ✔ **If you (or both of you, if you're married) didn't personally see your child prior to the adoption finalization in the other country:** According to the Bureau of Citizenship and Immigration Services (the government agency you'll be most intimately involved with when you adopt internationally; see Chapter 3 for details), the parent (or parents) must see the child before finalization in order for citizenship to be automatically granted. If this doesn't happen, you must refinalize back in the United States; then citizenship will follow. *Note:* In March 2003, the Immigration and Naturalization Service (INS) was absorbed into the Department of Homeland Security under the new name of the Bureau of Citizenship and Immigration Services.

- ✔ **If you live in Utah:** Utah doesn't recognize adoptions in other countries as legally binding. So if you're a Utah resident, it won't recognize your child's adoption until you finalize back home.

If you're adopting internationally, be sure to discuss the issue of refinalizing with your agency and an adoption lawyer in your state. Even if you don't fit into the two categories that make refinalization necessary, you may decide (or be recommended) to refinalize anyway.

Also keep in mind that the process for refinalization varies greatly from state to state, and sometimes even within the same state. Some states have developed special procedures specifically for refinalizations; others treat the refinalization exactly like the finalizations. If you're planning to refinalize your adoption, discuss the procedure with your attorney, as well.

What to Do after the Deed Is Done

Hallelujah! It's over! No more worries that someone may come and take your child away. You're a family, and your child legally has your last name. Now's the time to bask in the glow of the light at the end of the tunnel. You just have a couple more things to wrap up.

Celebrate!

Many families plan celebrations following their adoption finalizations. Depending on how old your child is, this celebration could be anything from a formal family dinner to an evening at a local kid-friendly restaurant to a trip to Disney World. Some families plan special things like sitting for a formal family photograph or mailing special announcements.

If your child is still an infant, he won't care much what you do as long as the bottle, the blankie, and Mom and Dad are nearby. He'll just go with the flow. If you're adopting an older child, planning the celebration is an excellent chance to include your child in the decision making. She may want to personally plan a celebration that reflects her own tastes, or she may not want to celebrate at all.

For an older child, this day may represent a final loss of the birth family. So let your son or daughter take the lead in how — or even whether — to celebrate.

Some parents of older children like to present their child with a gift to signify their new status. A ball cap or T-shirt with the child's new last name printed on it, an engraved gold bracelet or locket, or even a collectible figurine can become a treasured keepsake to remember the special day.

Going to court: What our hearts already knew

For me, going to court to finalize our adoptions was like our wedding ceremony. The adoption of our children happened in our hearts long before we ever went to court. The commitment of myself to my husband happened in my heart long before our actual wedding ceremony. Going to court and participating in the wedding ceremony are what we do in public, for the judge and lawyers (to make it legal), and for our families, so they can participate and be affirmed as part of the process. I enjoyed our adoption days, just like I enjoyed my wedding day, but in my heart, the knots had already been tied.

Christine Rembert

Get your child's Social Security number

Once you have your child's birth certificate (which was ordered on the finalization day and can take a couple weeks to a couple months to actually receive), you can apply for your kid's Social Security number.

To apply for the Social Security number, take the following paperwork to your local Social Security office:

- ✔ Your child's birth certificate
- ✔ Another form of ID for your child, like hospital or doctor records, baptismal records, day-care or school records, or your adoption decree
- ✔ Your own identification

All documentation must be original documents, not copies.

You can apply for the Social Security card by mail, but you have to mail all your original documents. They will be returned to you (or so they say).

You'll receive the card in the mail 10 to 14 business days after you apply. You may also be given a telephone number that you can call in a few days to find out your child's Social Security number.

Unless tax season is just around the corner, you probably won't give much thought to how long it takes to get your child's Social Security number. But if April 15 is fast approaching and you still haven't heard from Social Security, don't panic. Although as a rule you *do* need your dependents' Social Security numbers for tax purposes, if the number isn't available yet, you can enter a special code number in its place. Any professional tax preparer can guide you in this process.

Part III
Birthmothers and Birthfathers

In this part . . .

Birthparents, especially birthmothers, are important for a number of reasons. They share a genetic connection — and a history if you're adopting an older kid — with your child. Their decisions directly impact you and your family. Even if you don't have contact with them, your child will almost surely ask you questions about them. Instead of pretending that they don't exist or being overly concerned about the part they play in your adoption, you can accept their role in your child's life.

The chapters in this part explain who birthparents are, what role they can play in placement and adoption, and what you can do to acknowledge the connection they have to your child.

Chapter 13

God Bless the Birthmothers

In This Chapter

▶ Getting to know the birthmother

▶ Understanding how she makes an adoption plan

▶ Doing what you can to help her, now and as the years go by

Since before Moses — possibly the most famous adoptee in Western culture — children have been placed for adoption. And since before Moses' birthmother, Jochebed, women have made adoption arrangements. Yet until fairly recently (within the last couple of decades), birthmothers have traditionally been silent participants in adoption arrangements.

In the not-too-distant past, many unmarried women who found themselves in a family way — and without a quick marriage to look forward to — were often spirited away. Some went to stay with relatives; others went to maternity homes, where they stayed until they delivered their babies. When they returned home months later, many returned without the children they had given birth to. The maternity homes or the attorneys or doctors who knew the families arranged for the placements of the babies. The intent was to save the girl's, as well as her family's, reputation and to end, as quietly and discreetly as possible, an unfortunate and unmentionable episode.

Today, things are very different. The social stigma of having a child out of wedlock is pretty much gone — as is the idea that "good girls" wait for marriage and that "bad girls" mess around and get pregnant. And in an age when unmarried women can conceive and bear and raise children without stigma, most people understand that deciding *not* to parent a child you've carried — and cared for — for nine months can be the more difficult decision.

So whether you tend to regard birthmothers as saints or sinners, the truth is that most are simply ordinary women who make difficult decisions in difficult times. To help you understand who birthmothers are, this chapter debunks the myths about them, explains what they "get" out of making adoption plans, and offers suggestions for what you can do to help the person who has entrusted you with her child.

The Birthmother: Who She Is

There is no "average" profile of a birthmother. She can be any age or any race and can come from a variety of different socioeconomic backgrounds. The birthmothers I (Katrina) have worked with have been from 13 to 42 years old. They've been Caucasian, African American, Hispanic, Asian, East Indian, Native American, and of mixed races. They've been elementary school students, college students, school dropouts, and master-degreed. They've been unemployed, gainfully employed, or stay-at-home moms. They've been married and single, fat and thin, tall and short, wealthy and poor, urban and rural, and law-abiding or not.

A birthmother could be the girl next door, your cousin, your co-worker, or even your mother. She doesn't wear a scarlet letter to identify herself, and she's not easily recognizable. You probably know one.

One thing many birth moms have in common is that they gave birth to a child and then, at some point, made the difficult decision to allow someone else to raise that child.

Other birthmothers don't voluntarily relinquish their parental rights. Instead, their children are removed from their home by Child Protective Services. In these situations, the children become available for adoption following court procedures that terminate the birth mothers' parental rights. Like birthmothers mentioned previously, these women represent various ages, races, and socioeconomic levels. And, like other birthmothers, they find themselves in difficult circumstances and struggle with parenting their children.

These women, however, do not make an adoption plan; instead, they neglect, abuse, or fail to protect their children until someone reports them and their children are removed from the home. After the children are removed, the courts give the birthmother multiple "assignments" to prove that she's worthy of her children's return. She may be ordered to attend parenting classes, find employment, secure an appropriate living situation, participate in counseling, or do whatever else the court deems necessary.

Many overwhelmed birthmothers find these court-ordered mandates to be, well, overwhelming. In other words, they may not be able to successfully complete what the judge orders them to do. Eventually, these women lose all their rights to their children. (Head to Chapter 11 for information on what happens in these situations.) Although you can argue that these women made specific choices that led to the removal of their children, their feelings of grief, loss, guilt, and shame are quite real.

Myths you may have heard

If you're like many people, you may have some preconceived notions about who birthmothers are and why they make the decision they do. Following are some common perceptions that don't really hold up when you realize that there is no such thing as the standard "profile" of a birthmother:

Myth 1: Most are teenagers

Some birthmothers are teenagers, of course. But the average birthmother I (Katrina) see is in her mid-20s and is already parenting one or more children. These women understand what parenting a child requires emotionally, financially, and physically. They're wise enough to determine whether they can provide what their child needs, and they have the maturity to make a sacrificial decision to benefit their child.

Myth 2: She "doesn't want" her child

Most birthmothers want their children. They love their children. They just recognize that they may not be able to provide a good life for their child. Maybe they're too young. Maybe they don't have the necessary financial resources. Maybe they live in an abusive relationship or struggle with addictions. Maybe they're stressed to the breaking point or lack the stability they need to provide for a child. Whatever the reason, something in their lives prevents them from adequately parenting their child, and they do what good parents do: They see what their child needs and do what's necessary to provide it.

Even women who have abused or neglected their children often wish they could have their children returned. They may or may not understand what they did wrong or where they failed. If they do understand, they may still wish for "one more chance" to make things right. If they don't understand, they may feel victimized and angry.

Myth 3: They're monsters who don't care for their children

This is a common misperception about women whose parental rights have been taken away by the state. Although some women do, unfortunately, fit that description, most of these women love their children and want to do what's right for them. But even though they may recognize their inability to parent, they're not strong enough or don't have the resources they need to take the necessary steps to keep their child safe.

Many of these women were raised in abusive homes, with no role model for appropriate parenting or discipline, and find themselves repeating the same patterns they experienced so painfully as children. (These patterns could include physically or emotionally abusing their children, neglecting their children, or submissively allowing others to abuse or misuse their children.)

Books relating to international adoption

In international adoptions, you probably aren't going to have contact with your child's birthmother, probably won't have the opportunity to meet her or talk to her, and probably won't have any answers when your child begins to ask the questions that nearly all adoptees ask. And searches, explained in Chapter 19, will be that much more difficult for your child than for children adopted domestically. Two extraordinary books, *After the Morning Calm: Reflections Of Korean Adult Adoptees* (Sunrise Ventures, 2002) and *I Wish for You a Beautiful Life: Letters from Korean Birth Mothers of Ae Ran Won to Their Children* (Yeong and Yeong Book Company, 1999), give voice to the children and the birthmothers of international adoptions. Although specifically relating to international adoptions in Korea, the sentiments expressed in these works are universal.

After The Morning Calm is a collection of memories, reflections, and poems written by adults who, as children, were adopted from Korea. Edited by Dr. Sook Wilkinson and Nancy Fox, the pieces speak to the issues that many adoptees, of all backgrounds and situations, struggle with.

I Wish for You a Beautiful Life is a collection of letters written by Korean birthmothers to the children they placed for adoption. Taken from the files of birthmothers who resided at Ae Ran Won, a home for unwed mothers in South Korea, these letters offer insight into the pain and hope and love that these birthmothers feel for the children they let go. The letters are organized into thematic units with an introduction to each section that provides context. The book also includes a foreword that gives advice on how and when to share the sentiments and powerful emotions of these letters with older children.

Who she is to you

The birthmother is the person who gives you one of the greatest desires of your heart. She gave life to the child you love and are raising as your own. You may resent her. You may be jealous of her and wish that she didn't exist. But you mustn't lose sight of where you would be without her. Childless — or without the child you have.

If you've adopted an older child who experienced abuse or neglect, you're going to have a more difficult time having positive feelings for your child's birthmother. As your love grows for your child, so does your protectiveness and your sorrow at what he experienced. The reality is, though, that you can't do anything about the past abuse at this point. The damage was done, the state intervened, and now you're a family. Your child suffered and continues to suffer as a result of what he experienced. What he needs now is a stable home with supportive parents — parents who throw all of their energy into demonstrating the love, consistency, and commitment that their child has always needed. What the child doesn't need is any more negativity, blame, or anger. Let your own anger go (often easier said than done, we know), help your child deal with the feelings he has, and concentrate on the bright future you all have together.

The adoption triad

All adoptions involve three participants: you (the adoptive parent), the child, and the birthmother (and birthfather). You're all distinct individuals with your own needs, but you're also connected together through the adoption. This relationship is called the *adoption triad* (sometimes you hear the term *adoption triangle* used, too), and it represents the dynamics of the relationship between the three of you.

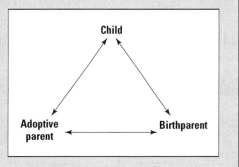

The birthmother is also important to you because your child will undoubtedly have feelings about her, whether or not they've ever met. (These feelings are explained in more detail in the following section.) If you adopt an older infant or child, your child may have a history with her and be working through the separation.

Who she is to your child

A young child might refer to his birthmother as "my birth mommy," "my birth lady," "the lady who grew me in her tummy," or many other variations. Some children refer to their birthmother by her first name. But, whatever they call her, she's an important person in their lives.

As they grow older, they may love her, hate her, miss her, long to meet her, feel abandoned by her, fantasize about her, or just try not to think about her at all. All of these feelings are normal, and the same child may experience all of them within a short period of time.

Older children who were removed from their homes because of abuse or neglect have many of the same conflicting emotions. You may think that these kids would hate their birthparents and be relieved and grateful to have been rescued from a difficult situation. Surprisingly, most of the kids just want to go home. Even if "home" was really bad, it was familiar, and the child knew what to expect. The children I (Katrina) have worked with in these situations usually recall their birthmothers with fondness and longing — even the children who I knew had suffered horrendous abuse. Many of the children fantasized that their birthmother would return for them. Even the kids who were well established in their new homes would say things to me like "When I go back to my birthmother . . . " or "When my birthmother comes back for me. . . ."

As adoptive parents, you need to understand that these comments come from the feelings of abandonment and pain that children are experiencing. At this point in their lives, they can't accept the fact that their mother is never coming back. Your continued love and your refusal to be rattled by their comments are very important in this situation. Professional counseling for you and your child may be helpful as well.

Making an Adoption Plan

At some time during her pregnancy, a birthmother decides to consider adoption for her child. At that point, she may read the ads in the Yellow Pages or newspaper, or she may receive a referral from her doctor or take the advice of a friend and eventually call someone to help her with her adoption plan. (Depending on who she's working with — agency or attorney, for example — she may or may not receive counseling and information about all of her options.) Following are the things she must do:

✔ She must decide what type of adoption she's comfortable with and how much openness she wants.

✔ She may select the adoptive family and choose to meet with them, or not.

✔ She has to plan her hospital experience and decide whom she'd like to share it with.

✔ In the midst of all of this planning and decision making, she also has to find a doctor, go for regular checkups, buy maternity clothes, and do all the other things pregnant women do.

As you can imagine, making an adoption plan during a pregnancy is very difficult. After all, most people don't set out to conceive a child so that they can place that baby for adoption. Birthmothers are like anyone else: They have their own dreams for their children and their own imagined versions of what building a family would be like. The difference is that growing within them or already born is the child that perhaps they've always wanted but, for whatever reason, don't feel that they can parent.

If you're adopting an older child, a birthmother whose parental rights have been terminated by the state doesn't make an adoption plan. In these cases, the judge and the case manager make all the decisions. For more on state termination of parental rights, see Chapter 11.

Information she's asked to provide

When a birthmother works with an agency or a reputable attorney, she generally has to provide quite a bit of information and answer many questions. Here are examples of the type of info she's asked to give:

- ✔ Identifying information, such as her name, address, birth date, and Social Security number
- ✔ Information about herself, such as her education level, marital history and status, and occupation
- ✔ Information about her health, including her complete medical history and whether she's had any previous pregnancies
- ✔ Information about the birthfather
- ✔ Her reasons for choosing adoption

Agencies also gather a complete social history. This history includes information on any other children the birthmother may have, her parents, her grandparents, and her siblings. In addition, she's asked the same types of questions about the birthfather's family. She is also quizzed about sexually transmitted diseases, HIV, and her alcohol and drug usage.

Gathering this type of information is a standard practice of reputable agencies and attorneys. In many adoptions, this information comprises the bulk of what you may learn about the birthmother, particularly if your adoption isn't open or if you adopt internationally.

If you're adopting an older child who was removed from his or her birthmother, you won't be getting information from the birthmother. In these cases, she isn't generally asked to provide additional information for the adoption of her kids. Instead, you'll receive the information in her file (the information that was gathered during the investigation of the abuse) and information gathered while her children were in foster care (things like their doctor reports, school records, assessments by counselors, and so on).

Services and aid she can (and can't) receive

Many birthmothers who work with adoption agencies receive support services from the agencies. These services include things like counseling, referrals to necessary services, and so on.

Occasionally, especially when you adopt a newborn, you may be responsible for financially helping the birthmother through the pregnancy. This aid is more likely if you adopt through an attorney (or a facilitator), but some agencies also expect you to help with birthmother expenses.

Each state has laws regarding what type of help birthmothers can and can't receive. The services most commonly allowed include payment of her hospital and medical bills, her attorney and legal fees, counseling expenses, her living expenses (housing and food costs, for example) during the pregnancy, and any traveling costs necessary for the adoption.

Be aware that many states don't specify what expenses are not allowed. Arizona's statutes, for example, state that any expense the court finds unauthorized or unreasonable is not allowed. Montana, however, has a statute that strictly forbids payments for vehicles, education, wages, or vacations.

Also remember that some states have a specific cap on these expenses; others allow whatever is "reasonable and customary." Some states limit the time following the birth (usually four to eight weeks) that these expenses can continue to be paid; other states have no such restrictions.

Be sure that the agency or attorney you work with knows all the adoption laws that apply in your situation. They differ from state to state, and sometimes (like when you adopt a child from another state), your state laws aren't the only ones that matter. Go to Chapter 7 for lists of questions you can ask the agency or attorney you're considering.

Chapter 4 gives you all the details on the financial help you may be expected to provide birthmothers, but keep in mind that most birthmothers aren't in this situation to make money.

The forms that she signs and what they mean

After the child has been born, the birthmother signs an adoption consent form (sometimes called a *relinquishment* form). Agencies and lawyers use their own versions of these forms. As a result, consents are sometimes several separate forms that the birthmother has to sign; other consents may be just one really long form.

A basic adoption consent form needs to give only the child's name and birth date, the birthparents' names, and a statement that says they're consenting to the adoption. Most agencies and attorneys add additional information to the consent or have the birthmother sign additional affidavits concerning certain information. Here are some examples of the other statements that may be attached to the adoption consent form (go to Chapter 11 for the complete details on the consent form):

✔ A statement that transfers custody of the child to the agency or the adoptive parents

✔ A statement that allows the agency or the adoptive parents to seek medical treatment for the child

✔ A statement that assures that the birthmother isn't under the influence of drugs or medication that would impair her abilities

✔ A statement that the birthmother understands that her decision is final and can't be canceled or revoked

Regardless what the various consent forms look like, they fulfill the same function: When the birthmother signs them, she is legally relinquishing, or giving up, her parental rights to her child. And if you think about how sweaty-palmed most of us get at the legal language of more-mundane contracts — like a lease agreement for a car or a consent form for an adventure cruise — you can perhaps understand how emotionally wrenching signing these papers is, even if you're sure that the decision is the right one.

When the decision becomes final

In many states, like Indiana, the birthmother's consent to the adoption is final on the date that she signs the papers. This means that, unless the birthmother can prove that she was coerced or lied to or that she had mental health issues preventing her from understanding what she signed, she can't simply change her mind and reclaim her child.

In other states, the birthmother has a certain period of time after she signs the papers during which she can change her mind about the adoption. In Maryland, for example, the revocation period is 30 days. This means that 29 days after a birthmother signs her adoption papers, she can ask for her child to be returned to her.

Who can and can't direct the adoption decision

The only people who can direct the adoption decision are the birthparents themselves. They need to decide once and for all whether they're going to place their child in the care of the adoptive parents. The agency may push, the lawyer may push, and the adoptive parents can promise whatever they want. But whether adoption is the right decision or not all boils down to what the birthparents think and what they feel they should or shouldn't do.

When the birthparents' rights have been terminated by the court, the child's fate is determined first by the judge who frees the child for adoption and then by the case manager or adoption specialists who interview and select the adoptive family.

Although these revocation periods are very scary, it's rare for a birthmother to change her mind about the adoption after the child has been placed. Most women take time to weigh their decision before they sign the papers, and they truly believe that adoption is the right choice for their child. Even though they experience grief, they usually still believe that they made the best decision.

Helping the Birthmother: What You Can Do

Birthmothers don't cease to exist after they sign the consent forms. They don't disappear, nor do they teleport to a distant galaxy. They're still around, and for many of them, the first weeks and months following the placement are the hardest. As they grieve, they go on — but without the child they carried and gave birth to and, if the birthmother made an adoption plan for her older infant or child, actually parented.

Regardless of how you feel about her — whether you agree with her life choices, like her personally, feel anger or jealousy toward her — you can't forget that the child you have exists because of her and, unless the state stepped in to terminate her parental rights, the decisions she made.

So do you owe her?

No, and yes.

No, because although she is connected to your child, her needs aren't the ones you're responsible for. You're responsible for your child's needs. But yes, because one of your child's needs is to be able to embrace his history, and his history is that of an adopted child.

Treating her with respect

The best way to help the birthmother is to respect her and honor her decisions. Depending on your particular adoption situation, you may or may not have personal contact with her. If you're adopting a newborn, for example, you may have an opportunity to be at the hospital while she's there; but if you're adopting an older child or a child from another country, you probably won't ever meet your child's birthmother. Of course, actually meeting her face to face isn't the only opportunity you'll have to treat her with kindness and respect. At some point, you're going to be talking to your child about her.

What you can do if you're at the hospital with her

If you're at the hospital with her, recognize her role as the mother of the child. Here are some suggestions:

- ✔ Give her the space she needs to really ponder her decision and to do what she believes is right. Don't hover and don't press.

- ✔ Follow her lead. Give her the time she needs with her child. She can demand time with her child if she needs to. Don't let it go that far. Ask her things like "Would you like us to leave you alone with the baby for a while?" or "What would you like us to do for the next few hours?"

    Don't swoop into the hospital room like you own the place. Even though this child may eventually be yours, it isn't your delivery, and it's not your hospital room.

- ✔ If she's named the baby and you plan to change the baby's name, don't repeatedly call the baby by the name you've chosen. Use the name she has chosen.

- ✔ Give her these few hours to mother her child in the way she would like to mother him. This is her time to show off the baby to those people close to her. Don't parade tons of family members in and out of the hospital to see the baby. You'll have years with this child. She may only have two days.

Bottom line: Be selfless, loving, and kind to the birthmother. That's what she is demonstrating to you. Buy her flowers, choose an appropriate card, make pizza runs, bring her some fuzzy slippers. She just had a baby . . . maybe yours.

When you talk about her with your child

At some point, your child will ask about her birthmother. What was she like? If you met her, what did she say? Was she pretty? Was she nice?

Believe it or not, these are the easy questions. Even if you don't know because you never met the birthmother, you can say something like "Well, look at *you*. You're pretty, so I'll bet she was pretty, too."

The harder questions are the ones like "Why didn't she want me?" "Why did she give me up?" and "Didn't she like me?" These questions compel you to talk about why she made the decision she did, which may bring up things about her lifestyle or her choices that you're uncomfortable with. The best tactic is to answer honestly but without judgment and to tell your child what he's old enough to understand. (Believe us, the questions will come up enough that you'll have the opportunity to add info as appropriate.)

Don't think that making your child's birthmother sound bad will make your child feel closer to you. It'll only make him feel bad about himself.

Keeping your promises

Promising frequent letters, pictures, or videos to your future child's birthmother is easy when you first meet with her. You want a child so badly, and she has the power to make that dream come true. Later, after you bring your child home, putting off doing what you said you would do is just as easy. After all, you're caught up in activities, and you're sleep deprived and exhausted.

What you may not realize is that the birthmother is also sleep deprived and exhausted. But instead of parties, visitors, and excitement, she's experiencing grief, loss, guilt, and emptiness. You have the power to help her through this time. Do it.

If you promise things and then don't follow through, the birthmother begins to worry that you're not the people you represented yourself to be, and she begins to fear for her child. Is the child safe? Healthy? Happy? Adding worry to her grief is cruel, and it may cause her to rethink her decision. See the next section for what you can do to help her work through her grief.

Helping her through her grieving process

If you agreed to send letters and pictures after an adoption, the time to start is soon after you take your child home. Right about now is when she's worried that you won't really love this baby or that you're just going to take her baby and run and refuse to honor your promises. Set her mind at ease. Here are some things that you can do:

✔ Send photos of a welcome home party, baby shower, gifts, loving family members, and so on to reassure the birthmother of her child's warm welcome. (Many adoptive families send a mixture of formal and casual photographs.) Some specific ideas that other families have used include

- Sending a little "brag book," an album filled with photos with captions or explanations on the back

- Sending larger professional photographs already framed for her enjoyment

- If you order the hospital baby pictures, ordering a larger package to share with the birthmother

- Purchasing an engraved locket for the birthmother with her baby's photo in it or, as a less expensive alternative, a plastic key ring with the child's picture on it.

✔ Write a letter expressing your deepest thanks and the love you feel for your child. If you've agreed to ongoing correspondence, reassure her of your continued commitment to keeping her informed.

✔ If you have the birthmother's phone number and have been in the habit of phoning her regularly, don't stop now. If you've developed a "friend-ship," don't take away that friendship right at the time she's grieving the loss of her child. The last thing she needs now is another loss in her life.

✔ Send weekly updates the first month following the placement. This first month is the most difficult for the birthmother. The frequency of your letters and the number of photos she receives directly correspond with how well she's able to cope with her decision.

✔ Send a video, with a year's worth of taping, once a year. These videos can include snippets of the birthday party, the egg hunt, the summer vacation, the trick-or-treating, and Christmas morning or the Hanukkah celebration. As the child gets older, you can include some film of the school program or the latest ball game.

✔ Some families like to send the child's school papers (those with a smiley sticker, of course) or drawings and crafts the child has made.

Many families hesitate to share their joy with the birthmother because they feel they should be respectful of her grief. Actually, most birthmothers want to see the joy they've given the adoptive family. Many birthmothers say the happiness of the adoptive parents is what helped them through their most difficult days.

Recognizing her role in your child's life

As much as you may wish it were so, you didn't give birth to your adopted child. Someone else had the honor of giving your child her physical features and genetic predispositions, carrying her for her first nine months, and then delivering her into this world. Then that person made the choice to allow you to parent this child. You just can't ignore this fact.

This doesn't mean, however, that you have to walk around feeling grateful to this woman every second of every day of your life. Nor are you just some kind of a "pretend" parent. You can allow yourself to settle into your parent-ing role and fall in love with your child. You can do all the things a "real" parent does because you *are* a real parent. As an adoptive parent, you just have additional responsibilities:

✔ You must tell your child her adoption story and answer all her questions in the years to come.

✔ You need to speak about her birthmother in a positive and respectful way.

✔ You must allow your child a safe place to express her feelings about her birthmother and reassure her that none of her conflicting feelings are wrong.

✔ You'll need a shoulder for your child to cry on and a stiff upper lip if she shuts you out. And you'll want to support her in any desire she has to reunite with her birthmother. See Chapter 19 for details on birthparent searches.

The other mother

From the moment I held each of my children in my arms, I've told them about their "other mother." We make no secret in our house about adoption. Rather, we want our children to be proud of who they are and be excited that they're adopted. Trying to hide the fact that a child is adopted only makes the child feel ashamed, as if being adopted is a bad thing. I always speak highly of my children's birthparents and reassure them that they've always been very loved by both of their mommies. I've also encouraged each of my children's birth moms to write a letter to their child, explaining why they chose adoption. That way, when my children begin to question the why's of adoption, I can let them read a letter from their birth mom that tells them exactly what their birth mom would want them to know.

Carl and Vicki Witmer

Chapter 14

Birthfathers and Their Role in Your Adoption

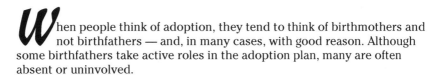

In This Chapter

▶ Understanding birthfathers' legal status

▶ Finding out what rights birthfathers have

▶ Locating fathers through putative registries

▶ Including the birthfather in the adoption plan

*W*hen people think of adoption, they tend to think of birthmothers and not birthfathers — and, in many cases, with good reason. Although some birthfathers take active roles in the adoption plan, many are often absent or uninvolved.

Nevertheless, even uninvolved birthfathers have legal rights, and you need to know what these rights are, when birthfathers can exert these rights, and what impact the birthfather's legal status can have on your adoption.

Defining the Legal Categories of Birthfathers

The term *birthfather* is used to denote a man whose child was placed for adoption. It sounds simple enough, but figuring out who the birthfather is can actually be more complicated than you think. Unlike identifying the birthmother, which is pretty straightforward (she's the one who gave birth to the child), identifying the birthfather isn't always as simple, for a variety of reasons. The main ones are

- ✔ **The reliability of the information that the birthmother gives:** Some birthmothers may not know who the father of the child is; some may lie about his identity; some may not name anyone.

- ✔ **The confusion surrounding some situations:** Obviously, the biological father is the man who supplies the sperm that actually creates the child, but what if the birthmother is married and the biological father isn't her husband? And this is a relatively straightforward complication; some situations are even more convoluted than this.

- ✔ **The categories of birthfathers:** In many states, fathers can fall into several categories. When more than one man can step forward as having an interest in the child, figuring out which one actually has the legal rights can be messy and take time. Other states try to simplify the confusion by narrowing the categories to just two.

To help you understand what role the birthfather — whoever he is — can play in your adoption, the following sections offer info on the categories he can fall into and tell you what his status means to you.

Obviously, your attorney or your agency needs to know all this stuff and the fine details distinguishing presumed fathers from alleged fathers from legal fathers from the man down the street. You *don't*. You can rely on your attorney or agency to give you the information, explain the finer points that affect your situation, and alert you to any risks associated with the birthfather's status. That's one reason why hooking up with a reputable agency or attorney is vitally important. If you need help in figuring out what to look for, head to Chapter 7.

The biological father

The *biological father* is the man who actually, physically, fathered the child. The birthmother may or may not know who he is. He may or may not know that he fathered the child. His identity may not ever be known for certain during the adoption proceedings. DNA testing is the only way to know for sure, and unless an adoption is challenged, DNA testing isn't usually used.

If a man pursues a plan to challenge an adoption and can prove (in the time frame outlined in the state statutes) that he biologically fathered the child, his rights to that child are equal to the rights of the birthmother. In short, this means that an adoption can't take place without his consent or having his rights terminated by the courts.

Of course, having these rights doesn't necessarily mean that the biological father would gain custody of the child. The judge would decide where the child belonged after taking many things into consideration. Considered first and foremost would be things like the genetic link and the biological father's innate rights to his child, but judges can take other things into consideration, too, like the man's suitability to parent the child.

To confuse things more, the biological father can be in any, some, or all of the following father categories.

The legal father

The legal father is the man who is married to the birthmother when the child is conceived. Whether this man is the biological father or not isn't important. In the eyes of the law, he is the legal father of the child: He has support obligations and all the other rights and responsibilities of a father. Because of his legal connection to the child (even if he doesn't have a biological connection), the legal father must also consent to any adoption, even if he hasn't had contact with the birthmother for years.

The legal father's rights to the child can be lost, however, and the child placed for adoption without his consent in the following situations:

- ✔ If he pursues custody and later tests prove that he didn't biologically father the child.
- ✔ If he can't be located or if he refuses to consent to the adoption and hasn't made any effort to parent (like paying support, visiting, buying gifts, or showing any interest in the child) after a six-month period. In this case, a claim of abandonment can be filed in court, his rights can be terminated, and the child can be placed for adoption without his consent.

The adjudicated father

The adjudicated father is the man the court deems to be the father of the child, based on DNA test results or as a result of a judgment in a paternity action. This category was much more important before DNA testing was readily available. Then, a judge would simply decide who he thought the father was and make it a court ruling. Of course, in these circumstances, a judge could have gotten it wrong and named someone the father who in fact wasn't. Now, with DNA testing, judges wait for the results to come back before ruling, which means that, in effect, the adjudicated father is also almost always the biological father.

The adjudicated father is rarely a player in an adoption because most adoptions take place soon after a child is born, and the adjudication process takes a long time. However, if a man is pursuing paternity of the child and hoping to be the adjudicated father, the adoption is placed on hold until his paternity action is resolved.

The alleged or putative father

A putative or alleged father is a man who *may* be the child's father but who wasn't married to the child's mother before the child was born and hasn't taken any legal action to prove he is the father of the child. He could be

✔ The person whom the mother of the child names as the father

✔ A person who comes forward and claims to be the father

In both instances, this person is referred to as the alleged father unless court proceedings determine something different (basically that he falls into another category or that he has no connection to the child at all).

Whereas legal or adjudicated fathers already have rights to their children and must be included in some way in the adoption plan, the alleged or putative fathers usually need to take some kind of action to make their presence known if they don't want to be ignored in an adoption.

Simplifying things? The Uniform Parentage Act

Just to confuse you more, many states have adopted the Uniform Parentage Act, which created just two categories of birthfathers: alleged and presumed fathers. (Talk to your agency or attorney to find out whether your state is one that has adopted this act.)

Under this act, you're an alleged father (see the preceding section for a definition of that) unless paternity can be "presumed." Paternity can be presumed if

✔ The man marries the mother either before or after the child's birth.

✔ The man claims that the child is his and/or he lives with the mother.

✔ The man has financially supported the mother and the child.

✔ The man has signed the birth certificate as the father.

A presumed father has the same rights as a legal father (see the earlier section "The legal father").

In an adoption, a presumed father's role depends largely on his relationship with the birthmother and whether he's the biological father:

✔ If he isn't her husband but *is* the biological father, his parental rights are terminated when he signs the consent forms after the child's birth.

✔ If he's the birthmother's husband but *not* the biological father of the child, he signs a consent form saying so (that he's her husband but not the baby's biological father).

✔ If the presumed father can't be located or won't sign the consent forms but fails to act as the parent of the child, the state can follow a legal procedure to terminate his rights.

Ready to scream yet?

Figuring out who's who

One of the problems that agencies and attorneys have with including the birthfather in the adoption planning is figuring out who he is, because doing so can be very complicated. A single man can fall into any of the categories: He can be both the legal, as well as the biological father, for example. Or he may be the biological father, but not the legal father.

The legal father, for example, has automatic rights to the child born to his wife, but he may not have been the man who actually fathered the baby. A woman may name a man as the alleged father of her child, but until his paternity is proven in court to support this claim, he may have no rights to the child. A judge may deem a man the adjudicated father and order him to begin paying child support — even though the man may know without a doubt that he was out of the country when that child was conceived. The biological father may not agree with the adoption plan, but he may have to undergo DNA testing to prove that he *is* the biological father before his concerns are addressed.

Add to all of that the fact that any of these potential fathers could choose to deny they are the father, leave town, or fail to offer the birthmother any emotional or financial support. Or they could all simultaneously claim to be the father and make known that they want to raise this child.

Because of all the variables surrounding birthfathers, ask your agency or attorney about how the birthfather's status may affect your adoption. Reputable agencies or attorneys will do all they can to understand the specifics that can affect your situation and to protect you if they have reason to believe that a man with rights to your child is likely to challenge the adoption or reappear and claim his rights.

Understanding the Birthfather's Rights

Many adoptions take place without involving the birthfather in any way. He might not receive any counseling, choose the adoptive parents, meet the adoptive parents, see the baby, or sign any papers. But regardless of his participation, he has the same rights as the birthmother. In other words, a birthfather is that child's father unless he voluntarily relinquishes his rights as a parent or has his rights terminated by the court.

All of this is well and good — provided that the man who fathered the child is aware that he has a child and is available when the adoption decisions are made so that he can be involved. But what happens when a man doesn't discover until after the fact that he fathered a child and that child is now in an adoptive home? Or when he hits the road and isn't around to give his consent to the adoption plan that the birthmother makes? These situations, and others like them, directly impact what has to happen before the child becomes available for adoption and how much risk is involved. The following sections tell you what you need to know.

All reputable agencies and attorneys follow certain procedures to ensure that the birthfathers, if they can be located, are aware of the adoption plans and know their rights. And if the birthfathers can't be located, these agencies and attorneys make sure *you're* aware of the risks involved going forward. Anyone who tells you not to worry about the birthfather because he's not around, doesn't know about the pregnancy or adoption plan, or just "isn't interested" in what's going on is playing with fire — and the house that may burn down is yours. Every adoption that proceeds without the birthfather's consent carries a degree of risk. The particular situation determines how much risk. Don't let anyone tell you otherwise.

Legal risk adoptions

Most agencies and attorneys welcome the birthfather's presence and participation in making the adoption plan. Why? Because if the father knows about the adoption and is in agreement with it, and if he signs the necessary legal papers to consent to the adoption, he can't challenge the adoption at a later date.

Still, many adoptions proceed even if the birthfather can't be found or doesn't sign consent forms. These situations carry a degree of risk because of the chance that he may reappear and claim his parental rights to the child. In fact, the less involved the father is in the adoption planning, the more legal risk is involved in the adoption. To protect you in these situations, agencies and attorneys do the following:

✔ **Inform the birthfather of the adoption plans:** The adoption is less likely to be challenged if the birthfather cooperates and participates in the planning. Even if the father isn't in agreement with the adoption, he still needs to be kept well informed of the events. Otherwise, he can come back later and claim that everything took place without his knowledge.

✔ **Try to locate missing birthfathers:** The best possible scenario for you is to have the legal father and/or anyone presumed to be the biological father informed and involved of the adoption plans. This can't happen if no one knows who the father is or where to find him. To address this issue, agencies and attorneys search putative father registries and publish notices in places they think he may be. See the section "Being notified of a pending adoption" for details on how they do this.

✔ **Make you aware of the birthfather's attitude, cooperation level, and involvement in the adoption plan and explain the risks involved:** Once you know the full situation, you can make a decision about whether you're prepared to take those specific risks.

Every adoption carries an element of risk. When the birthfather has been absent from the mix, the adoptive parents have to live in fear that he may emerge to challenge the adoption. If you move forward with an adoption in such a situation, be certain that your attorney takes all the necessary legal steps to provide you with as much protection as possible.

Being notified of a pending adoption

To avoid a situation in which an absent or uninvolved birthfather steps back into the picture and challenges the adoption, attorneys and agencies do what they can to inform the father of the adoption and his rights. That way, if he's inclined to assert his parental rights, he can do so before a child gets placed in an adoptive home. How agencies or attorneys notify the father depends on whether they know who and where he is.

Name and whereabouts known

Most agencies and attorneys routinely serve legal notices to the father during the pregnancy. This notice informs the birthfather of the pending adoption and tells him what he needs to do if he wants to stop the process.

After receiving the notice, the birthfather can't later claim that he was unaware of what was transpiring. In addition, he has to act within a certain period of time (which differs state by state) if he wants to stop the adoption. In most states, not acting is the equivalent of consent.

Name known; whereabouts unknown

If the father's name is known but his whereabouts are unknown, some states require the agency or attorney to make reasonable efforts to locate him. So what constitutes "reasonable" effort? The answer differs by state and, often, by judges within a state. It often includes things like making phone calls, writing letters, and so on.

States that offer a putative father registry (discussed later in this chapter) may not require any effort to be made to locate the birthfather. In these places, the burden falls on the man to know whether he may have gotten someone pregnant and to take steps to retain his parental rights, if he wants them.

The amount of time that a man has to respond to the notification also varies by state. Usually it's a few weeks. If he can't be located or doesn't respond within that time frame, the adoption moves forward.

Now, here's the $64,000 question: If your agency takes these steps but still can't find the birthfather and the adoption proceeds, can the man appear later and, with the claim of not knowing what was going on, reclaim his rights? The answer to that question depends on the laws in your state. In some states, he may get a hearing; in other states, he may not. If you're in this situation, ask your agency or attorney to explain what happens if an absent birthfather reappears.

Nobody knows nothin'

When the birthmother refuses to name the father or when she doesn't know who the father is, obviously, no one can serve him with a notice, and no arrangements can be made for him to sign legal adoption consents. As a result, these adoptions carry the most legal risks.

In these cases, the agency or attorney checks the putative father registry (explained in the section "Putative Father Registries," later in this chapter). If no name is found on the registry, the attorney or agency places legal notices in a publication (usually local newspapers) notifying the public that this adoption is about to transpire and that the father of the child must come forward if he wants to stop the adoption proceedings.

Ask your agency or attorney about the following policies:

- **Where adoption notices are published:** The guidelines vary by state. Some states don't have any specific guidelines. Usually, the notice has to be published in the city or state where it is believed the father resides.

- **How long the notice has to run:** This policy varies by state, but expect the notice to run for a few weeks.

> ✔ **Whether adoption notices are still published, even if your state has a putative father registry:** Although states with a putative father registry may not require that you publish, many attorneys still recommend that you do.

If the birthfather doesn't come forward, he loses his parental rights.

Legal challenges he can initiate

Any man who believes that he has fathered a child who is being placed for adoption can take legal action to prevent the adoption from taking place.

One of the first things the birthfather can do is sign up with the putative father registry. This registry, which is described in more detail in the following section, allows men who think that they may have fathered a child out of wedlock to be notified about any potential adoption proceedings. If the man is notified that an adoption is being planned, he can retain an attorney to represent him and file a petition to establish his paternity in court. Then, the court would order DNA testing and make a ruling on the man's paternity suit based on the results. If the DNA evidence shows that the man isn't the child's father, he loses any claim he has to the child, and the adoption proceeds. If the DNA results support the man's claim, another hearing is scheduled to begin deciding the matter of custody of the child. These court proceedings are lengthy and can continue for years with all the appeals that are allowed.

A man who wants to establish his paternity must do so in a timely manner. What constitutes timely is determined in each state's laws, but it's usually within the 30-day period following the birth of the child. Keep in mind, however, that judges have a lot of leeway and can do pretty much whatever they want. If, for example, a man is one day late filing his papers, one judge may rule that he didn't file in a timely manner; another judge may say, "Well, he's only one day late" and hear the petition.

Putative Father Registries

In the past, agencies and attorneys have had the burden of trying to locate the father of the child and securing his consent before proceeding with an adoption plan. This task was sometimes impossible. He may have left town or gone into hiding. He may deny he had a relationship with the birthmother. She may not know who he is. She may disclose that several men could possibly be the father of her child. In response to this difficult state of affairs, many states have initiated legislation to shift the burden from the agency or attorney and onto the birthfather himself.

In states with registries, the birthfather must make his presence known by registering with the putative father registry within a certain time frame. Like just about everything else in adoption, this time frame varies by state. Usually, a man has to register within 30 days of the child's birth or within 30 days of the adoption petition being filed in court. If he doesn't, then his parental rights are terminated, or his consent to the adoption is implied.

In these registries, possible biological fathers provide identifying information so that they can be notified in the event that court proceedings are pending for an adoption of a child that he fathered or court proceedings are pending to terminate his parental rights. In addition to helping them retain their rights as fathers, registering with a putative father registry can also give these men the responsibilities of a parent, including paying hospital and medical expenses as well as paying child support.

Here are some other things to know about putative father registries:

- Once a child reaches the age of 1 year, the registry no longer applies. In those cases, actual notice must be given to the father before his rights are terminated.
- These registries don't apply to adjudicated fathers (see the earlier section "The adjudicated father" for a definition) or men who have established a parent/child relationship.
- The registries are usually maintained by the state's health department.

Most states have a registry available. Ask your agency or attorney to find out whether a registry is available in your state.

Birthfathers as Part of the Adoption Team

Birthfathers, unfortunately, are frequently not a part (or a participating member) of the adoption team. It's been my (Katrina's) experience that even when the birthfather is in agreement with the adoption, he may be reluctant to get involved or participate in the process. The majority of the adoptions I have been involved with have not included the birthfather's participation.

Still, it would be wonderful if birthfathers always participated in the adoption plans and decision making. The following sections outline some ways they can be included.

Being supportive of birthmothers

Having the birthfather participate in the adoption planning and process can be an immense help to the birthmother. He can share the burden of making the adoption decision, choosing the family, meeting the family, and so on. His presence also means that the birthmother has someone to talk to and to share her experience with.

Even if the birthmother and the birthfather are no longer a couple, they can share in the planning for the child they created together. Although the birthmother may receive counseling and may have a supportive social worker, nothing takes the place of the birthfather because he and she, in many ways, are experiencing the same loss.

Attending meetings with the birthmother

When the birthfather attends meetings with the birthmother and the social worker of the agency, the agency gains valuable information that may otherwise not be available. With information from the birthfather himself, the agency may be able to receive a more complete medical and social history. This is also an opportunity for the birthfather to be fully informed of the adoption process and his role in it. When the birthfather is a regular participant in these meetings, he is also a participant in all of the decision making.

As long as the couple's relationship is one of respect and appropriate interactions, the birthfather is also always welcome to attend any of the meetings between the birthmother and the adoptive parents. When the birthfather attends these meetings, he has the peace of mind about the appropriateness of the family. The adoptive family benefits as well, because family members can get to know their child's birthfather, and they can later share this information with the child.

Signing the consent form

Like birthmothers, birthfathers (if they're available and willing) can sign the consent forms. In many states, the child has to be born before the birthfather can consent to the adoption.

In some states, however, the birthfather can give his consent to the adoption before the child is born. If his identity and whereabouts are known and he doesn't want to sign the consent forms, the agency serves him with a legal notice before the child's birth. This notice usually gives him 30 days to respond. If he doesn't respond within the time frame, his rights to the child end — even if the child hasn't been born yet.

If the father is willing to sign the consent forms for the adoption, every effort is made to accommodate him. He can come to the hospital and sign his consents at the same time the birthmother signs hers. Or someone can meet him at his home, work, or wherever. I (Katrina) have taken fathers' consents in parked cars, in restaurants, in a McDonald's parking lot, in a mall, at a park, and once, standing outside in the pouring rain — whatever is necessary.

The father signs consent papers that are similar to the ones the birthmother signs (see Chapter 11 for details about the content of consent papers), but his papers may not be as lengthy, or he may not have as many separate affidavits to sign. Usually, he has to sign the papers in the presence of a notary public.

Requesting pictures and letters

The father of the child can ask for pictures, letters, and videos, just as the birthmother does. Usually the same arrangement is made for both birthmother and birthfather. When this is the case, the adoptive parents often send the same letter to each of them, with copies of the same pictures.

Birthfathers

We have adopted twice, and our experience with birthfathers was very different each time. In our first adoption, our child's birthmother didn't give any information about the birthfather. This caused some delays in our timeline, because our attorney worked hard to provide all the notice we could. In our second adoption, we adopted a sibling group. The birthfather knew the children had been born. Our attorney visited the birthfather, but although he didn't object to the adoption, he didn't want to participate either, so he didn't sign the consent forms.

Hindsight is funny. The reality is that the first adoption was more risky; the birthfather had no knowledge of the child and couldn't make any decisions about his desire to be a parent. I *felt,* however, more concerned about the second adoption. When I started to worry, I spoke with the professionals at our agency. They helped me understand the second birthfather's behavior. I must say that all told, we didn't spend a lot of time worrying about the birthfather. We trusted the process and our agency, prayed all the time, and bonded with our children.

Christine and Maurice Rembert

Chapter 15

Keeping in Touch: Meetings and Contact with the Birthmother

*A*s more adoptions become open or semi-open, the barriers that kept adoptive parents separate from birthparents have fallen. Although some adoptions today are closed, most aren't. In infant placements, how open an adoption is depends on the wishes of the birthmother, the policy of the agency you work with, and the comfort level of the adoptive family. Although these same things can play a part in older child adoptions, more often the openness of the arrangement depends on the age of the child, what led to the child's availability for adoption, and whatever court orders the judge hearing the case deems necessary.

This chapter explains the type of contact that can be arranged in both infant and older child placements and examines some issues you'll want to think about before you decide on how much contact you want with your child's birthmother.

Obviously, how open your adoption arrangement is determines to some extent how big a role your child's birthmother has in your life. (For the specifics about the different types of adoption arrangements, turn to Chapter 2.) But don't fool yourself into thinking that if you have a closed arrangement (that is, no contact or identifying information has been shared) that you don't have to deal with birthmother issues. You do. Part IV covers many of the issues you'll face as an adoptive family, and one of the biggies is your child's questions about where she comes from, what her birthmother was like, and why she made an adoption plan.

Getting to Know You: Contact Prior to Placement

When you adopt nowadays, you can expect to have some contact with your child's birthmother before a child is placed with you — even if that contact is only through your social worker. That's because most adoptions today are open or semi-open, rather than closed. Still, how much and what type of contact you have depend on the arrangement you've made with the birthmother. Common types of contact are

- **Profile sharing:** Birthmothers receive your profile as well as the Dear Birthmother letter you may have written. (To find out what a profile is, head to Chapter 9.)

- **Meetings:** In most agency adoptions, birthmothers are asked whether they want to meet with the family they have chosen. In open adoptions, these meetings may become visits that you arrange yourselves in the time leading up to the baby's birth.

- **Phone calls:** In some cases — particularly with attorney-assisted adoptions — you and the birthmother may converse over the phone.

The following sections explain what type of contact is commonly involved in the different types of adoptions.

The definitions for semi-open or open adoptions may differ from agency to agency. Also, adoptions fall on a continuum from fully closed to totally open, so the exact line where an adoption changes from one category to another is often fuzzy.

No contact, no way, no how: Closed adoptions

A few birthmothers still prefer closed adoptions, in which they have very little involvement in the overall process. In these adoptions, the birthmother frequently asks the social worker to select the adoptive family rather than provide her with profiles to read. She may not even want to hear a description of the adoptive family. Nor does she meet the family or have communication with them following the adoptive placement.

The women who request these adoptions may do so for the following reasons:

✔ They may feel that making the decisions about their child's future family is too big of a burden to bear.

✔ They may find the entire process too painful or stressful.

✔ They may believe that if they have less involvement in the process, they'll experience less pain as a result.

If your child's birthmother prefers a closed adoption, you probably won't have any contact with her. The women who choose closed adoptions are rare. Most often, women prefer a semi-open or open adoption arrangement, explained in the following sections.

Negotiating an agreement: Semi-open and open

In a semi-open or open adoption, the birthmother is more involved in the adoption process itself and, to a large extent, directs the adoption decisions. She can decide things like how much involvement she wants in the selection process, what characteristics she wants in the adoptive family, and how much contact (both before and after the placement) she would be comfortable with.

Both open and semi-open arrangements can involve meetings, ongoing contact, regular correspondence, and so on. The main difference between the two is whether you trade identifying information:

✔ In an open adoption, you know the first and last name, phone number, and possibly address of your child's birthmother; and she has the same information about you.

✔ In a semi-open adoption, you know each other's first names, but beyond that, you don't have identifying information like last names or addresses. (Some people also share phone numbers, pager numbers, or e-mail addresses.) All written correspondence between the two of you goes through the agency.

The following sections explain the type of involvement the birthmother has in these adoption arrangements and some of the contact options that may be available to you.

Choosing a family

After the birthmother tells the agency how involved she wants to be in the selection process, what she's looking for in an adoptive family, and how much contact she wants, the agency gives her profiles of families who fit her criteria.

She reads these adoptive parent profiles and selects a family. Some women stop there. Many others, though, want to meet the family they've chosen.

Meeting the family

If the birthmother wants to meet you, the agency will call you to tell you that you've been selected and to schedule a time for you and the birthmother to get together.

Meetings can take place in an office, a restaurant, a home, or any other place convenient for the birthmother. The adoptive family usually travels to her.

Whether you're expecting an open or semi-open adoption, having a social worker present for the first meeting is helpful. She makes the introductions and can guide the discussion. During this first meeting, you and the birthmother will talk about the following:

- ✔ **What kind of contact you're each hoping to have:** See the section "Trading Info after Placement," later in this chapter, for the type of contact you can have with the birthmother after your child comes home.

- ✔ **How (or even whether) you'll be involved during the pregnancy:** You might make arrangements for regular visits during the pregnancy or no more visits at all. The birthmother may invite you to accompany her to doctor's appointments and to the labor and delivery of the child.

    You can accept or decline these invitations; the important thing is to be honest about what you really plan to do.

Meeting your child's birthmother can be a nerve-wracking experience: What do you talk about? Do you hug her — or not? What will she want to know, and what kinds of questions will she ask? *What if she doesn't like you?* Although meeting a birthmother can be intimidating, it's an opportunity that you should take if you have it. Following are some pointers and things to think about:

- ✔ **The birthmother is probably as nervous as you are.** And the same questions that plague you are probably plaguing her: What if they don't like me? What will they ask? and so on.

- ✔ **Take the birthmother's lead.** When my husband and I (Tracy) met my older daughter's birthmother, I didn't know what the proper "etiquette" was. Sit near her? Sit across from her? Shake her hand? What? After our social worker made the introductions, we all sat down, each of us in a separate seat around the coffee table — anyone walking in would have thought that we were waiting for the carpet samples to be pulled out. But at some point during this meeting, the awkwardness disappeared, and I found myself sitting on the sofa beside her, holding her hand while we talked. Three days later, I brought home my daughter, whom I had first felt kick in her birthmother's stomach.

✔ **Consider bringing in a family photo album when you meet with the birthmother.** Having an album gives everyone something to focus on early in the meeting, and it gives you an excuse to sit by the birthmother because you'll want to point out and explain the pictures to her. By the time you've finished looking at the album, your nerves have calmed down, and she has a better idea of what your family is all about.

✔ **Remember that meeting a birthmother doesn't mean that you've been selected.** Although most birthmothers select the first family they meet, other birthmothers feel like they need to meet with a few families before they make a decision. In addition, some birthmothers may select a family and then, after meeting with the family, change their minds. The best thing you can do is to recognize that until a child is placed with you, nothing is guaranteed. Be hopefully optimistic but prepared if things don't turn out the way you'd like.

✔ **The birthmother may bring other people with her to the meeting.** Birthmothers can bring whomever they want to these meetings: mothers, sisters, fathers, grandmothers, and best friends. (Of course, they usually only bring one or two at a time.) Some of these people remain silent during the meeting, others may ask a few questions, and some may totally take over the whole meeting. These people are there as support for the birthmother, but they can add another dynamic to an already emotional situation.

A special meeting: Reassuring the siblings

When we were approached by our adoption worker at the hospital to tell us that our birthmother had signed off on the consent forms, she also came with an additional message: "Her other children would like to meet with you." To say that we were both a little hesitant would be an understatement. Our adoption worker reminded us that the decision was strictly ours. Neither of us had given much thought to meeting her children. We had been told of a possible meeting with her mother and sister, but to meet the other children — that was something different. We decided that we would meet with them and attempt to help them with the questions that I was sure they had.

Not really knowing what to expect, we expected the situation to be extremely uncomfortable and very awkward. Instead what we found were two beautiful, well-behaved children, a girl, age 11, and a boy, age 8. They wanted to know about us, how we lived, and if we had other children. Would we love him like they and their mom would? Would he have his own room? Could they send him pictures of them, and would we tell him about them later in life? Is he going to be okay? Would they ever see him again? Would we send pictures of him throughout his life? His biological sister even asked if we could send her a picture of him for her birthday. After answering all of their questions and putting their minds at ease, our son's biological siblings had a better understanding of the situation that was taking place. My husband and I were glad that we took the time to meet with them. We realized that they were as scared as we were and trying

(continued)

(continued)

to understand something that even we had a hard time understanding.

In keeping with our promise, we have sent pictures and letters keeping in touch with his biological family. In return, we have received pictures of his biological siblings. When he is older, we will tell him of the day we met.

Leon and Tonna Thomas

Ongoing contact

In many semi-open and open adoptions, the contact you have with the birthmother may continue beyond the first meeting. Maybe you and she will stay in touch throughout the remainder of her pregnancy. Maybe you'll be involved in the delivery. Your degree of involvement depends on how involved the birthmother wants you to be and your comfort level.

When you discuss ongoing contact during the pregnancy, keep these suggestions in mind:

- **Establish boundaries that you're both comfortable with.** Only you and the birthmother can know an appropriate boundary for your unique situation. What may work for some people may not work for you.

- **Be willing to reevaluate and discuss the amount of contact you have if you or the birthmother begins to feel uncomfortable.** Following are some common situations that may require another heart-to-heart:

  - Calling too frequently. Although your first thought here may be that you don't want the birthmother calling you every day, remember that you also may be tempted to overstep this boundary and call her too frequently. So think twice about adding the birthmother's number to your speed dial list.

  - You, as the adoptive parents, taking over the pregnancy, by making (or trying to make) the birthmother's decisions, not giving her the space she needs, and so on.

  - The birthmother asking for favors, like drive me here, drive me there, baby-sit my kids, loan me money, and so on.

If you find yourself having to address issues like these, use your social worker as a resource. She can help you and the birthmother resolve these uncomfortable situations and come to a compromise that works for both of you.

- **Don't initiate a lot of contact if you don't plan to continue that contact after the placement.** If the birthmother comes to rely on you as a friend or support person, your withdrawal from her after the birth is another loss she has to endure.

Trading Info after Placement

Semi-open and open adoptions frequently include regular correspondence between you and the birthmother. What constitutes "regular correspondence" depends on what you agree to. Some families correspond at scheduled times; others wing it. Some arrangements specify that certain types of information be shared over a certain period of time; others leave this schedule open.

Looking at types of contact

In semi-open adoptions, the correspondence is generally written, with the agency acting as an intermediary. You send letters to your agency, for example, and the agency forwards these to the birthmother. The birthmother, likewise, sends her response to the agency, which then forwards it to you. In this way, confidentiality is maintained. The correspondence usually includes the following things:

- ✔ **Letters and notes from the adoptive parents:** These letters are your way of sharing information that you think the birthmother would like to know, things like how your child is growing, whether she's happy, and how your family has welcomed her. Often, you may find yourself responding to a letter that the birthmother has written you.

- ✔ **Photos and videos of the child:** In addition to the letter they may write, many families also send photos or videos of their child. Chapter 13 has suggestions for the types of photos and videos that you may want to share.

- ✔ **Pictures and letters from the child to her birthmother:** If your child has a lot of questions or feels a yearning to connect to the woman who gave birth to her, letting her draw pictures and write notes to her birthmother may meet her needs.

- ✔ **Letters, photos, and possibly gifts from the birthparent to your child:** Receiving these gifts can be a concrete reminder to your child that her birthmother hasn't forgotten her.

In addition to all of the preceding stuff, open adoptions also often include some type of agreement for visits. These visits can range from a scheduled, once-a-year get-together in a public location (like the zoo or a park) to casual, spur-of-the-moment drop-in visits and everything in between.

The key to all of this is finding an arrangement that meets your *child's* needs, and your child needs the following:

> ✔ **To know where she belongs:** Your child belongs with you and in your family. Nothing — and not even contact with the birthmother — threatens that. Nor should it threaten you.
>
> ✔ **To feel at peace with where she came from:** When the only information you have is a giant question mark and a mom or dad who can only answer your questions with "Well, dear, as far as we know . . . ," all sorts of thoughts creep in to fill the void.

For help figuring out what kind of contact will be best for your family, head to the section "Agreeing to Contact: Things to Think About," later in this chapter.

Making changes to the game plan

Before the baby's birth is when you usually agree on the type of contact you have with the birthmother following the placement. One challenge with this approach is that it's hard for both parties to really know what will work best for everyone, especially this early in your acquaintance. In reality, relationships develop over time.

The thing to keep in mind is that your relationship may change and agreements regarding contact may need to change along with it. The key here is the word *agreement*. Changing the parameters of the relationship is okay when everyone agrees to it. Other than a mutually agreed upon change, the only other time you should veer off the path of the agreement is if the contact with the birthparent becomes stressful or traumatizing for the child. Of course, doing little extras above and beyond the agreement is always a welcome change.

Agreeing to Contact: Things to Think About

Nearly all parents are possessive of their children — and you'll feel possessive toward your child. You're the parent. You know what's best. You're in charge. No one can possibly love your child as much as you do, and so no one, other than you, can claim that place in your child's life and heart. So when you think about what kind of contact, if any, you're willing to have with your child's birthmother, the question you have to ask yourself is "Am I meeting my needs or my child's?"

Obviously, the answer to that question depends on what your child needs. But the fact of the matter is, although some kids have no curiosity or desire to know about their birthparents, most kids do. When you think about the kind of contact you'd be comfortable with, remember that you're not preserving or creating a parent-child bond between your child and his birthparent. You're helping your child connect to his past, giving him an opportunity to find out about a person who played an important role in his life, and helping him feel okay about it. When you think about it, those are the things that parents do.

The following sections give you some things to think about as you decide what's right for your family.

Deciding what's best for your child

Although you may hope that your child will be uninterested in matters regarding her birth family, she may surprise you. Most children who were adopted spend a lot of time thinking about their birthparents and the situation leading to their birth and subsequent placement. Many children wonder, "Why didn't she keep me?" "What does she look like?" "Does she ever think about me?" "Where is she now?" and more. Photos, letters, phone calls, or even visits can help to fill this void.

If kids don't have the facts, they may spend time fantasizing about what might have been true. Even well-adjusted, well-loved, and secure children have this curiosity. If you or your child can have some kind of ongoing contact with the birthmother, this contact can provide your child with the answers he seeks.

I (Katrina) never dreamed I would be interested in contact with my children's birthparents. But, by the time my daughter was 7 years old, I wished desperately for that opportunity. My daughter was asking all the preceding questions and more. Because she was born in Korea, we had no contact with her birthmother, and therefore, I had no answers for her questions. Having a daughter in need and no way to ease her distress makes you a firm believer in openness in adoption.

Additionally, I receive calls regularly from adoptive parents asking whether there's a way to initiate contact with a birthmother in a closed adoption arrangement. In each case, the parents are seeking contact in order to meet their child's needs.

Adoptive parents who resist openness in adoption are sometimes fearful of the familiarity. They fear it may lead to some kind of kidnapping plot or court battle initiated by the birthmother. Families who have agreed to openness report that the contact with the birthmother can actually help alleviate those fears. As a relationship develops, the birthmother ceases to fit the image of the big bad wolf waiting to pounce and instead becomes a real person — often, a person who seems content with the adoption arrangement and who expresses her gratitude for it.

Another thing to consider is that ongoing contact with the birthmother provides ongoing information regarding family health issues. Your daughter needs to know if her birthmother develops breast cancer in her 30s.

Considering your comfort level

Your initial reaction to the idea of contact with the birthmother may be "She made her decision; she doesn't have any right to ongoing information!" That's parental possessiveness talking. And it misses the bigger issue: You don't continue contact for the benefit of the birthmother. You continue it for the benefit of your child. Here are a few things to think about:

- ✔ Many parts of the adoption experience are uncomfortable for the adoptive parents (think home study, for example) and for the birthparents (think signing consent forms). But the best interests of the child should prevail. Even if contact makes you uncomfortable, don't reject it out of hand. It may help your child.

- ✔ Contact doesn't mean weekly Sunday dinner together unless you both want it to mean that. Come to an arrangement that you can follow through with; see the earlier section "Trading Info after Placement" for details. If it isn't obvious why living up to your end of the agreement is important, skip to the next two sections.

- ✔ If you're still not comfortable, try to find out what other experts say about openness in adoptions. Also talk to families who have open adoption arrangements. Although you may not experience a complete conversion, you may gain enough insight to help resolve your conflicting feelings. Here are some resources you may find helpful:

    - *The Open Adoption Experience,* by Lois Ruskai Melina and Sharon Kaplan Roszia (published by Perennial)

    - *Dear Birthmother, Thank You for Our Baby,* by Kathleen Silber and Phylis Speedlin (published by Corona Pub)

- ✔ Obviously, you need to be comfortable and secure as parent of your child. You don't want anything to make you feel inferior or inadequate or like you're simply playing a part. You need to realize that no enemy or threatening "other" wants to steal your child away — physically or emotionally. Remember that your child's birthmother is not an opponent — she's a resource for you as your child's parent.

Keeping promises

When someone gives you a great gift, you don't turn around and slap that person in the face. Remember that this woman helped you become the parent of your child, and honor the promises you made to her. (For more information on birthmothers, see Chapter 13.)

If you begin to think that the contact you've agreed to is no longer in your child's best interests, share this information with the birthmother or with the social worker at the agency and try to come up with another arrangement that does work. Don't just cut off all contact.

Your treatment of the birthmother may someday come back to haunt you. And we're not talking karma here. Your child may grow up to search for his birthmother someday and, after connecting with her, could learn that you didn't honor your promises to her. Information like that could damage your relationship with your adult child. If this possibility still isn't enough to make you follow through when you're inclined not to, read the next section.

Legal stuff

Many agreements for contact are just good faith agreements. Although they're not legally binding, the expectation is that both parties will honor the arrangement they made. Some states (California, Minnesota, and Rhode Island are three examples), however, have passed laws that allow for enforceable agreements. Called *post-adoption contact agreements,* these detail the type and frequency of the contact agreed upon. A copy of the agreement is usually filed in court, along with the petition to adopt.

Not complying with the legal agreement doesn't mean that the adoption can be overturned or invalidated. After all, all consents or voluntary relinquishments specifically state that the birthmother (and birthfather, if he's involved) has given up *all* parental rights. But it does mean that, if either party feels the other isn't honoring the contract, one person can take the other to court to enforce it.

Arranging Contact in Older Child Adoptions

When you adopt an older child (who is available for adoption because the birthparents parental rights have been terminated by the state), the judge determines what kind of contact you have with your child's birthmother. In most instances, especially involving abuse and neglect, a judge may have determined that contact between the birthparent and the child isn't in the child's best interest.

This isn't always the case, however. Counselors or therapists may determine that having some type of continued supervised contact is in the child's best interest because, in their view, although the birthparent wasn't able to appropriately parent her child, she may still have something positive to offer. After considering such a report, the judge may decide that ongoing contact with the birthparent is in the child's best interest. In other cases, the judge may make arrangements for the child to have consistent visitation with siblings who've been placed in other homes. (In addition, the child may have developed close bonds with foster parents and desire continuing a relationship with them.)

In these situations, the contact with the birth family has usually been ordered and is already taking place when you first hear about the child. As a part of the adoption arrangement when you adopt, you agree to continue the contact.

Although no official mechanism is in place to make sure you follow through with these arrangements, you want to honor the agreement for a couple of reasons. First, if members of the birth family don't receive the visits they've been promised, they can report it. Second, if you disobey a court order, the judge can order a bench warrant for your arrest. And, really, this is no fun. If you come to feel that the contact in an older child adoption is no longer beneficial to your child or you want to modify the arrangement, discuss the matter with your social worker. She can tell you what steps you need to take to have the arrangement reviewed and possibly amended.

Maybe it would be simpler for you if this contact were discontinued. But your child has already experienced many losses in the past. Make whatever efforts you can to preserve any healthy relationships or connections that remain.

Part IV
Issues Adoptive Families Face

The 5th Wave   By Rich Tennant

"Our decision to adopt is based firmly on our desire to parent, our belief in the adoption process, and our commitment to building a family. Of course, it also takes the embarrassment out of riding the 'Wild Teacups' at amusement parks."

In this part . . .

Most, if not all, adoptees and their families face certain common issues relating to adoption. This part delves into these issues and offers suggestions and ideas for how you can handle them in a way that helps your children feel good about themselves and their place in the family and in the world.

Chapter 16

All in the Family: Issues You Deal with at Home

* *

In This Chapter

▶ Sharing the adoption story

▶ Answering the "Who's my real mom (or dad)?" question

▶ Helping your child deal with feelings of rejection

▶ Handling race and cultural issues with your child

▶ Anticipating issues you may deal with as parents of older adopted children

▶ Being aware of issues associated with international placements

* *

All parents prepare for the day when their child looks at them with big, inquiring eyes and wants to know where babies come from. Most parents, having abandoned the stork-and-cabbage-patch stories, opt for honesty — or as close to it as they're comfortable getting with a 5-year-old — and answer in more or less technical terms: Mommy's tummy. For obvious reasons, that answer doesn't work for adoptive families. But it's one of the first of many questions you may have difficulty finding an answer for. Other questions may include

> Who's my "real" mom (or dad)?
>
> Why didn't she want me?
>
> Why don't I look like you?

These and other questions are ones that your kids are going to ask as they try to understand how they fit into your family. Adopt an older child — a child who has been part of his birth family or who has been in the child welfare system for possibly years — and the issues you'll face may be even more challenging. This chapter helps prepare you for the things that you're going to be grappling with as your children try to figure out why they are where they are and how they got there. For tips on dealing with issues that the outside world throws at your doorstep, head to the next chapter.

Once Upon a Time . . . The Adoption Story

Some people put the adoption story in the same categories they assign other "difficult" topics (think sex and drug use). You know these categories; we've all encountered them. They're the "I'm going to wait until they're old enough" category and the "things we seldom talk about because I'm uncomfortable with the topic" category. But you shouldn't treat the adoption story as something you discuss only when you absolutely, positively can't find any way to avoid it. (Frankly, you shouldn't treat the other topics like that either, but that's beside the point.)

The adoption story is your child's story, and as such, it's something to share and celebrate and help your child understand. And you can't do that with a one-time talk, and you certainly can't do it if you feel uncomfortable when the subject comes up. Remember, you want your child to understand and feel good about how he came into the world and how he came to be a part of your family. Keep this advice in mind:

- Embrace your child's story. It's private, but it's not a secret.

- The adoption story is your child's story, and she can share it with whomever she wants.

- Not everyone has the right to know the story, and other people's curiosity doesn't justify their need to hear it. It's for you (and your child when he's older) to decide who gets what info. Head to Chapter 17 for information on what to share with others.

Don't pretend that your child came to you in a different way than he or she did. And don't obsess that this "difference" is important. It's not. It's more mechanics and logistics than anything else. I (Tracy) remember hearing a story of a woman who took her family to a friend's church one Sunday. In making introductions, the friend introduced the woman's daughter as the woman's "adopted daughter." Without missing a beat, the woman took over the introductions. "And this," she said to the pastor, "is my vaginally delivered son."

So when do you tell your child that she was adopted? What do you tell? How do you tell it? And what do you do if the adoption story includes tough-to-handle information? These are questions many adoptive parents wrestle with, especially for their first child. So if you're grappling with these things, you're not alone.

When to tell and how

The best time to start telling your child about her adoption is as soon as she arrives. Talk honestly about the adoption when she's present. Don't whisper about it behind her back. Use the word "adoption" in her presence (it's not a word to be ashamed of). If you handle it correctly, "adoption" can be a word your child is proud of and feels comfortable with.

Incorporate your child's adoption story into your bedtime story routine. He'll love it. After all, he is the star of that story, and what child wouldn't enjoy hearing about how much he's loved and how much joy and excitement he's brought to your life?

Here's an example of an adoption story:

> Once upon a time, Mommy and Daddy really wanted a baby, but no babies ever grew in Mommy's tummy. So we called the 123 Agency and asked them if they had any babies who needed a mommy and a daddy. They told us about a lady named Susie who had a very special baby growing in her tummy. Susie loved her baby very much, but she couldn't be a mommy right now. She was looking for a good mommy and daddy for her baby . . . and on and on and on.

Always end the story by telling your child how much you love him and how happy you are that you could adopt him. He won't understand the word "adopt" at first. As he grows older, he'll ask what that word means, and you'll have an opportunity to go into greater detail.

The goal is to have your child grow up knowing about the adoption. You never want your child to carry a memory of the "day he found out." See the sidebar "'I have something to tell you'" for reasons why.

In addition to telling your child her story, many wonderful children's books are available that depict adoption. You can find a list in Chapter 20. Read these stories to your child and then add a statement like "That's what happened when we adopted you!"

If you correspond with the birthmother, casually mention, "We received a letter from Susie today; she says she misses you" or "Look at this gift Susie sent you." Occasionally, your child will ask again, "Who is Susie?" You can answer, "Remember? She is the lady who grew you in her tummy" or "Your birth mommy."

Sharing the information casually is very easy to do, and the kids do the rest for you. They ask age-appropriate questions as they grow up, and you just supply the age-appropriate answers. The key is to find that magic balance between openly discussing your child's adoption and yet not focusing on it.

"I have something to tell you"

If your spouse, parent, or close friend were to take you aside and say, "I have something to tell you," what would your reaction probably be? If you're like most people, you'd out and out panic. If you're not the panicky kind, you're at least going to be concerned. The reason? Because life-altering, foundation-shaking news tends to follow these six little words.

So imagine what it must feel like to a child (or teen or young adult) to have his parents sit him down, take a deep breath, and say, "Dear, we have something to tell you," followed shortly by the revelation of his adoption, followed by the reassurance that "It doesn't make any difference."

Of *course*, it makes a difference.

You've just told your child that he isn't who he thought he was. And neither are you. You've created a divide in his life: who he was before he found out and who he is now. An adopted kid. And, no matter how much you try to assure him that it doesn't matter, that you love him the same, yadda yadda yadda, he's probably going to wonder what else you haven't told him.

So don't delude yourself into not telling or waiting to tell because you consider adoption a serious and complex issue that small children can't understand or because you think that, since adoption doesn't make any difference to you, it shouldn't make any difference to your child.

Of course, adoption is complex and difficult to understand, but by sharing the knowledge in a loving way and elaborating on your child's story as he grows and asks, you have the opportunity to help your child see adoption as *you* see it.

What to tell

When you share the adoption story, you tell the truth, and you always answer your child's questions honestly. It's important for children who were adopted to know that they can fully trust the information they receive from their parents.

Families often question how they can be honest with their children about difficult situations, such as date rape. One way to handle that is to just give little pieces of information. When your child asks about her birthfather, for example, you could say, "Your birth mommy didn't know him very well." Just that simple answer usually satisfies a young child. When your child gets older and asks why, you can answer, "Because she didn't think he was very nice." You can answer future "whys?" with "Because he wanted her to do things she didn't want to do" and then "He wanted to touch her private places." You get the idea.

Eventually, when the child is more mature, he'll ask the question that leads to the date rape explanation. Although it may sound like horrible information for a child to have, it is the truth. Most adult adoptees are seeking the truth.

I (Katrina) have actually had adult adoptees tell me that hearing the difficult details has enabled them to finally justify in their minds why their birth-mother chose adoption. The prettier the adoption story, the harder it is for them to understand why she made an adoption plan.

Who's Yer Daddy (or Mommy)? Dealing with the "Real" Parent Issue

We don't know any adoptive parent who has escaped the "real" parent issue. If it doesn't come up with outsiders (see Chapter 17 for info on that), then it will definitely come up with your children.

Although I (Katrina) carefully talked to my children about their "birthmother" or "birth mommy," all my children used the term "real parent" at one time or another. This was the term used by their peers and, unfortunately, other adults they came into contact with. And although I (Tracy) have never used the term *real parent* to indicate my children's birthparents, one day when we were talking about our old house, my older son (who was 4 when we moved and 7 when we were having this conversation) remembered that house as the one where, as he put it, his "real mommy lived."

So you're going to hear the term somewhere, very possibly from the lips of your child. Sure, it takes you aback a little when it comes from the mouth of your babe (and ticks you off when it comes from someone else). This is one of the relatively minor things you're going to have to deal with, however, and it's not something to get hung up about.

Simply correct your child's use of the term, but never in an angry way. A casual "Oh, you mean your birthparent?" or a joking "Are you trying to say I'm not real?" will probably work just fine (those responses have worked for us). (You can use the same approach with other adults, but in those situations, you get the bonus of being able to add a little attitude.)

Handling Feelings of Rejection

All parents want their children to feel special and loved and wanted. Parents who give birth to their children simply have to say things like "Your father and I waited so long for you!" or "The happiest day of my life was the day you were born" and their child can bask in the glow of being cherished and adored.

Well, your child is cherished and adored, too. And heaven knows, you probably waited a long time for her, and the day she came into your life was the day you did cartwheels. So when you tell the adoption story, you focus on the good things: Your child was wanted. Your child was loved. Your child was meant to be yours. And then your child starts asking questions that let you know that your pretty story isn't enough to soothe her curiosity: Why did she (the birthmother) give me away? Was something wrong with me? Didn't she want me?

No matter how pretty you try to paint the picture of your child's adoption or how vehemently you say that the birthmother wanted and loved your child, your child probably will still experience her adoption as a rejection. My (Katrina's) son once told me, "You might not call it abandonment, but it feels like abandonment to me."

When these feelings come up

Some children seem to think about these issues at all ages, while other children don't vocalize these things at all. (Remember, though, that not bringing it up *doesn't* mean that your child doesn't have these feelings.)

I (Katrina) receive many calls from parents of 7- and 8-year-olds who say that they're dealing with these issues at home. Adolescence is usually another difficult period.

Sometimes, anniversaries — your child's birthday, for example, or the anniversary of the day the child was removed from his home — may be difficult for the child.

Dealing with your child's pain

If your child's adoption causes her to feel pain and loss, you can take several steps to help her. First, be honest with your child about her situation. Although you want to give age-appropriate answers, don't sugarcoat things simply because *you* don't want to have to deal with them. Second, be open to whatever your child feels and don't try to persuade her to feel differently.

Although you may try to explain to your child that her birthmother made the decision out of love, don't expect your daughter to "buy" it. Your child may be angry at her birthmother, and if you continue to "defend" her, your child may feel you aren't being supportive. Sometimes, the best thing to say is "Yes, I know you are hurting, and I am sorry" rather than launch into the whole "You know she loved you soooo much" routine.

As hard as it is, you need to realize that no answers will truly soothe your child's longings. Part of the package of being adopted is having feelings of longing or hurt. I (Katrina) have never talked to an adult adoptee who believed that he or she had survived the adoption experience unscathed. (I'm not saying that such a person isn't out there; I'm just saying I haven't talked to one — and I've talked to several hundred adoptees.)

One of the worst feelings imaginable is to see your child in pain and not be able to do anything about it. It's a feeling of helplessness like no other. Most families get proactive when this happens and take some of the following steps to offer relief to their child.

Accepting your child's feelings and remaining nonjudgmental

If your child shouts, "I hate my birth mom; I wish she were dead!" say, "I know it hurts, honey." Don't say, "Oh, you don't mean that!" Even harder, your child may shout, "I hate you! I wish I lived with my birthmother!" Respond again to the pain your child is feeling: "I know you are hurting; I wish I could make it better."

Keeping the communication lines open

You want your child to talk to you, to share his feelings — whatever they are — so that he doesn't have to feel them alone. You may not be able to make things better, but you *can* support him as he struggles with issues he faces. Often, however, adoptees don't tell their parents about their feelings, especially the painful ones. Many are afraid that these feelings will hurt their parents or make the parents feel like they've failed. Where do these kids get this impression? Frequently and unfortunately, from their parents, who often don't even realize that they're erecting barriers.

So when the topic comes up, don't flinch, don't grimace, don't sigh, don't ignore it, and don't give any other outward sign that your child can interpret as discomfort or reluctance to talk. Although your heart may be palpitating and your mind may be racing, outwardly you need to be calm and responsive. You, after all, are the grown-up, and do you really want your child protecting *you*?

Using available resources to help your child

If your child is feeling a longing for his birthmother, you may be able to help. If you have any contact with the birthmother, ask her for photos for your child. Ask her to write your child a letter. Allow your child to write back or draw a picture. Ask her to send the child some token to let your child know she's thinking about him.

One birthmother I (Katrina) know bought identical Christmas ornaments for her child and herself. She explained that every year when they put that ornament on their trees, they would know they were thinking of each other. Another birthmother explained that she would be holding a rose in every formal photo she had taken in the future. When she sent the photos to the adoptive family, they would know the rose represented her love for her child.

Some families have initiated actual meetings with the birthmother as a result of their child's longings. These parents report positive results and a lessening of their child's sadness.

If contact with your child's birthmother is simply not possible, you can introduce your child to other children who were adopted. Seeing and knowing others like yourself can be comforting. And being able to talk to someone who really understands can be invaluable. If you're interested in getting in contact with other adoptive families, consider joining an adoption support group. To find support groups in your area, call your agency, look in the Yellow Pages, or head to Chapter 21 for a list of support groups and information on finding one in your area.

Any happily-ever-afters?

Some children (especially those in closed adoptions) continue to long for their birthparents and want to know the facts surrounding their birth and adoption. These children are the most likely to initiate a search (head to Chapter 19 for information about birthparent searches). Other children, struggling with their feelings of rejection, decide early on that they want nothing to do with their birthparents and tend to reject them in return. These kids don't want to talk about their birthmother and would rather not be confronted with evidence of her existence.

Many adoptive families notice differences in how their children process their adoption experience and can make a good guess as to who will search and who will not.

People generally want fairy-tale endings, where everyone rides or walks or dances into the sunset, where all pain and grief and loss are resolved, and where the future holds nothing but good. If that's your expectation, whether you're adopting or not, you have some reality issues to deal with.

The happily-ever-after for children who feel rejected is, ultimately, acceptance: accepting themselves, accepting how they came into the world, accepting how they came to be with the family they're in, and accepting that they had nothing to do with the decisions that were made. Essentially, it's being able to accept the pain of loss, accept the love of family, and move on to a full, rich life.

Additional resources for parents

All parents need help from time to time or want to tap into the opinions of experts or others who have traveled down the same road. Fortunately, you can find all sorts of resources about adoption, from the general to the very specific. Here are some books you may find helpful:

For parents who adopt older children: If you are thinking about adopting, are in the process of adopting, or already have adopted an older child and want information and insight in how to deal with some of the challenging issues you may face, *Adopting the Older Child* (Harvard Common Press, 1979), written by Claudia L. Jewett, may help. Jewett, a nationally known family therapist who has raised ten children, seven of them adopted, explains the transitions that you can expect with older child adoptions. From the honeymoon period through the testing phase to integration into the family, Jewett describes what adoptive parents can expect and gives advice on handling the situations that may arise.

For parents who adopt children of a different race: *Inside Transracial Adoption* (Perspectives Press, 2000), written by Gail Steinberg and Beth Hall, covers many issues and challenges that multirace families face (like racism in America, the myth of color blindness, feelings of belonging, and so on). This book offers insight into how to build close, loving families and raise children who are comfortable in both their adopted and birth cultures. Much of the information focuses on the children of color adopted into Caucasian families.

For parents whose children feel grief for their birthmother: *Twenty Things Adopted Kids Wish Their Adoptive Parents Knew* (Dell Publishing, 1999), by Sherrie Eldridge, is built on the premise that most, if not all, adopted children experience grief and loss as a result of being separated from their birthmother and that they must experience and deal with this pain in order to move beyond it. The people best able to help? The adoptive parents. In *Twenty Things,* Eldridge explains this grief, how it can manifest itself, and what you can do to help your child heal.

For people whose extended families aren't supportive: Not everyone who hears about your plans to adopt is going to be thrilled with the idea. Some will have a few minor reservations; others may be downright hostile. In *Adoption Is a Family Affair! What Relatives and Friends Must Know* (Perspectives Press, 2001), author Patricia Irwin Johnston, MS, explains the hows and whys of adoption in easy-to-understand language, sensitively but forthrightly addresses the objections some people have, and suggests ways that they can be supportive of your decision.

As parents, *you* need to accept the fact that adoption is a lifetime journey, full of hills and valleys, and no end. As much as you may long to take the journey (and the hurt) for your children, you can't. But you can walk beside them to support them when they need it and comfort them when they hurt. Just knowing that you're there can make a big difference to them.

Special Issues in Transracial and Transcultural Adoptions

When you adopt transracially, you adopt a child of a race different than yours. Adopting transculturally means that your child comes from a different culture than yours. If you're one of these families, you're going to have — in addition to the regular, run-of-the-mill adoption issues — other issues to deal with that are unique to your situation.

You hear it all the time: "Things are so much better today!" "There just isn't as much prejudice as there use to be." "Everyone is equal now." Yes, things are better, but don't fool yourself that there isn't still a long way to go. And don't think that just because your neighbors ooh and aah now over how cute your baby is that they'll want her to grow up and date their son. A lot of prejudice is still present in the United States, and your family is going to be a lightning rod for bolts of bigotry.

The race issue

Children are not chameleons. They don't change color to match their environments. To ignore your child's racial difference is to do her a great injustice. As soon as your child enters school (if not before), she'll be questioned about the racial differences in her family. You need to provide your child with coping mechanisms to handle the curiosity and questions from others.

Celebrating diversity

Several books celebrate the differences among people. Here are a few that you may want to take a gander at and share with your kids:

✔ *The Colors of Us*, written and illustrated by Karen Katz (Henry Holt and Company, 1999): A little girl, on a walk with her mother, learns that brown isn't just brown. It's a myriad of different shades, each unique and beautiful.

✔ *Bein' with You This Way*, written by W. Nikola-Lisa and illustrated by Michael Bryan (Lee & Low Books, Inc., 1994): Written as a child's playground rap, this book celebrates the ways that people are both different and the same. The high-spirited verse and the expressive drawings will actually make you want to dance around the yard with your children.

✔ *Black is brown is tan*, written by Arnold Adoff and illustrated by Emily Arnold McCully (HarperCollins Children's Books, 1973): Winner of the National Council for Teachers of English Award for Excellence in Poetry for Children, this book celebrates a transracial family.

Helping your child cope with questions

What can you do when people ask questions related to racial differences? First, educate your child that she doesn't have to answer personal questions if she doesn't want to. I (Katrina) once overheard a young child asking my daughter a series of questions that included "Who is that lady with you?" "Where is your real mom?" "Where did you come from?" "Can you speak Korean?" And on and on and on. I could tell by my daughter's curt answers and her body language that she was not enjoying the exchange. It was also obvious that these questions were repeats of previous conversations with other children. I later tried to explain to my daughter that there's nothing wrong with saying, "I don't want to talk about that" or "That's personal."

If your child does want to answer questions, work with him to decide what he might say. My (Katrina's) son says he always went through the same "routine" when he met new people. His pat answers included "I was adopted when I was 6 months old," "South Korea," and "Those *are* my real parents." He has stated that he liked to get the exchange over with and out of the way early on in his relationships.

Dealing with people who are hostile

Becoming an interracial family may make your family less popular. You may be surprised to see family, friends, or neighbors react negatively to your choices. Sometimes complete strangers even have opinions. You may encounter curiosity, nosiness, rudeness, prejudice, bias, and hostility, and maybe all of these on the same day! Even nice people can really get on your nerves. You can only take so much of people approaching you to tell you "how wonderful" you are.

How you handle these people and these situations may change with your mood, but always keep in mind that your child will learn how to react by watching how you react.

Here are some suggested responses to racist comments:

- ✔ "I am offended by what you just said."

- ✔ "I am sure you don't mean what you just said. Because it would be cruel to say something like that in front of my child."

- ✔ "What do you mean by that?"

- ✔ "Why did you say that?"

- ✔ "Why do you feel that way?"

- ✔ "Short of listening to my dog howl along to 'The Star-Spangled Banner,' that is just about the most asinine thing I've ever heard."

When hostility is blatant or potentially threatening, removing yourself from the situation may be your best option. You certainly aren't going to be successful in changing those attitudes, so arguing won't help. Having a good sense of humor can help when encountering the truly ignorant people.

Preparing your child

A lot of the work related to dealing with the race issue needs to be done at home, not on the spur of the moment in the middle of an altercation. Some things to do:

- ✔ **Talk to your children about racism.** Explain your theories of why people act this way.

- ✔ **Make sure that they understand that stereotypes, racism, and discrimination are wrong.** Educate your children that they don't deserve to be treated badly.

- ✔ **Talk together about comments or behavior they may experience.** Discuss possible responses to these situations.

- ✔ **Always remind your children that you're there to help when needed.** If they feel threatened or afraid, tell them to come to you for help.

- ✔ **Intervene when necessary but honor your child's request if he begs you not to get involved.** Sometimes an enraged parent can be more humiliating than the original problem.

I (Katrina) spent time with my children role-playing different scenarios. We practiced what to do if a "bad" person called us names or was rude to us. We all took turns being the bad person and the victim. The kids enjoyed the game and did very well. Then one day, they watched in horror as I grabbed a poor little boy by the arm, pulled him down the sidewalk, pounded on his door, demanded he be punished, and then burst into tears. All because I heard him call my son a "Chinese monkey-face." Obviously, Mommy needed more practice!

You're going to react differently on different days, depending on your mood, the situation, whether your child is with you, and any of a number of other things. When you're in a patient mood, you may try to answer ignorant questions in a friendly way that also educates the questioner. When you're in an impatient mood, you may be curt and a bit less friendly. And, let's face it, occasionally, you're going to lose it entirely: You may embarrass your kids, scare the neighbor lady, and cow everyone else into silence. But take heart: Years from now, when you and your children sit around your kitchen table talking about how crazy things were when they were little, you can bet that little episode will be one your kids will retell, with equal touches of amusement, embarrassment, and pride.

I can't believe they just said that!

Don't believe that people can say really stupid things? Here are some examples that folks have shared:

✔ A good friend shopping with an adoptive mother at the mall, both with babies in the stroller: "It doesn't embarrass me to go shopping with you now. I hardly even think about it anymore."

✔ A family member: "How dark skinned are Korean kids anyway?"

✔ A stranger in the mall: "Did you marry a Chinese man?"

✔ A grandmother: "Isn't their skin greasy?"

✔ A student: "I want to go to the prom with you, but my dad says it would make everyone uncomfortable."

✔ A man at a family funeral: "We like it out here; we like to keep it white. Know what I mean?"

✔ Many people everywhere: "Are these your children?"

Head to Chapter 17 for advice on how to respond to comments like these.

Dealing with family and friends

Zero tolerance is a catch phrase frequently used to describe the policy that parents should follow to protect their children. It means that you will not tolerate anyone devaluing, ridiculing, or embarrassing your child. You can take the intent a step further to mean that you will not tolerate any racially or ethnically biased remarks about anybody. Zero tolerance is an easy policy to follow with strangers, but not so with friends and family.

Even though doing so is hard, if you notice problems occurring in conversation or the actions of your friends or family, you must address the situation. If someone says something blatantly racist in your child's presence, you should challenge the remark. Your child is listening. If the problem is ongoing, take time to talk to this person alone. Describe how his remarks make you feel and how they affect your child. Ask for this person's help in protecting your child. If the person doesn't take your comments seriously, you may have to explain that you can't bring your child into situations where she's not treated with respect.

Here are examples of actions or speech that will hurt your children:

✔ Telling racial jokes that degrade your child

✔ Making comments that imply your child isn't really part of the family

✔ Excluding your child from gifts or giving unequal gifts to your child

✔ Openly hesitating to touch or show affection to your child, *or* frequently touching your child and examining him as if he were a novelty

✔ Acting as if they don't trust your child

✔ Frequently suspecting or blaming your child

Always ask yourself the question "How is this behavior affecting my child?" If your relationship with family or friends is hurting your child, and if your pleas for change are unheeded, end the relationship. Your child must come first.

How could you do this to me?! What to do when your kid's the one who's hostile

Sometimes, the person who may feel hostile toward the transracial mix of your family is your child. Don't be surprised if, one day, your child is the one who gives you grief over the race issue. Why?

Well, first, you're his parent. If a kid needs to lash out at someone, who better than you (or a sibling, friend, or the family dog)? Second, you put him in this situation. When he was a baby, did you ask *him* if he wanted to grow up in an all-(pick a race) house?

Kids who grow up in transracial environments have a lot of advantages and opportunities that kids who live in isolated environments don't. But they also have to find a way to feel comfortable in two worlds, which can be hard if they don't exist in either one completely. If you adopt transracially, you have to find a way to unite races and cultures for your child's sake so that she feels comfortable in both worlds. Following are some suggestions to accomplish that goal:

✔ Make sure your child has same-race role models.

✔ Take advantage of opportunities you have to experience and embrace your child's culture.

✔ Make sure that the literature in your house — children's books, adult books, and so on — is representative of the diversity in the world.

See the later section "Honoring the culture of origin" for specific suggestions.

Not everything is about adoption; hostility is normal for birth kids, too. Your kid hassling you may simply be his way of showing you that he knows where your buttons are and he likes to push them.

Cultural genocide: The position statement of NABSW and federal law

Years ago, the National Association of Black Social Workers (NABSW) took a strong stance opposing transracial adoptions. The organization called these adoptions a form of "cultural genocide." Many agencies stopped placing children transracially as a result of this censure. Since this time, a federal law has been enacted that changed everything. In 1994, the Multiethnic Placement Act (MEPA) was enacted. This act prohibits the use of a child's (or adoptive family's) race to delay or deny the child's placement. The federal law requires any agency receiving federal funding (therefore, all public agencies) to place children in available adoptive homes regardless of the race factor. Many agencies previously opposed to transracial adoption now practice it, enabling them to remain eligible for federal assistance. You rarely hear the genocide argument now.

Honoring the culture of origin

When you adopt transculturally, you have an obligation to your children to educate them about their culture. Because you don't "possess" their culture, you can't "give" it to them. But you can expose them to it, teach them about it, and help them learn to appreciate it. In order to accomplish this, you first need to educate yourself:

- ✔ **Do a personal inventory.** How much diversity is noticeable in your life and in your home? What foods do you eat, what music do you listen to, what books do you read, what magazines do you subscribe to, and how do you decorate your home? If everything is looking pretty bland, mix it up.

- ✔ **Learn about your child's history, read books, and cultivate friendships.** If your child is coming from China, for example, buy chopsticks, Chinese cookbooks, and Chinese art and music. Attend festivals, expos, and events that reflect your child's culture. Learn to love and appreciate this culture so that you can share that love and appreciation with your child.

- ✔ **Notice those around you where you live, shop, and worship and in your school district.** Make changes as necessary so that your child will be comfortable. Consider race and culture when selecting physicians, child-care givers, beauticians, and so on. For example, if your child is African American and one of the first-grade teachers is African American, request that teacher for your child. Take every opportunity to expose your child to individuals representing her race or culture.

A leap of faith

As our children have grown, we have tried to find ways to embrace their culture. When our oldest son was 14 months old, we discovered that our town had a Baptist church with a primarily African American congregation. We didn't know anyone there, and we hadn't been invited, so we took a leap of faith and just showed up there one Sunday. They greeted us with hugs, smiles, and a warmth that was completely unexpected. They were quite naturally curious about our son, but they didn't ask us to explain our family — they just accepted that we were a family and embraced us without hesitation. We went back the following Sunday, and the Sunday after that.

Here it is two years later, and the members of our church are closer to us than some of our family members. They have given us support, encouragement, and, more important than anything, acceptance. They were there when our youngest son was placed with us; they were there when my husband and I were baptized; they were there when my mother left a 30-year marriage and moved in with us; and they are there for us for whatever we need, unconditionally. Several members of the church come and get the boys and keep them for the day or overnight to give us a much-needed break.

What better way to immerse your children in their own culture than to step out on faith and truly embrace members of their community. Heritage festivals are great, and adoption support groups are a great way to meet other interracial families. To truly give your children the support they need in our society, however, they need to have positive role models of their own race who are as close to them as family. As parents, we can offer them love, understanding, and a happy home, but we can't teach them what it's like to be a part of their cultural group because we just don't know.

I encourage all parents who have adopted transracially, or who may be considering that possibility, to really think about ways they can help their children to bond with people of their own cultural group. Seek out people who can offer your children a positive, yet realistic, view of what it means to be a part of that group. It really is one of the most wonderful gifts you can give to your children, and I can assure you it will enrich your life at the same time.

Ilene Watson

Special Issues Faced by Parents of Older Adopted Children

No matter how your older child came to be in your home, you can bet that she's going to have issues with trusting adults and feeling safe. This child has probably moved around a lot, has probably seen other children move in and out of her foster homes, and has experienced the "rejection" resulting from the separation from her birthparents. So as a parent of an older child who is going through all of this, you're going to have your own special issues to deal with.

The relationship with their birth mom

Most children feel love for their birthparents, whether they admit it or not. This is a good thing. You want your child to have the ability to love others. The love that children feel for their parents is not a rejection of you, so don't react as if it is. Remember, you're not competing with the birth mom. Humans have the ability to love many people simultaneously. Offer your child a safe place to express how she feels, and she'll feel closer to you for it.

If contact with the birthmother (or birth family) continues

If your child continues to have visits with members of the birth family, try to be upbeat, supportive, and cooperative. Keep remembering, your child's love for her birthparent doesn't detract from her love for you.

If you're having a hard time with the concept of your child continuing to visit her birthmother, think of this. The fact that you live with your spouse doesn't mean that you no longer love your parents. No matter how wonderful your spouse is, you probably still get excited at the prospect of visiting your parents. Now, if someone were to suggest you move in with your parents, you may be horrified at that idea. In fact, you may believe that there is no way you and your mother could live under one roof together. However, again, you love your mother and want to see her.

When the visit is over, your child may have many conflicting feelings: love, anger, and grief, all bundled together. Your child has to experience and work through these feelings in order to accept the realities of her situation. Protecting her from experiencing them may not be the healthiest approach.

However, if your child is having serious traumatic responses to the meetings, they may need to end. Seek professional advice to make the decision. Most adoption visitation agreements allow for the visits to end when they cease to be "in the best interests of the child."

If contact with the birthmother should have ended . . . but didn't

Even a judge decreeing that the child is to have no more contact with his birthmother doesn't mean that your child will necessarily follow the rule. Many older adoptees already know their birth moms' phone numbers and addresses. And if they're determined to remain in contact (many kids, in fact, continue to call their birthmothers long after contact was supposed to have ended), you can't do much about it. Even if you forbid your child to use the phone at home, she can find another phone to use somewhere else.

Some families treat this ongoing contact as any discipline issue and enforce consequences. But such a call is probably a result of the pain the child is experiencing. Talk to your child about his birthparent and what he was hoping to accomplish with his call.

Unhappy pasts: Prior abuse and neglect

When you adopt an older child, your child has probably been the victim of abuse or neglect (the reason being that most older children who are available for adoption have been removed from their homes by the state after allegations of abuse or neglect have been substantiated). Your child will probably be a child who doesn't feel safe and who lives in fear.

Your child may lie, steal, yell, or exhibit aggressiveness, withdrawal, depression, bed-wetting, impulsiveness, anger, and more. What you need to remember is that these behaviors are probably just symptoms of the real problems: her inability to trust and her fear. Instead of focusing on behaviors, you can work on building trust and alleviating fear.

Remember, talking and touching are two ways to reach your child. Give lots of reassurances, explanations, and praise. Talk to your child about how he's feeling and, to some extent, how you're feeling. Initiate pats and hugs, if your child will allow. If not, try to engage your child in other activities that include physical touch, things like wrestling, basketball, or reading while sitting close to each other. Head to Chapter 11 for more information on what you can do to help your child adjust to her new home and to you.

Some things to keep in mind:

- ✔ Your child's scars may never heal completely, and she may always long for the people she has lost. What you can look forward to is seeing her attachment to you grow and her fear subside. You can make a positive difference in this child's life.

- ✔ Don't be afraid to be honest with your social worker when discussing your family's adjustment to an older child adoption. She expects you to have some difficulties, and she may be able to help. At the very least, she can listen with nonjudgmental ears. The last thing she wants to do is remove this child from your home and move her once again. She's rooting for you.

- ✔ As always, seek professional help for any child who is hurting.

History of broken attachments

Children with a history of broken attachments are frequently children who find it difficult to attach. Although much is said about reactive attachment disorder (RAD) and attachment disorder (AD), discussed in more detail in Chapter 18, many questions are still unanswered. The research often disagrees on the exact causes, the criteria for diagnosis, the best treatment, and the prognosis. Here's what the researchers do agree on:

> ✔ Many children with a history of neglect suffer from this disorder.
>
> ✔ Symptoms may range from mild to severe.
>
> ✔ Traditional parenting approaches are usually not successful with these kids.

In addition, these children are often "charmers" with those outside the family circle, which prevents the parents from receiving the support, understanding, and assistance they need.

If your child is diagnosed with an attachment disorder (explained in more detail in Chapter 18), you need to seek help from a therapist familiar with the characteristics of these children. Also, seek out a support group of families dealing with this disorder in their family.

Special Issues Faced by Parents of Children Adopted Internationally

When you adopt an infant from another country, you rarely adopt a newborn. Instead, your child will usually be at least a few months to a year old, sometimes older. If you didn't specify infant on your application, your child, obviously, could be any age. The reason this information is important is because your child will have lived and grown in a culture that's different than yours. In addition to being a phenomenally enriching situation, it can also be challenging. The following sections explain some of the issues that families like yours typically deal with.

Special health issues

What type of medical issues you have to deal with depends largely on the resources available in your child's birth country (or the resources available in the region where your child was born or cared for) and the common medical practices available there.

Some diseases and conditions that have been eliminated or are easily treated in the United States are still prevalent in other countries. Whereas a cleft palate, for example, is not a major medical issue in the United States, where treatment is available and common, it may be a major medical issue in your child's birth country. Here are some medical issues you may face with an internationally adopted child:

✔ Because of the possible lack of adequate healthcare, it's not unusual to see children with developmental delays, low weight or small stature, malnutrition, or parasites.

✔ Your child may not have received immunizations or may have undiagnosed health problems.

✔ Many times, you'll get no medical history from the birthparents.

✔ Your child may have experienced poor prenatal care or no care at all.

✔ If your child was deprived emotionally or socially, he may be at high risk for an attachment disorder. See Chapter 18 for more on that condition.

Creating additional problems is the fact that some information about the child's medical tests, exams, and reports may not be entirely reliable.

When you face this situation, be sure that your child's pediatrician is aware of the circumstances surrounding your child's adoption. She can perform necessary tests and immunizations, guide you in overcoming any developmental delays your child may experience, and direct you to specialists for additional help, if necessary.

Other things you may encounter

Although many special issues you're likely to encounter with children adopted internationally relate to the care they receive in their birth countries prior to their adoption, you may find yourself working through these issues, too:

✔ **Language barrier:** Obviously, if your child comes from a country whose language you don't speak, you're going to be facing a language barrier. Even a very young child may know a few words in his native language (up, potty, mine, no, and so on). By learning a little of your child's language as he learns yours, you can reduce the communication gap.

✔ **Questions about your child's age:** You may not know your child's actual birth date. This scenario is most likely if the country has experienced significant political or social upheaval and the records are lost (or not adequately kept) or if your child was abandoned. In this case, your (or your agency's) best guess is the best you can do.

✔ **Cultural issues:** Your child may react to cultural expectations or beliefs that you know nothing about. Or he may exhibit behavior that in America would be deemed rude or disrespectful (like not looking someone in the eye who is speaking to you) but that in his birth country is the proper etiquette. For this reason, learn as much as you can about your child's culture of origin and, if possible, join a support group of families who've adopted children from your child's birth country.

I (Tracy) read of a woman who, years ago, adopted a 3-year-old from Vietnam. Once back home, the daughter would periodically wet the bed. The mother tried all the regular remedies but to no avail and resigned herself to the fact that her daughter was just a very sound sleeper and would have to outgrow the problem. Then one night, after staying up unusually late, the mother peeked into her daughter's room and found her wide awake and peeing on the bed. When she questioned her daughter, the child answered with the Vietnamese word for "ghost." Come to find out, ancestral ghosts are part of the Vietnamese culture, and this little girl thought one had visited her. The sight of the ghost scared her enough that she didn't want to get out of bed, even though she had to go to the bathroom.

✔ **Initial adjustment issues:** Your agency may inform you of common behaviors — night terrors, excessive clinginess, and so on — that your child may exhibit due to the major change that he's just been through.

Consider creating a lifebook for your child. This book is essentially a scrapbook detailing the events of your child's life. Commonly used for children in foster care, these books contain photos, mementos, and information about placements and the birth family. You can adapt this idea to help your internationally adopted child. The story in the sidebar "Sarah's lifebook" illustrates what a valuable tool these books can be to help your child adjust to her new life.

Sarah's lifebook

We adopted our daughter, Sarah, when she was 3½ years old. I made Sarah's lifebook a priority when we returned home and had it done very quickly. I felt this was important because Sarah is a bright and articulate child, and the transition she had to make to a new family, a new culture, and new home was undeniably overwhelming. She left behind a foster mother who loved her dearly, an orphanage in which Sarah herself had responsibilities and felt very needed, and the Chinese culture of which she was very proud. Her lifebook helped her to visually see the transition she was making while, at the same time, honoring her past. It helped her to sort through information that she could not make sense of alone. And it helped her emotionally to know that we supported her continued relationships with the people she loved in China while showing our family coming together.

Even before she could speak English, Sarah would flip through her lifebook and speak in Chinese about the pictures from her orphanage. As she began to speak English, I wrote down everything she could tell us about the pictures. When she went through the expected periods of grieving, she would get out her book and bring it to me to share. Then she went through a period where she seemed indifferent to her book on the shelf. Now she selectively decides when and with whom she will share it . . . usually close friends or teachers. Her varying levels of interest in her lifebook have helped me to know where she is emotionally in regards to her adoption and attachment.

(continued)

(continued)

Arguably, I went out of my way after Sarah's adoption to make contacts with her caretakers and foster mother in order to get more information about her early life in China. The effort was worth it because what they provided me through their letters is priceless. I have added their words to her lifebook in a story format. I continue to add each letter that we receive to the back of her lifebook so that Sarah can see her ongoing story and the relationships that we still value with the people who loved her in China.

Her lifebook has been a wonderful tool!

Charlotte Ottinger

Chapter 17

Beyond the Family: Dealing with Outsiders

. . . .

In This Chapter

▶ Sharing (or not sharing) the adoption story outside your family

▶ Responding to hurtful questions or remarks

▶ Handling issues that will probably come up at school

▶ Helping your child keep a positive attitude about adoption

. . . .

*W*hen your child is a baby, you're omnipotent. You decide what she hears, what she watches, and what she's exposed to. If anything hurtful comes her way, you magically deflect it or absorb it yourself so that your child remains happy and oblivious to life's crueler moments. Nosy inquiries? Gone. Unkind comments? Vaporized. You're more effective than popemobiles and Secret Service agents combined.

And then your child grows beyond the protective sphere you so successfully erected, and your power to protect her is gone. She's going to have to deal with people and situations on her own.

That doesn't mean, however, that you're out of a job. After all, not being able to protect your child doesn't mean that you can't show her how to protect herself. You are your child's staunchest ally and biggest supporter. With your help and example, she can develop the skills she'll need to deal with the things the outside world will throw at her.

For the questions and comments you and your child are likely to hear, this chapter gives you suggestions on how to respond to some, deflect others, and educate the people who say thoughtless things.

Who to Tell What about the Adoption

Imagine yourself at a restaurant with your spouse and baby. You're juggling the accoutrements of parenthood — sippy cup, baby crackers, and portable toys — and a stranger with an insipid smile approaches, leans toward you, tips her head toward your squirming bundle of joy, and asks, sotto voce, "Did you conceive her in the missionary position?"

Of course you can't imagine that. People don't ask those things because they know that *how* you conceived and delivered your child is a private — and special — family affair.

But substitute the question "Did you adopt her?" in the above scenario, and you can imagine it pretty easily. Adopt a child, especially one who doesn't share certain of your physical characteristics — like race — and some folks feel absolutely no compunction at all inquiring in public places about private matters.

How do you deal with the adoption issue? Some people, like your child's pediatrician, need to know about the adoption. Others, like the neighbor down the street, don't need to know but will probably ask. So whom do you tell? How do you tell it? And how do you respond to strangers who seem to think that their curiosity alone warrants an answer? This section gives you ideas.

People who already know

Some people, like your close friends or work associates, probably already know about your child's adoption. What they know, however, depends on how close they are to you and what you want to tell them. You're probably going to share private details with your intimate friends, for example, and only more general information with others. As you share your information, keep these things in mind:

✔ **General discussions have a tendency to become very personal.** When the topic of adoption comes up, even if you're not talking specifically about your child's adoption, some people may assume that no details are off limits and will ask personal questions that you aren't comfortable answering. Some responses that can get you off the hook with as little awkwardness as possible include

- "I'm sure you can understand why we would want to keep that private."

- "We're saving that information for our child, when he asks."

✔ **Just because you've shared *some* information about your child's adoption doesn't mean that you have to share *all* the information about the adoption.** Figure out for yourself what you want to share and with whom you want to share it. Then don't feel compelled to answer questions beyond that, even innocent ones that spring from honest curiosity rather than nosiness.

✔ **Even friends you love say careless things.** Sometimes these remarks reveal ideas that may fundamentally offend you ("Wouldn't they rather be with their own kind?" "It's too bad you can't have your own kids."). Other times, they reveal nothing more than a poor choice of words. A close friend of mine (Tracy's), when she saw a portrait of my sons, said, "They look like brothers." Knowing how she feels about my children, I didn't question for a minute her intention or her real meaning, but I corrected her nonetheless. "They *are* brothers," I said. And she thanked me for not introducing a new orifice into her anatomy.

People who need to know but don't

Some people won't know about your child's adoption unless you make a point of telling them. So whom do you purposefully tell? Anyone who needs to know. Obviously, your child's doctor or pediatrician is number one on this list. Even if you've adopted a healthy infant or child, it's still important that your pediatrician know of your child's history of adoption. Here's why:

✔ Internationally adopted children are at risk for different illnesses or conditions than U.S. doctors usually test for.

✔ Many adopted children don't have complete medical histories.

Be sure to explain to any doctor when a specific medical history is unknown. Although you may be tempted to just check no on the health history form that includes all those questions about specific conditions, don't. If you really don't know, your doctor needs to know that.

✔ Children who were adopted at an older age may have experienced abuse or neglect that could impact their developmental growth.

In each of these situations, your doctor can provide the best medical care if she is fully informed.

Any counselors or therapists working with your child also need to be made aware of your child's adoption. Sometimes, children having behavioral problems are really just struggling with adoption issues, and your child's counselor or therapist needs to be aware of this possibility.

You know what I mean

We imagine that nearly all adoptive parents hate these five little words: "You know what I mean." You hear this response in scenarios like these:

> **Them:** I thought she was your own kid.
>
> **You:** She is my own kid.
>
> **Them:** You know what I mean.

Or

Them: I couldn't do that to my kid.

You: She made this decision out of love.

Them: You know what I mean.

"You know what I mean" isn't a question, asking for understanding. It's a statement that essentially says, "You're just objecting out of convention. But deep down, *you know what I mean.*"

No, we don't know what you mean.

To figure out who belongs in the need-to-know category, ask yourself whether your child could benefit from this person's knowing. If having a better understanding of your child would improve your child's situation in some way, then tell the person. If there's no way the child could benefit, then you don't need to tell anything.

People who ask

People generally don't ask about adoption unless something makes them suspect that you didn't give birth to your children. Sometimes that "something" is that you and your children are of different races. Other times, that something is how close in age your kids are. My (Tracy's) three younger kids, for example, are each eight months apart. Once people do the math in their heads, they generally ask whether we adopted.

People who ask questions about your family generally fall into two camps: those who have a genuine interest in adoption and those who are curious. The people who are simply curious will drive you crazy. For some reason, they think their need to figure out why your family looks the way it does overrides any other consideration. They'll ask you, "Is he adopted?" or "Are they your own?" wherever and whenever they feel like it, without any thought to how this may make you or your child feel. Head to the section "Dealing with Tactless Neighbors, Friends, and Nosy Strangers," later in the chapter, for ideas on how to respond to these people.

The difference between nosy and non-nosy questions

So how do you know whether the question is a nosy one or not? Consider these examples of a nosy and non-nosy question:

✔ **Nosy question:** Did you adopt your children?

✔ **Non-nosy question:** Did you adopt your children?

Look the same. Sound the same. So how do you know?

The key isn't so much *what* they say, but *why* they want to know. This common question ("Did you adopt your children?") isn't a problem if the questioner also has adopted, has family who

adopted, or knows someone trying to adopt and just wants to talk about or share a common experience. But some people asking this question are just Jerry Springer types seeking any dirt they can find. They look to you to provide their entertainment for the evening. One really good way to filter the nosy from the non-nosy is to answer with "Why do you ask?"

People who have a genuine interest don't hesitate to answer. You'll hear things like "Well, I was adopted," or "I've been thinking about adopting," and the like. People who are just being nippy will give you a confused look.

But if you're approached by someone who has a genuine interest in adoption (and isn't just curious about your family), you can use this opportunity to be an advocate for adoption. If you think about it, the more people who are informed and educated about adoption, the better life will be for your child and your family. If you have the time and the inclination, answer sincere questions of the non-nosy type. When you answer questions, keep these things in mind:

✔ Try to move the conversation away from your individual child and onto adoption in general.

✔ Use your positive adoption language skills (see Chapter 1) and recognize that your children are watching and learning.

✔ Sometimes you might want to offer to discuss the topic at another time when the children aren't present.

If your child shares your race, most people who see your family won't question how it was created. They'll assume that your children were born to you. And that in itself can make for some pretty interesting conversations. You don't want to explain your family's origins with complete strangers, but you don't want to lie, either. I (Tracy) have found that, usually, you can simply answer the questions without elaborating. When my older daughter was an infant, for example, the first thing people generally noticed about her was her coiffure. She had been born with a head full of stick-straight brown hair that stuck up all over her head. One day another young mother came up to me and asked whether I had experienced heartburn before my daughter was born, because she had heard that women carrying babies with lots of hair generally have heartburn. I smiled and answered her honestly: "No, Sarah had not given me heartburn before she was born." (Of course, if this woman were to ask me the same question now — whether my daughter gave me heartburn — I could honestly say that I pop Tums like lemon drops.)

What should remain private

When you talk to your child's doctors or teachers about your child's adoption, you don't need to tell them everything. You only need to tell them what they need to know. Doctors, for example, need to know about anything related to medical information, like whether your child was exposed to drugs (prescription or otherwise) in utero. Teachers need to know about anything that could impact your child's ability to learn, like whether English isn't her native language. (For more information on the types of things you're going to deal with when your kid heads off to school, head to the section "Dealing with Adoption When Your Child Hits School Age," later in this chapter.) Basically, you're winnowing through all the info to pull out only what applies.

Keep the specific details of your child's family information private. Sometimes the child's story may include difficult things like drug or alcohol exposure, the birthmother's promiscuity, or dysfunctional family situations. Keep these things in confidence for your child. It's her information to share with whom she wants, not yours. Having others know any lurid details of the birth family's situation can be embarrassing for your child.

Dealing with Tactless Neighbors and Friends and Nosy Strangers

Anyone aware of your family's experience with adoption will be curious about it. If you've adopted transracially, it will be apparent to most people that you have adopted, and therefore, most people will be curious. You may discover that you routinely notice stares, looks, whispers, comments, and questions when your family goes to public places. Having a sense of humor is an absolute necessity, and an abundance of patience also comes in handy. Good humor and patience only go so far, however. When the questions are intrusive or inappropriate, you may have to take another approach.

Dealing with offensive comments

You may want to address specific offensive remarks. You may want to challenge obvious prejudices about birthmothers, adoptees, or adoption in general. How you challenge these prejudices depends on several factors.

Who's offended you and how important a relationship with that person is

Dealing with offensive remarks made by people you don't care about is easy. Dealing with these kinds of remarks from close friends and family members is what's tough.

With strangers or people who aren't important to you, you can respond to a rude remark in the following ways:

- ✔ **Ignore the comment (and the people) and then talk about the incident with your child later.** If your children are around when the comment is made, you don't want them to misinterpret your silence for either embarrassment or agreement. See the later section "Whether your child is present when the comments are made" for details.

- ✔ **Respond at the time of the incident in a manner that makes your point and ends the conversation.** A cold "We happen to feel differently," "I'm sure you didn't mean to imply what you just did," or "This is not a topic for discussion" generally either stuns or cows rude strangers, and that's all you need to move on.

- ✔ **Put the culprits on the defensive.** Turn the tables. If a busybody comes up and asks, "Is she adopted?" try asking a question of your own. "Why do you ask?" or "Do I know you?" is usually a pretty effective way to leave the busybody sputtering for an answer.

With family and close friends, many other things impact how you respond. Some people are worth educating. Ideally, you want to help them recognize and abandon their prejudices. Sometimes, just getting them not to voice these feelings around your kids is all you can hope for. If neither of those options is possible, you may end up in the unhappy position of having to choose: your relationship with these people or your kids' emotional well-being. And that really isn't a choice at all.

The intent of the remark

Is the sentiment behind the remark offensive, or just the phrasing? Having a 70-year-old great-aunt say that your son is just the cutest little Chinese baby she's ever laid her eyes on is quite a bit different than having that same aunt say that she wouldn't trust "one of their kind" any farther than she could throw them. In either instance, of course, you have to deal with the comment, but whereas the first remark may warrant a gentle correction, the second may require that you evaluate whether this particular aunt is one you want to spend any time with at all.

The situation and circumstances you're in

Where you are and what you're doing when the comment is made can impact how you respond. Dealing with your parents' friends at your folks' 25th anniversary party may require different strategies than dealing with your own friends and their significant others at the neighborhood bar.

You want to pick the strategy that best meets your objective, whatever that is. If you want to foster understanding or increase sensitivity, a yelling match probably isn't your best bet. If a particular incident hurts you to the core, you may decide that you need a few days to get your thoughts together before you respond at all, and then you may decide to write a letter rather than have another face-to-face confrontation.

Whether your child is present when the comments are made

Remember a couple of things if your child overhears someone's comment. First, kids are pretty in tune to the undercurrents of situations. Even if they didn't hear the specific comment, they'll notice if you're uncomfortable or upset, and they'll want to know why. Second, don't assume that, because you know that the jackass spouting off is a moron, your kid knows that, too. A child hearing something negative about him- or herself has a tendency to believe that the remark is true and that other people feel that same way. Finally, your child takes her cues from you. Although you may want to lunge across the table and eviscerate the offender from gullet to groin, you need to remember that you have a child at your elbow, watching and learning.

So keep these things in mind when you have to deal with these situations in front of your kids and when you have to help your children understand what happened:

- ✔ **Try to stay calm.** You don't have to be nice, but, if you can, be civil. An angry parent creating a scene at the mall may be more embarrassing to your child than a rude comment from a stranger.

- ✔ **Put the burden where it belongs: on the offender.** Someone else's prejudice isn't your problem. It's the offender's problem. You just get the unpleasant task of cleaning up after him. So when you talk to your child about how some people have bigoted notions, don't make the conversation about your child or your family. Make the conversation about how wrong these ideas — and the people who espouse them — are. You want your child to understand that she isn't the problem; they are.

- ✔ **Don't personalize the incident to your child.** Although the offender may be reacting specifically to your child or your family, don't say, "He doesn't think you should be in our family." Instead, say, "He's not a very nice man. And he doesn't understand families very well."

A trip to the store

As the proud Caucasian parents of two African American sons, we have been joyfully immersed in the world of parenting. More importantly, we have taken several leaps of faith and have immersed ourselves in another culture. This may seem like an easy thing to do — let me assure you, it isn't. We live in a very rural area in southern Kentucky and weren't sure how this whole transracial parenting thing was actually going to play out once it happened. During our home study process, we read every article, pamphlet, and personal account we could get our hands on so we would know what to expect.

When the agency called to tell us that our son had been born, we were ecstatic. We raced to the hospital to see him and were amazed at how beautiful he was. He was easily the most adorable baby we had ever seen.

We had our first family outing to a department store when Cameron was 2 days old. A very nice clerk noticed the infant carrier attached to our shopping cart. The canopy was up on the carrier, and she couldn't see the baby. She was telling us all about her newest grandchild as she edged around the cart to get a peek at the baby. When she finally made it to the front of our cart, the conversation went something like this: "How old is he?" "Two days." "Oh, gosh. Let me see. Well, isn't he . . . he just has the black . . . black . . . blackest hair, doesn't he?" All the while she's looking at my husband and me with our fair skin, blond hair, and blue eyes with a look of utter confusion on her face. It was all we could do to keep a straight face while we explained that we were just blessed with the adoption of our son and were stocking up on baby supplies. She congratulated us and quickly scurried away.

When we got to the car, we absolutely lost it. We couldn't stop laughing. At that point, we knew that our senses of humor would get us through just about any situation that came our way.

Ilene Watson

Smart answers for stupid questions

Some questions, just by their phrasing, make answering pretty darn easy. When people ask, "Is he your own?" the answer is simple: yes. It doesn't matter that these people are really asking, "Is he adopted?" Just because they think that oblique phrasing makes the question more palatable doesn't mean that you have to answer the unspoken question, particularly if their only reason for asking is their own curiosity. Here are some other phrasings of the "Is he adopted?" question that you can easily answer:

✔ Is he your real kid?

✔ Are you his real parents?

✔ Is he yours?

Just answer yes with a smile. It may or may not satisfy them, but their satisfaction isn't your concern. And who knows? You may be treated to watching
them as they try to process this info and, if they're particularly determined,
hunt around for another way to ask the same question.

Not all questions or comments are this easy to respond to, though. Some are
personal, some make offensive presumptions, and some are just plain out of
line. The following sections list a few comments that we've encountered and
give you some advice on things to think about when you respond, especially
if your children are present when the comment is made or the question is
asked.

The main thing to remember is that we're all adults. We can handle these situations ourselves. Our children, on the other hand, may be dumbfounded,
overwhelmed, or hurt by these kinds of encounters. Take the time to teach
your child how to field questions and comments. Set a good example. Role-
play and discuss options for different situations. Make sure that your child
learns appropriate responses for inappropriate questions or comments. The
more prepared they are, the more confident they will be.

Is she adopted?

This question is a tough one for a couple of reasons. First, the question
implies that something about your child doesn't quite fit with this person's
preconceived notion of what a family looks like. And no one has the right to
make your child feel separate from her family. Second, it's a personal question, and strangers aren't entitled to inquire about personal things. Finally,
the adoption is your child's story. She should get to decide when she wants
to bring it up and what people know about it. People who blurt this question
out presume that that right is theirs.

Having said that, adoption is something to celebrate. You don't want your
children to think that you would hesitate to acknowledge their adoptions or
that there is anything to be ashamed of. So decide what answer makes you
most comfortable. I (Katrina) usually answer yes. If I'm feeling less friendly, I
might say, "Why do you ask?"

This question — Is she adopted? — can also be awkward to answer if you've
adopted more than one child but only one child seems to elicit this attention
from others. This generally happens if one of your children is of a different
race or ethnicity. For example, I (Tracy) have had people single my African
American daughter out of the family and ask, "Is she adopted?" I usually
respond by saying, "Actually, several of my children are adopted." And if the
next question is "Oh, who?" I say, "I don't remember."

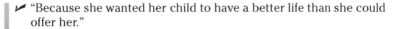

Yes, yes, a *thousand* times yes!

I (Tracy) come from a family built through adoption. Some of us were adopted into the family, and some of us were born into the family. There are six of us kids in all, of various ages, sizes, and shades, and my parents. Our family came to be at a time when integrated families were fairly uncommon, and so we were accustomed to being the object of stares and questions and comments.

One year at back-to-school night at our elementary school, one of our teachers asked my parents, "Are all these children yours?"

My father, who doesn't suffer fools lightly, answered simply, "Yes."

The teacher continued. "No, I mean are they all your *own* children?"

My dad: "Yes."

"Your real kids?"

"Yes."

"No, your *real* kids?"

"Yes."

Finally the teacher looked to my mother for help. "He's joking, right?"

My mother, who has the social grace of Miss Manners and generally goes out of her way to make people feel comfortable: "No."

How could a woman give away her own flesh and blood?

This question is a particularly hurtful one for children to hear. It implies that the child wasn't wanted and that the birthmother was a selfish person. The best way to answer this question is to make a simple, general statement. Here are a couple of examples:

> ✔ "Because she wanted her child to have a better life than she could offer her."
>
> ✔ "Out of love and sacrifice."

Don't get into the specifics of your child's adoption history. If the other person tries to probe further, simply say, "That information is private."

Who are his real parents?

You can get pretty creative with this one, and how you respond probably depends on your mood and how inclined you are to educate the other person. You can say, "We are" or "Last time I checked, I was pretty real." If you want to educate the person, you can correct the person's phrasing: "Do you mean, who are his birthparents?"

Of course, then you get to the question itself. Before you answer, you need to decide whether this is information this particular person needs to know. Usually, the answer is a big, fat *no*. In which case, you can simply say, "Sorry, but that information is private."

You must be really special people (to have adopted)

It sounds like a compliment, and the people who say it mean it as a compliment, but there's just something offensive about the presumption that it takes a special person to adopt or that raising children born to someone else is a feat that only the stout of heart should attempt. A good response to these kinds of statements is "No, we were selfish. We just wanted to be parents."

I (Tracy) have been told that I'm special, that I've done something most people couldn't do, that there's a special place in heaven for me — and for what? Because I wanted to be a mother and became one. If that's the requirement for a special place in heaven, I figure I'll go to Florida instead. It's probably less crowded.

They (the children) should be so thankful!

This statement is akin to the "You must be special people" sentiment you hear (see the preceding section). The best answer? "Oh no, we are the ones who are thankful for the opportunity to have them in our lives."

Dealing with Adoption When Your Child Hits School Age

When your children hit school age, your sphere of influence shrinks exponentially. They'll hear things you don't want them to hear, see things you don't want them to see, and say things you couldn't imagine coming from the mouth of your babies. And *that's* what every parent goes through. As an adoptive parent, you need to be prepared for a bit more.

Although your child's adoptive status might make her different than some of her classmates, it probably won't cause much of a stir. These days, the kids at school have moms, dads, stepmoms, stepdads, mom's significant other, and dad's partner to contend with. Some children are being raised by foster parents, grandparents, or other relatives. Most people probably won't be that interested in just one or two adoptive parents.

To share or not to share: That's always the question

Deciding whether or not to share your child's adoptive status may be out of your hands. Some children are so excited about their "story" that they happily share it with everyone they come in contact with. In transracial or transcultural families, it may be obvious to others that your family was formed by adoption.

With your child's teacher

In some instances, you need to inform your child's teacher of the adoption. Definitely talk with your child's teacher if your child was placed at an older age, was adopted from another country, is new to the English language, or has experienced frequent changes in living situations or school systems. In any of these situations, the teacher needs to be aware that your child may benefit from extra classroom help, testing, or tutoring. At the very least, the teacher needs to be aware of the challenges your child is facing.

Even if your child doesn't fit into those categories, you may still want to discuss the adoption issue with her teacher. Kids spend so many of their days in the classroom, and so many lessons and discussions relate to families and human relations (see the later section "Topics that are likely to come up" for details); you may want to schedule some time with your child's teacher to discuss the issues that may be important to your family. You may, for example, want to consider doing the following:

- ✔ Ask the teacher whether she would consider incorporating adoption into any lessons she has planned about families. (If you need to, make sure that she understands that you aren't asking her to discuss *your* child's adoption.)

- ✔ If the teacher is responsive to your suggestions, you could provide her with some information regarding positive adoption language (see Chapter 1 for information on that).

- ✔ Discuss any issues that concern you, such as assignments that you feel should be handled with sensitivity. The section "Topics that are likely to come up," later in this chapter, covers some of the more ubiquitous classroom lessons that can make adopted kids feel awkward.

- ✔ Ask to be informed if your child is being questioned by classmates so that you can discuss the subject at home.

With schoolmates

Some adoptive parents prefer to be proactive in protecting their child from hurtful remarks or questions. They may pick a day to talk to the classroom about their child's adoption. Specifically, in situations when the child has recently arrived from another country, such a presentation may be helpful. The thought process is that, if the children understand what has occurred, they won't make fun of your child for being "different." Instead, they'll welcome her and be eager to help her learn the ropes.

Other adoptive parents may indicate their willingness to come to school and share information about adoption as a part of the children's educational experience. Just like firefighters visit schools during Fire Prevention Week, adoptive parents may want to volunteer to speak during November (National Adoption Month).

Before you do anything, however, consider how your child feels about having this information shared. If your child is excited about being adopted and can't wait to share his story with friends, then go for it. If your child is shy, doesn't want to be the center of attention, or is uncomfortable talking about his adoption, let it go.

Apart from your involvement, allow your child to share what she wants, when she wants, to whomever she wants. It is her information, after all.

Topics that are likely to come up

When your child heads to school, you probably have already anticipated having to deal with the adoption issue with classmates and friends. You may have even considered sharing information with the teacher. But you may be taken by surprise when your little one comes home singing a song titled "I'm Gonna Climb My Family Tree and See What Makes Me Me" or when your teen comes home angry or hurt because a class discussion on *Silas Marner* led to a discussion about adoption that turned into a free-for-all.

The following sections outline some of these class projects and discussions that you're probably going to have to deal with.

The family tree

Veteran adoptive parents may shudder at the thought of the famous family tree assignment. This assignment keeps popping up, in various forms, from elementary through the high school years. Adopted children (as well as children of blended families and children in foster homes) never know quite what to do with this assignment. If they complete the family tree with just the information from their adoptive families, they're ignoring a big chunk of history that makes them who they are, including perhaps a racial or cultural difference. If they complete the assignment with information only from their birth family (assuming that they have the information; many adopted children don't), they would be ignoring all the contributions of their adoptive families.

Talk with your child's teacher about the conflicts that arise and see whether she would be open to modifying the assignment. Adoptive parents and educators have developed many creative ways to tackle this project. Here are just some examples:

✔ Very young children can do the assignment by drawing and naming the people they live with inside a line drawing of a house. Older children can connect their house to other houses filled with people they identify with.

✔ Another option for the older child uses the tree metaphor. The child is identified as the trunk of the tree, with the branches available for the adoptive family names. The child uses the root system of the tree to add known information about the birth family. See Figure 17-1 for an illustration of such a tree.

✔ Some teachers offer all their students the option of doing the tree assignment for a fictional family or even a historically significant person (Abraham Lincoln, for example).

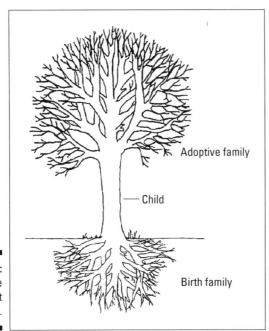

Figure 17-1:
Family tree with the root system.

The abortion debate

Many high school teachers choose the abortion issue as a topic for debates or discussion. What those teachers may not realize is how this debate can be sensitive for children who were adopted. When classmates argue things like "If she doesn't want the baby, she shouldn't have to have it" or use terms like "unwanted pregnancy," adopted children may have a strong reaction. And who can blame them? A loaded discussion like this can turn very personal very quickly.

I (Katrina) received a call of apology from my son's high school English teacher. This teacher explained that the student's debate about abortion was heated and had gotten, in her words, "a little out of hand." She realized that my son had a strong emotional reaction to this debate and that he had taken the comments personally. Unfortunately, two years later, I had the same call from the same teacher. This time it seems my daughter had a similar reaction. Imagine that!

Other stuff

Other assignments that can be difficult for your child are lessons in genetics. You know the one: The child is asked to trace back how he got his blue eyes, black hair, and so on.

Geography or history lessons that cover the country of your child's birth can also be tricky. It is important that the teacher speak respectfully of the people, government, or culture of your child's birth country. Of course, the teacher should be doing that with any lesson she teaches.

The traditional "bring in your baby picture day" may be difficult for children who have no such pictures.

You can head some problems off at the pass by talking with your child's teacher so that he or she can make such assignments meaningful to your child, but that approach works best in elementary school when your kid still thinks you showing up at school is a cool thing. By junior high and high school, most will just prefer that you let them handle these issues on their own.

Dating

The kids for whom dating may be an issue are those who were adopted trans-racially. Although these kids are pretty well received as playmates for children of different races when they're small, as soon as they're old enough to date (or think about dating), things have a tendency to change. This change first becomes apparent during the junior high and high school years, when things like dances, basketball and football games, and other school events give kids an opportunity to pair up.

When my (Katrina's) son asked a girl from school to the senior prom, she accepted his invitation. The next day she came back to school and was embarrassed to tell him that she couldn't go with him after all. Her father (a local minister) said that if she went to the prom with him, it would "make everyone uncomfortable."

Dating may continue to be a big issue for kids until they reach college age. By that time, the people interested in dating them are less likely to be interested in what their parents think.

Helping Your Child Deal with Negative Perceptions of Adoption

Your child will frequently encounter negative perceptions of adoption. They are everywhere — on television, in movies, in the newspaper, in their classroom, and in their community. The best way of combating this negativity is to help your child develop a positive outlook and a strong sense of self-worth.

Bastard Nation

Not everyone has warm and fuzzy feelings about adoption. Along with all the positive literature regarding adoption, a lot of negative adoption information is available as well. Some individuals or groups feel that adoption is a horrific act and that adopted children are the victims. Some people believe that adopted adults can never resolve the loss of their birthmother and will not be able to respond to others in an emotionally healthy way. Some people believe that housing children in orphanages would be preferable to placing them in adoptive homes. Some people think that adoptive families are an artificial attempt to reproduce a "real" family and can never be successful. But for every angry, resentful, unhappy adult adoptee, there are many successful and happy ones.

One radical group that stands out is the Bastard Nation. This group of adoptee activists advocates for fully open adoption records to every adult adoptee. They believe that each adult adoptee should have the right to receive all the personal information included in his or her birthmother's file, even if she doesn't want the information disclosed. The members of this group state that they are proud to wear the "bastard" title and refuse to feel shame at being born out of wedlock or in having been adopted. This group is politically active and promotes legislation to achieve "equal rights" for adoptees. The Bastard Nation wants all states to open all adoption records to adult adoptees "on demand, without condition and without qualification."

Sharing positive feelings about adoption

Adoption is a very personal experience. Each person who is touched by it has his or her own feelings about it. I (Tracy) know how I feel about adoption. I hope that my children, when they're adults, will feel the same way about adoption that I do. But I realize that they may not. And that's okay. No one can tell you that adoption is or isn't a particular thing. For some people — adoptive parents and adopted children alike — it's a great joy. Some people see adoption as a wound they have to recover from. For others, adoption is a combination of the two.

What you can do as an adoptive parent is to show your children *your* view of adoption. Help them see its wonder, its specialness, *and* its ordinariness and learn to accept the parts about it that can be painful. Here are some ideas:

- **Celebrate your child's adoption day.** The celebration can be as simple or elaborate as you want it to be, but the purpose is simple: to commemorate a very important day for your family.

- **When the topic of adoption comes up, share your feelings about it with your child.** You don't have to write odes to make your point. Just speak from the heart.

- **Discuss negative portrayals that your child encounters.** When you see a depiction of adoption that you think is hurtful or offensive, discuss the portrayal with your child. Help your child recognize that not all people understand adoption and that sometimes, because they don't understand it, they say silly or ignorant things.

If your child has concerns about adoption — like whether it's forever or why she was placed for adoption — help ease her mind:

- Stress to your child that her adoption is permanent.

- Acknowledge that the birthmother made the adoption plan out of love, but be careful. Some experts believe that, if you stress how much the birthmother loved the child and use that love as an explanation for the adoption, the child may fear *you* will love her that much as well.

- Make sure that your child understands that there is nothing wrong with her that caused her to be adopted.

- Don't let your child believe that adoption was a less desirable way for you to become a family.

- Reassure your child that you understand she may have some sad feelings about her adoption and that she can always talk to you about those feelings.

Adoption day

I was adopted, and my parents always remember my adoption day. This was important to me as a child because it helped me feel extra special about my being part of my family. My husband and I have three children, all of whom were adopted. Our kids are still young (age 3 and infant twins), but we talk about adoption day when it comes each year, and as the children grow, we plan to have bigger celebrations. Our oldest child was able to come to the adoption day of his brothers. I think he has fond memories of court (because he got presents), and he has a point of reference for discussions about what his adoption day was like.

Christine Rembert

Making the adoption story just one part of his history

Adoption is an important part of your child's history, but it's not the most important part. It's not the reason he is who he is. It's not the thing that makes him good (or bad) at baseball or the thing that makes him quiet or outgoing. It won't (or shouldn't) be the deciding factor in how he grows to manhood or what kind of person he becomes. It's just a fact of his life, like his green or blue or black eyes. It has its place in his make-up; it will probably be important or impact him at various times in his life, but it isn't the most significant part of him. So don't let it be.

Not everything that happens happens because of your child's adoption. So celebrate it when it's time to celebrate it. Discuss it when your child wants to discuss it. Recognize when it *is* a factor and be open to your child's feelings. And then let it go. Let your kid be who he is, without driving yourself crazy thinking that everything he is can, in some way, be traced back to the adoption.

Discussing the issue when your child needs to

Adoptive parents have to walk a fine line between making sure their child knows and understands the facts of her adoption and yet allowing her to be a "normal" kid.

Although you want to take every opportunity offered to you, when you're going to have heart-to-hearts, timing is everything. Sometimes kids just want to be kids. They have important things to do, like participate in a soccer game, go to a friend's house, play in the dirt, or whatever. They won't always appreciate being sat down for a serious talk about important matters.

So listen to your child and follow her lead. When she wants to talk about it, talk about it. When she wants some space, give it to her.

Some kids will come to you and ask you outright whatever they want to know. Other kids may never come to you directly and ask you to tell them all the facts of their adoption. But they'll probably give you clues that let you know they're thinking about it. A conversational tidbit like "Bobby asked me why my real mom didn't keep me" may be the perfect opportunity to explore that subject.

Don't make the mistake of thinking that the bedtime story you told your child at 3 years old will be all the information your 8-year-old needs. If your child never gives any signals, you may need to initiate conversations to check out how she's doing. Here are some examples of things you can say to give your child the opportunity to discuss her feelings, even if she's not inclined to bring the topic up herself:

- ✔ "You have such pretty hair. I wonder if your birthmother has hair like yours. Do you ever wonder about things like that?"

- ✔ "I love you so much! I am glad we were able to adopt you. Do you remember your adoption story?"

- ✔ "I bet your birthmother thinks about you a lot. Do you think about her?"

- ✔ "Look at these pictures I just found! This is the day we saw you for the first time. I remember. . . ."

With each of these intros, draw your child out. Find out what he remembers about his story. Sometimes he may remember things that never happened or will fill in the blanks with fantasy. If that's the case, gently remind him of what really happened. Ask whether he has questions. As your child gets older, add more details. Describe the birthparents and the situation that led them to make the adoption decision. Ask your child whether he feels sad. Reassure him of your love and acceptance of his feelings.

Chapter 18

What Can Go Wrong and What You Can Do

In This Chapter

▶ Figuring out what to do if the adoption is challenged

▶ Recognizing the risk factors that can lead to disrupted adoptions

▶ Dealing with unforeseen health and behavioral issues

*L*isten to the adoption news stories that get the most play, and what are you likely to hear? The horror stories of the adoption world, that's what. The stories that scare the bejesus out of anyone who's thinking about adopting, in the process of adopting, or parenting the child he or she adopted. If news stories are your only exposure to adoption and adoption issues, you're probably under the impression that few human endeavors are so fraught with danger and heartache as adopting a child in the United States.

The truth is, the vast majority of adoptions are successful, and most adoption stories have happy endings. It is also true, however, that things sometimes can, and do, go wrong. A birthmother may change her mind, a birthfather may reappear and claim his rights, your child may have major health problems you didn't know about, and so on. This chapter helps you keep the risks in perspective and explains what you can do when the worst happens.

I Want My Baby Back: Challenges to Placement

Most adoptive parents worry that one of the birthparents will at some point change his or her mind and demand his or her child back. Part of the worry stems from the process itself. Your adoption isn't final until a judge says it's final (explained in Chapter 12), which leaves you to worry during the placement period that something out of your control will happen to disrupt your family. This worry is often made more pronounced by the news coverage of some of the high-profile cases, such as the stories of Baby Richard and Baby Jessica, in which adopted children have been returned to their birthparents after lengthy court battles.

Although challenges to placement can happen, it happens very infrequently. Just in terms of numbers (how many adoptions occur annually versus how many of them get challenged), your adoption is very unlikely to be one that falls into this category. The National Council of Adoption estimates that less than 1 percent of adoptions are contested by a birthparent who seeks the return of the child.

If the birthmother changes her mind

Yes, all birthmothers *can* change their minds, but most don't. If a birthmother changes her mind, she'll usually do so in the days and weeks immediately following the placement of her child. This is the time when her grief is at its most intense and when her emotions are raw from all that she has been through. Here are some things that you can do proactively to protect yourself from such a challenge:

- ✔ **See that your child's birthmother has received adequate counseling.** If she fully understands her options and the legal implications of her actions, she's more likely to be at peace with the decision she makes. Ongoing counseling can also help her through the emotional period following the child's birth.

- ✔ **Work with a reliable agency that has a good reputation for ethical practices.** When selecting an attorney, choose an attorney with experience in adoption law. When the t's are crossed and the i's are dotted, you shouldn't have anything to worry about. Chapter 7 explains how to find good agencies and attorneys.

Even these precautions, however, aren't a guarantee that nothing will go wrong. How successful a challenge to placement is depends a lot on the timing of the challenge and the specific situation regarding the adoption.

Before she signs consent forms

It's not uncommon for a birthmother to change her mind about her adoption plan after her child is born. Many times, a birthmother will try to logically and methodically plan for her child's future during her pregnancy, but then, when the child is born, she's overwhelmed by her emotional response to the child. One look at the baby and she may say, "What was I thinking?" Be prepared for this possibility. Try to be supportive of whatever the birthmother decides.

Babies Richard and Jessica

In the early 1990s, two adoption custody cases featured quite prominently in the news. One involved a child called Baby Richard. The other involved Baby Jessica.

In the Baby Richard case, Baby Richard's birthmother, Daniella Janikova, told his birthfather, Otokar Kirchner (whom she believe had abandoned her for another woman), that the child she was carrying had died. She refused to identify the birthfather, and four days after Richard's birth, she relinquished her parental rights. Jay and Kimberly Warburton adopted Richard. Later, Daniella Janikova and Otokar Kirchner reconciled, and Otokar learned of his son. He challenged the adoption (which by this time had been finalized in an Illinois court). Although Illinois law required that a father demonstrate an interest in his child within 30 days of the child's birth, Otokar argued that he didn't know he had a son and therefore couldn't have known that he had to claim him. Two lower courts ruled against Otokar's claim, but the Illinois Supreme Court overturned the adoption, claiming that Otokar had been deceived and that the adoptive family hadn't looked hard enough for the birthfather before proceeding with the adoption.

In the Baby Jessica case, the birthmother (Cara Schmidt), a resident of Iowa, lied about the identify of her child's birthfather (Dan Schmidt). She named someone else. The adoptive parents, Jan and Robert DeBoer (residents of Michigan), took custody of Baby Jessica, believing that both birthparents had consented to the adoption. Before the adoption was finalized, Dan and Cara Schmidt reconciled and sought to regain custody of Jessica. The Iowa court ruled that the DeBoers had to return Jessica to the Schmidts. A Michigan court entered a custody ruling in favor of the DeBoers. Eventually, the Michigan Court of Appeals ruled that the lower Michigan courts had no jurisdiction in the case, essentially overturning the custody award to the DeBoers. Jessica had to be returned to the biological parents. The legal wrangling took years. When it began, Jessica was an infant. By the time the battle ended, she was a preschooler. TV cameras caught the transfer of a screaming and crying Jessica as she was taken from one set of parents to be placed with the other.

If the birthmother changes her mind before she signs her consents, you can do absolutely nothing about it. She is under no obligation to place her child with anyone. Kidnapping is never a good option.

After she signs consent forms

Occasionally, birthmothers change their mind after they sign the consent forms. Whether her change of heart actually affects your adoption and what happens next depend on the adoption laws in your state.

In states without revocation periods

If the birthmother lives in a state that has no revocation period (that is, the consents are legally binding as soon as she signs them), there is very little she can do. Her rights to her child end with her written signature on the legal papers. In order to "undo" the adoption in these situations, the birthmother usually has to prove either of the following:

- ✔ That she signed the consents because she was deceived or coerced
- ✔ That she signed the consents when she was mentally impaired and unable to understand the implications of her actions

If a birthmother decides to challenge the placement, she must hire an attorney, who files a petition on her behalf.

The point at which you learn of the challenge depends on the policies of your agency. Some agencies inform families as soon as the problem comes up. Some withhold initial information of a potential problem until they know how big a problem it really is. If the case actually goes to court and a hearing is scheduled, you'll definitely be informed because you're going to be a party in the case.

If the birthmother can prove that she was coerced, lied to, or mentally impaired, the judge then makes a decision about who should have custody of the child. Some judges may take into consideration the best interests of the child, but if the family participated in the fraud or coercion, it's a pretty safe bet that the child would be removed from their home.

What can adoptive parents do? Not much until after a determination has been made. Then they should get a good lawyer and appeal the court's ruling. Keep in mind, however, that if the birthmother was the victim of a crime (for example, she was coerced or her child was stolen) and the adoptive parents received her child as a result of that crime (even if they had no part in the deception), then they're probably going to lose the child. This is one reason why working with ethical, reputable people is absolutely necessary. Refer to Chapter 7 for details on finding someone you can trust.

In states with revocation periods

If the birthmother lives in a state that has a revocation period, she can reverse her decision and ask for her child to be returned at any time during that period. In these cases, the child will be returned to her, with no questions asked. But once the revocation period ends (usually between one and three months after the child's birth), the consents become legally binding, and she has no recourse other than that discussed in the preceding section.

If the birthfather challenges the adoption

When an adoption is contested, the birthfather is usually the one doing the contesting. The birthmother is required to consent to the adoption before the child is placed with the family. The birthfather doesn't always sign those consent forms, and this leaves him in a better position to put up a challenge.

The main thing to be concerned about regarding challenges by a birthfather is whether your agency or attorney gave due diligence in trying to find him, *prior* to the adoption moving forward. What constitutes "due diligence" depends on the adoption laws with each state.

In states that have adoption registries (which I explain in detail in Chapter 14), the burden falls on the father to make his existence and his connection to the child known. In these states, a man can register as a father of a child and retain the right to be notified of any adoption actions. If a father doesn't register his interest in his child, he can't later contest any adoption proceedings.

In states without these registries, the burden falls on you (or the adoption agency or attorney who is facilitating your adoption) to locate the birthfather and inform him of the adoption plan. In most cases, these procedures include things like notifying known birthfathers of adoption actions, conducting searches for absent birthfathers, and publishing announcements for unknown birthfathers. (For details on these procedures, head to Chapter 14.) In most cases, these procedures safeguard the adoption.

AWOL birthfathers who reappear after the fact

If an absent birthfather reappears in any state that has a registry and tries to challenge the adoption, he'll discover that he has lost his right to contest an adoption if he failed to register. If the state isn't one that has a registry, he'll probably discover that the adoptive family (usually through the family's agency or attorney) had published a legal notice to him informing him of the adoption and giving him a deadline to respond. If the deadline has passed, there isn't much he can do. Once the adoption is finalized in court, he'll have a very hard time challenging it.

The birthfather has the best chance of challenging the adoption before the court finalization (head to Chapter 12 for information on that). After the finalization occurs, the birthfather likely has to prove one of the following:

- ✔ That he was lied to or coerced into signing consent forms (assuming that he knew of the placement and agreed to it)
- ✔ That no attempt was made to locate him (in a state without a registry)

As a rule, birthfather rumblings before finalization are the ones to be most concerned about. Before finalization, the judge can be sympathetic and hear the birthfather's case, even if the agency or attorney did everything right *and* the birthfather failed to do what he needed to do to protect his rights. After finalization, the burden falls on the birthfather.

After some very well-publicized cases (see the sidebar "Babies Richard and Jessica" in this chapter for details) in which courts have returned children to their birthfathers, most states scurried to enact new legislation to safeguard adoptive families. Talk to your attorney or the social worker at your agency to find out what safeguards are in place in your state.

Birthfathers who oppose the adoption from the beginning

Whether a challenge can even be made depends on the legal category of the birthfather. Before a man can challenge an adoption of his child, he must be one of the following:

✔ The *legal* father, that is, the man married to the birthmother at the time the child was conceived

✔ The *presumed* father, the designation given to men in states that have tried to simplify the various birthfather categories to two: alleged and presumed

In order for the challenge to move forward, a presumed or legal father has to prove that he is the biological father. (We know that it's confusing. Head to Chapter 14 for the mind-numbing details.)

The guys who fall into these categories have the same rights to their child that the birthmother does. The adoption can't take place unless their parental rights are terminated, either by signing adoption papers or by court action (which usually stems from the man having abandoned the child).

If an *alleged* father (defined as a man who hasn't established a legal claim to the child) wants to prevent an adoption, he first has to take some legal action to prove his relationship to the child. But just coming forward and proving a relationship is usually not enough to stop a planned adoption. Most courts want to determine whether it's in the child's best interest for the birthfather to retain his rights and halt the adoption. The father is usually required to complete an assessment process similar to the home study for adoptive parents (see Chapter 9 for information on home studies). This report for the court discloses his income, child-care arrangements, criminal history, and so on. The judge takes this information into consideration before ruling on the case.

What you can do

If your adoption is being challenged by a birthparent, you're going to have tough times and tough decisions ahead of you.

Few things are more stressful than having your adoption contested. Dealing with this stress has all the implications for your family, marriage, health, finances, and mental stability that other major stresses (such as a death or divorce) do. But something to consider is the fact that this stressful situation can last for years before it is resolved.

Gather your resources

First and foremost, find an excellent adoption attorney. Chapter 7 explains how to hunt for a reputable attorney. To find one who has experience handling challenges, focus your questions in that area: Ask for details about the cases they've handled, the outcomes, and so forth.

Then amass as many personal resources as you can:

- ✔ You may want to hook up with other families who've been through what you're going through now.
- ✔ Work with a therapist to guide you in how to handle things with the child.
- ✔ Seeking support and counsel from family, friends, church members, and others often makes the process more bearable.

Decide: Fight or relinquish?

If your child's birthparent challenges the adoption, you have to make a very hard decision: fight for your child or relinquish. In making this decision, the most important thing you must consider is your child's well-being. The decision may seem like a no-brainer ("Of course, our child is better off with us!"), but it's really not. All of the following can make an impact on your decision:

- ✔ **Your chances of winning the case:** Your attorney can advise you of your chances. The thing to remember is that, although you may want to fight no matter what, if your chances of winning are slim, you may just be postponing the inevitable.
- ✔ **The financial commitment:** A contested adoption can lead to lengthy court procedures that may continue for years before a final decision is made. Adoption agencies are not financially able to pay the legal expenses in these situations. The birthparent contesting the adoption is required to retain an attorney to represent his side, and the adoptive parents need to retain an attorney to represent their interests. For this reason, some families make the decision to voluntarily relinquish the child once they discover that the adoption has been contested.
- ✔ **The length of time the court proceedings go on:** These court battles can go on for years. Your child may be an infant when the fight begins, but could very well be a 4- or 5-year-old when the action is finally resolved.

✔ **The intent and persistence of the birthparent doing the contesting:** A birthparent who is determined to reclaim her child is a much bigger danger than one who lobs the challenge more out of convention than commitment. For example, one birthfather we know, when the case manager approached him with the consent forms, claimed that he wasn't going to sign because his girlfriend (not the child's birthmother) wanted the baby. When the caseworker explained that he would need to retain a lawyer to prove his relationship with the child before he could have the child, he decided that the challenge was too much work and signed the consent forms.

✔ **The appropriateness of the lifestyle and parenting abilities of the contesting parent:** This information — whether your child's birthparent is capable and loving or not — can definitely play a role in your decision.

Barring deceit or coercion, a birthparent usually has to undergo a home study before the court decides to remove a child from his adoptive home and return him to his birthparent. In many cases, if the court determines that the birthparent is unfit, the adoption can proceed.

✔ **The devastation the loss of the child would cause the family:** No one can answer this but you. But here's something to keep in mind: Your pain isn't the most important thing. Yes, your heart will be broken into a thousand pieces, but if you can spare your child the same heartbreak, you should.

What happens after

Obviously, if you win the custody battle, you can heave a huge sigh of relief and get on with your life.

But if custody is returned to the birthparent, what happens next depends on the judge. Usually the court hears testimony from a child therapist or psychologist, who advises the court on the best transitional plan for the child. Remember, however, that although this witness may recommend some visits for a while before an abrupt change, the judge has discretion to do as he pleases.

In most cases, following any transitional period, the adoptive parents don't see the child again. Visits are up to the birthparent, and by the time the trial is over, the birthparent and the adoptive parents usually aren't feeling too friendly toward each other. Jessica and Richard (see the sidebar "Babies Richard and Jessica" in this chapter) didn't get any visits from the adoptive parents, nor did the Internet twins (see Chapter 2).

If a therapist insists that the children have ongoing visits with the adoptive parents, a judge may consider ruling that an agreement take place. Many experts believe, however, that the child won't bond with the new parent if he remains in contact with the old one, so these visits aren't likely.

Explaining the loss to your other children

You've already lived your nightmare. If you have other children, you now have to explain it to them. This explanation is especially difficult if your other children are adopted, too, because, in addition to grieving the loss of a sibling, they may fear that they'll be taken away, too.

If you've probably told your children that adoption is for always, you now get to add "except when it isn't."

Just be honest with your other kids but reassure them that you don't think it would ever happen to them. (Hopefully, you have enough info on the other birthparents to know that such a challenge won't happen.)

Things Don't Work Out: Disrupted Adoptions

Technically, a disrupted adoption is different from the dissolution of an adoption: The term *dissolution* is used for situations in which an adoption that has been finalized in court doesn't continue. A *disruption* of an adoption is when the child has been placed in a home for the purpose of adoption (the birthmother may have signed legal consents), but the family hasn't yet attended the finalization hearing. Many agencies and families, however, use the term *disrupted* to refer to both scenarios.

In either case, the result is heartbreaking. The adoption, which probably began with a lot of hope and commitment, falls through.

How likely is this scenario to happen to you? Not very. Some studies show that fewer than 2 percent of overall adoptions disrupt. However, you need to be aware that some adoption situations carry more risk than others. When you look only at adoptions of older children or children who came from an institution or foster care, the number of disruptions increases to 10 or 20 percent. No, they're not good numbers, but even adoptions that carry the most risk are more likely to be successful than not.

Recognizing the situations most at risk

Most experts agree that specific factors can increase the risk of an adoption disruption. Included are placements that involve the situations explained in the following sections.

Children who have experienced abuse or neglect

These children are more prone to having emotional or behavioral problems than children who don't experience abuse or neglect.

Children who have emotional or behavioral problems

Defiance, sexual acting out, cruelty, and destructive impulses are some specific behaviors that can increase stress levels in the home.

Older children

The older a child is at the time of her placement, the more connected she is to the birth family and possibly more resistant to bonding with a new family.

Children with a history of multiple placements

This category includes any child who has lived in more than one family situation. A child with many past placements may not have had an opportunity to bond with caregivers. If the child hasn't had an opportunity to form attachments to her caregivers, she may struggle with attachment issues or have an actual attachment disorder (see the section "Undisclosed or unforeseen conditions," later in this chapter, for details).

Children who have already experienced an adoption disruption

Having experienced the pain of one disruption, a child is even more wary of bonding and less trusting of the new family's commitment. They're also at increased risk for acting out behaviors as a way to test their new adoptive parents ("I will be as bad as I possibly can be so that, if you aren't going to keep me, I'll find out before I care.").

Children placed with an adoptive family from foster care or an institution

A child who has experienced a lack of permanence, commitment, or stable home situation may be uncomfortable in a permanent, committed, and stable home. A diagnosis of reactive attachment disorder (RAD), explained in the later section "Undisclosed or unforeseen conditions," often seems to be a factor in disrupted adoptions.

Inexperienced or unprepared adoptive parents

All children who've been adopted have special needs that result directly from their adoption. Examples include the need to have any feelings of loss or rejection validated, to be able to integrate their adoption history into their sense of self in a healthy way, and, if the adoption was transracial or transcultural, to comfortably exist in both cultures. (See Chapters 16 and 17 for more on these issues.) Some children — older kids and kids with medical or emotional challenges, for example — may require even more help in dealing with the myriad issues they may face. Adoptive parents who don't recognize these needs or who don't prepare for them are at a disadvantage in helping their children.

Adoptive parents with rigid parenting styles

Parents adopting children at risk must be prepared to have their lives turned upside down for a while. They must be flexible and able to go with the flow. Some misbehaviors must be overlooked as you choose your battles. If you have strict rules and require good behavior from your children, you probably should adopt an infant.

Adoptive parents with unrealistic expectations

This category refers to unrealistic expectations about your child, about yourself, about your family and friends' reactions, and so on. Sure, all parents want things to go well. They want the kids to be happy and well-behaved. They want the house to be clean and presentable. They want to be able to deal calmly and appropriately with every parenting issue that arises. In the utopia that adoptive parents may dream up, their children never question their belonging, never act out (and if they do, simple love and understanding alone are enough to solve the problem), never get hurt by unkind words or perceptions, and never long to know or form a relationship with their birthparents. If you have these kinds of unreasonable expectations, you're setting yourself and your kids up for disappointment.

Protecting yourself and your child

Even if your adoption falls into a high-risk category, you can take some actions to help ensure that your family can not only survive the tough periods but also thrive.

Being honest with what you can and can't handle — before you commit to a child

You need to honestly evaluate what you're prepared and willing to deal with. In nearly all adoptions, your agency will inform you of any known risks or conditions so that you can make the very personal decision about whether a particular placement is the best one for you and your family. If you aren't prepared or don't feel that you can best parent a child who is profoundly deaf, for example, don't let guilt or a feeling of obligation make you say yes when you really want to say no. (Chapter 8 explains some issues you may want to think about when you decide what you can and can't handle.)

Once you say yes to a child, you're committed to that child for the long haul. Your needs are no longer the most important ones to consider. Your child's needs become paramount.

When you adopt a child from the at-risk population, you and your family should possess specific characteristics. Flexibility (in place of rigidity), realistic expectations, commitment, strong support systems (family and friends), and religious affiliations are some examples of the glue that can help hold a family together.

Knowing what you're getting into

The best prevention of adoption disruption is advance preparation and education. When you have been adequately prepared and know about the resources available to help you, you're able to better handle the difficult situations. Here's some advice on amassing the info you need:

- ✓ First and foremost, get all the medical history available for your child. If your child is an infant, request medical records and lab reports from the hospital.

- ✓ If your child is older, request information about school performance or testing, previous placements, family history, incidences of abuse or neglect, and any records of counseling or interventions. If you're adopting an older child domestically, talk with foster parents about behavioral issues and request an adequate number of *pre-placement visits* (the schedule of visits that take place between adoptive parents and an older child before that child actually moves into their home).

- ✓ When you adopt internationally, ask for every piece of information available. Take medical information and reports to your doctor for her interpretation.

Be aware that some countries require an identified medical concern on the child's documents and may fabricate one so that the child can be placed. Check with your agency about specific policies or cultural attitudes that may affect the child's reports.

- ✓ If your child has specific medical or behavioral concerns, read everything you can get your hands on about it. Talk to other parents struggling with the same issues. Identify community resources available to you and your child.

Tapping into post-adoption services

Post-adoption services can be a valuable tool for protecting your adoption. Check with your agency to see whether it offers any specific services for you. If not, here are some ways to help your family cope:

- ✔ Make use of educational materials and literature pertinent to your situation.

- ✔ Locate and attend seminars that may help you understand your child's specific challenges and treatment options.

- ✔ Join support groups or develop supportive relationships with others who let you vent and be honest about your feelings.

- ✔ Seek appropriate counseling. This counseling may include both individual and family sessions.

- ✔ Seek out respite care for your child to give both of you a much-needed break.

  Respite care is anything that allows the parents some breathing time away from their child. A family can step in and offer overnight or weekend visits for the child. Summer camps, sport camps, or mommy's day out programs can be a lifesaver. Connect with other families interested in trading baby-sitting nights. Some public agencies have formal respite programs that use foster parents to provide respite for adoptive parents who need a break from a challenging child.

Don't ignore warning signs

If your family is under stress, take some action. Don't wait until the situation is out of control. Warning signs that you need some help include the following:

- ✔ You're not enjoying your child.

- ✔ You're overwhelmed by your child's issues or behaviors.

- ✔ You find yourself constantly criticizing or complaining.

- ✔ You fantasize about a life without your child or you wish you had never adopted him.

Admittedly, any parent may feel all of these ways on a particularly bad day. We're talking about a pattern of behavior here. If you experience any of these feelings frequently or for long periods of time, get help.

What happens when the adoption falls apart

Sadly, some adoptions do fall apart. Some families choose to permanently end their relationship with their child. For whatever reason, they decide that they don't want any further involvement with the child. The dissolution of an adoption is like divorcing the child, but this situation includes no visitation arrangements.

Sometimes families recognize that they're unable to love/parent/bond with their child but realize that someone else may be able to. In other cases, families are at the end of their rope because they have exhausted all of their health insurance benefits and can't provide the care their child needs. In these cases, parents may decide to relinquish their legal rights to their child in order for their child to receive needed services or treatment that the parents can't afford.

Legally, once the adoption is final, if you want to disrupt the adoption, you have to sign adoption consent papers, just as if you were a birthparent, in order for the child to be placed with someone else. That's assuming that you have someone waiting in the wings to adopt the child. Most of these parents don't. If you're in this situation, call private agencies until you find one that has experience in this area and can guide you on how to proceed.

What it means to the child

A dissolution is a huge rejection for the child — almost as huge as the birthmother consenting to the adoption (or failing to fight for them). Once a child has had a disrupted placement, she'll have more resistance to bonding, attaching, or trusting in the next home she's in. With each disruption the child experiences, the greater the chance that the next placement will disrupt as well.

Still, many children from disrupted adoptions can go on to be re-adopted and flourish in their new homes. Adoptive families who re-adopt children tend to have more realistic expectations and are better able to cope with disruptive behaviors.

Non-options

When you're desperate, you may come up with all sorts of ideas about how to relinquish a problem child. Here are some options that you shouldn't take: They can lead you into very hot water:

You can't give the child to the Office of Family and Children; that would be an abandonment of the child. These offices don't take children from harried parents; they only remove them for abuse or neglect reasons.

Some families get on the Internet and find families to take their children. I (Katrina) know one family who brought their Russian daughter to Indiana from their home in Texas and just handed her over. Legal paperwork transpired later. This was illegal because interstate compact regulations (explained in Chapter 3) were ignored. In another case, adoptive parents took their child from Indiana to another state the same way and then had to go back and get her after they talked to a lawyer and realized they had broken the law.

What it means to the family

When you disrupt an adoption, you're going to face a huge amount of guilt, shame, embarrassment, and a feeling of failure. You have to face family, friends, co-workers, and your community and explain why you don't have your child anymore. Other adoptive parents will often judge you very harshly.

Problems You Didn't Know Existed

When you adopt, you do have the opportunity to discuss and decide what health issues, emotional issues, and so on that you feel comfortable and are willing to deal with. But adopting a child isn't a guarantee. Reputable agencies and attorneys disclose any information they have about the child being placed, but they don't know everything, and no one has a crystal ball that can tell what issues you may end up facing in the future: The happy toddler you brought home may have behavioral issues you didn't know about, the child whose birthparents were honor students may have a learning disability, or the child you thought was healthy may develop childhood cancer.

If your agency or attorney deliberately withheld information from you, take the necessary steps to file a complaint. Speak with the director of the agency, the bar association, the state licensing office, the Better Business Bureau, or all of the preceding. Don't let the matter go; you could protect other families from experiencing this same trauma.

Health issues

One risk in adoption stems from the fact that medical information is often incomplete. A family history of mental illness, heart conditions, and even genetic conditions may be unknown or unreported by the birthmother. When you choose to adopt, you accept this risk as a known factor in adoption. No one likes it, but you must accept it if you plan to adopt.

Similarly, no one can predict what health issues you may encounter as your child grows. Healthy children become ill, develop lasting impairments, or develop lifelong medical conditions. Yet, just as you make a commitment to accept your birth child whatever the future holds, enter into an adoption with the same attitude.

Undisclosed or unforeseen conditions

Once you bring your child home, you may discover problems or conditions you didn't know existed. The following sections explain two conditions — reactive attachment disorder (RAD) and oppositional defiant disorder (ODD) — that are especially challenging to deal with and that have been featured fairly prominently in the news, especially in regard to international adoptions and adoptions of older children.

These conditions represent a real challenge to families, and a high number of disrupted adoptions involve children with these disorders (see the earlier section "Things Don't Work Out: Disrupted Adoptions" for information on disrupted adoptions). If your child is at high risk for these conditions, if your social worker indicates that your child has been diagnosed with these conditions, or if your child exhibits several of the behaviors associated with them, *pay attention.* Children with these problems need serious help, and you can't provide it if you ignore the problem or don't prepare yourself for what lies ahead.

Reactive attachment disorder (RAD)

Bonding is absolutely necessary for a child not only to thrive physically but to develop emotionally as well. Simply being cared for — fed, held, and talked to — enables an infant to develop trust ("when I cry, my mother comes; someone out there will take care of me and meet my needs"), and feel affection or reciprocal feelings ("when I smile, my mother smiles; when I hold out my hand, my mother takes it; what I do connects me to another human being"). These are the foundations of later human relationships and feelings.

Reactive attachment disorder (RAD) is a mental disorder that occurs when an infant isn't able to bond with his primary caregiver and who, therefore, has not developed these basic human characteristics. Children at high risk for this disorder include the following:

- Children who have suffered severe neglect
- Children who have been moved from one environment to another without having the opportunity to bond
- Children who have been raised in institutional settings that lack the resources to adequately care for their emotional as well as physical well-being

If your child experienced these situations (moving frequently from one home to another in domestic adoptions or growing up in an orphanage in international situations), you need to be aware that your child is at risk for this condition.

Children with RAD have a hard time forming lasting, meaningful relationships. They are often unable to feel real affection or love for others and lack empathy for others. Some people describe children with RAD as not having a conscience. Following are some of the symptoms displayed in children with RAD:

- ✔ They're superficially charming and may be overly affectionate with strangers.

- ✔ They're cruel to animals or people and may be fascinated with blood, death, and gore.

- ✔ They're bossy and manipulative, often playing people off of each other. They often have difficulty making and keeping friends.

- ✔ They may have language and speech problems, as well as other developmental delays.

Children don't outgrow RAD, but with proper treatment (usually involving both counseling and behavior therapy), they can learn to form normal human attachments and live a normal life. Without proper treatment — or with treatment that comes too late (many experts say that too late is after the child is 12) — the child's antisocial behaviors can become more pronounced.

Oppositional defiant disorder (ODD)

Oppositional defiant disorder (ODD) is a mental disorder that's associated with bad parenting or abuse situations and is characterized by long-lasting hostile or defiant behavior that includes several of the following:

- ✔ Frequently loses temper

- ✔ Often argues with adults

- ✔ Actively defies rules and requests

- ✔ Annoys people on purpose and is easily annoyed by them

- ✔ Is often resentful and angry and blames others for their own misbehaviors

- ✔ Is spiteful and vindictive

Although most people associate these behaviors with sullen teens, we're not talking about normal, annoying, oppositional teenage behavior. We're talking about *extreme* behaviors. And this disorder isn't limited to teens; even small children can exhibit them. In fact, most parents begin to notice ODD behaviors when their children are between 1 and 3 years of age.

Some kids outgrow ODD, and some kids' symptoms lessen as they get older, but some kids battle it their whole lives. Treatment options vary, depending on whether another condition (depression, ADHD, and so on) is also present. With ODD alone, treatment usually involves behavior modification. With other conditions present, treating the other condition usually takes precedent.

Your responsibility: Deal with it

Certainly dealing with any condition or ailment that threatens your child or that can have lifelong ramifications is horrible, but your child isn't a defective toaster that you can take back or exchange. If you have agreed to bring the child into your home for the purpose of adoption, and/or you have finalized your adoption, you need to seek out services to try to make this adoption work.

If the safety of the other family members is a concern, you may decide that the child can't be allowed to stay in the family home. Yet even if your child needs to be institutionalized, she still needs someone to refer to as her family. She needs visitors, cards, letters, and phone calls. These things could make a difference in the child's progress.

The thing to remember is that, once you have adopted your child, you're responsible for her. In fact, because of your act of adopting her, you are all she has. Stand by your child, seek out appropriate services for her, and make any necessary arrangements for her.

Unforeseen problems don't occur only in adoptive families. Families who give birth to their children also deal with unexpected or unforeseen conditions and illnesses. As parents, you should demonstrate the same commitment to your adopted children as you would to your birth children.

Chapter 19

In Search of . . . Birthparents

M any kids who've been adopted eventually begin a search for their birthparents. Sometimes they simply want medical information. Other times, they want answers to questions only these people can answer. A few want to build a relationship with the people who gave them life. Whatever the reason leading to the search, you may wonder what you can do to help your child, worry about how the search will end, and possibly have conflicting feelings about your child's need to find his birthparent.

This chapter explains birthparent searches: what they are, why they may be important to your child, and how to go about finding a birthparent. It also explains what you can do to help your child through the search and beyond.

Why Kids Seek Birthparents

Most adoptees live their lives without having answers or access to some very important information. Basic, fundamental knowledge that children born to a family take for granted remains secret or unknown for many adopted children. Many of these kids eventually search for their birthparents.

This search can drive seemingly well-adjusted parents into a state of panic. Did you not love your child enough? Were you not good enough parents? Does the search mean that your child doesn't love you? The thing you have to remember is that your kid isn't trying to hurt, reject, or abandon you. In fact, the search isn't even about you or your parenting or whether you were stingy with the freeze pops. It's about your child and her need to know about herself.

Did they love me?

Not long ago, I was asked for about the hundredth time, "Why?" Why did I want to find my birthparents? The way people view a search sometimes amazes me. More than once, people have voiced their disgust that I would want to find the people who would "just get rid of me." Over the years, this made an impact on me, and I began to wonder what my birthparents' reasoning could be. I was frightened that I had simply been rejected, and so I put off my search until I was 27 and felt ready to handle the outcome.

Somewhere along the way, I figured out that, in this day and age, someone had to love me just to have me. There had to be love in the decision to carry me for nine months and then give another family your most precious gift. There had to be love involved when placing the name Serena Rochelle on my birth certificate, knowing the family receiving this gift would change it. I was right!

Last year, I met both biological families, maternal and paternal. I have such closure, knowing that the decision that had been made was so right. I now thank my parents constantly for adopting me. Just knowing why — and knowing that there is someone out there who looks like me — is so fulfilling. Gone are the days of walking down the street wondering if I am passing my mother. I also received a gift more precious than I could imagine: two half brothers and a stepsister, all of whom I cherish.

The outcome of my search was wonderful, an answer to my question: "Did they love me?" Yes, they did, and in making that one, selfless decision to give my parents the gift of their child, they gave me the gift of a better, more stable childhood.

Amy Young-Gray

Kids who search want answers. They want to know who they look like and who they inherited certain traits from. They want to have up-to-date health information. They want to see the person who gave birth to them and then allowed them to be raised by someone else. They want to know why all of that took place. Some also have a strong desire to connect emotionally with their birthparents.

I (Katrina) have conducted many searches and facilitated many meetings between adoptees and birthparents. I have never had an adoptee ask me to do a search because he despised his adoptive parents. In contrast, the majority of adoptees asking me for a search report that they have a close and loving relationship with their parents. Many fear, however, that they might hurt their parents by initiating a search.

The Search Is On

Some children start asking questions from the get-go. As soon as they hear the birthmother part of the adoption story, they make pretty clear that they want to find this person and will ask all sorts of questions about her. Other kids don't verbalize their questions, but that doesn't mean they don't wonder and won't someday begin a search.

Whether your child is chomping at the bit to find his birthparents or just mildly curious about them, keep in mind that specific events in your child's life may trigger his need to search. Things like a marriage, a desire to have children, the birth of a child, a specific health problem, or the death of a loved one can cause your child to consider searching, even if he had never seriously considered it before. The following sections explain how someone who wants to search can go about it.

Following is some general information to know about searches:

- ✔ Every state has its own adoption law governing the release of identifying information to adoptees and birthparents. These laws aren't intended to make anyone's life difficult, but they are intended to protect people's privacy. As such, you need to follow specific procedures in order to access adoption records or information.

- ✔ Either party — the birthparent or the child — can conduct a search.

- ✔ Most laws stipulate that only adults (not minors) can conduct a search. So in every state you need to be either 18 or 21 to conduct a search.

- ✔ Adoptive parents can't conduct a search on their child's behalf. If you need to find your child's birthmother for life-and-death medical reasons, you can petition the court to have a Confidential Intermediary (C.I.) appointed to find the birthmother for you.

Who ya gonna call?

The person you call to initiate a search depends on your adoption arrangement. If you're part of an open or semi-open arrangement (explained in Chapter 2), you can simply contact the birthmother, either directly or through the agency that facilitated the adoption. If your arrangement was closed, the steps are a bit more complicated.

The majority of open or semi-open adoptions took place less than 21 years ago, and most registries require the adoptee to be 21 before utilizing it. So currently, when people talk doing a search, they're usually talking specifically about closed adoptions.

For closed adoptions

When you want to conduct a search, the best place to go is the agency that handled the adoption. Don't expect the caseworker or manager to simply hand over the information, though. Even if the person on the other end of the line has access to the information you're looking for, she can't, by law, give it to you. What she can give you is information on how to do a search. Many agencies have people on staff who know the law and what's required to do a search. They may also have someone to actually do the searches. If they don't, they can usually direct you elsewhere.

How you find whom you're looking for depends on the search procedures available in your state. Some states have search registries, explained in the section "Registries and how they work," later in this chapter. Some states simply require that you complete an application process before they give you the information you're seeking. See the later section "A note on open records states" for details on this option. Other states may provide neither of these avenues, and then you can either use a privately run search registry or launch an out-and-out, bona fide search, explained in the later section "When registries don't work: An out-and-out search."

Laws differ from state to state, so your first step in a search really is to contact one of the following: the agency that did your adoption or any other licensed agency, your local Office of Family and Children, or an attorney. Any of these should be able to either inform you of the laws you need to follow (or direct you to someone who can) or tell you what steps you need to take to launch your search. Your city may have a triad support group available. These groups often have experience in searching and can offer support and information helpful to the search process.

For open and semi-open adoptions

In an open or semi-open adoption arrangement, adoptees don't need to do an "official" search, because the two parties (the child and the birthparent) already have a way to contact each other. If your adoption is open, you can simply contact the birthmother directly. In fact, if you have a completely open adoption, with visits and regular communication between your child and his birthmother, you don't really need to conduct a "search" at all. Your child probably already has a lot of the information that children in closed adoptions (and sometimes semi-open adoptions) don't have.

In a semi-open adoption, you contact the birthmother through whatever avenue you've used to pass along and receive updates — usually through the agency. Some people, for example, exchange e-mail addresses as a start and then disclose other identifying info later. Some agree through letters to register with the state registry (see the section "Registries and how they work" for information on those). Some arrange through their calls or letters to meet at an agreed upon location.

Registries and how they work

All kinds of registries have been established to handle inquiries about birthparent searches. There are registries that are run by the state, registries through specific agencies or individuals, registries online, and registries specifically for international adoptions or other unique groups.

In the states that have search registries (listed in the sidebar "States with registries"), search registries are handled by one of the following: State Health Department, family courts, the Department of Human Resources, Child Protective Services, Division of Family Services, or the Department of Social Services.

Basically, all registries work like this: They match birthparents and adoptees through information that each provides. This info can include things like birth date, gender, place of birth, and so on. Although many state-run and online registries are free, some charge a (usually) nominal fee for their services, usually between $20 and $40. The following sections explain the main types of registries.

You can also use registries to search for siblings. Online registries enable you to search for anyone. State registries may have rules governing sibling searches. For example, Indiana's state-run registry doesn't allow for sibling searches unless the adoptee is younger than the siblings being searched for. Nebraska allows for sib searches, without such restrictions.

Voluntary registry

A voluntary registry is an online registry where you post your info (usually gender, birth date, and place of birth) and whom you're looking for. For example, people who don't have their birthmother's name would say, "I am looking for my birthmother." Others, especially in some of the older cases, do have their birthmother's name and can use that for the search. (Keep in mind though that having the name Lisa Brown at your disposal from 35 years ago is usually not that helpful. She has probably changed her name, maybe more than once, and you probably don't have any idea what city she was from or where she lives now.) After you enter your information, you read other listings for a match.

Although these types of registries can be quite successful — especially if the other party is also actively searching for you — here's one word of caution: You may find a match and later discover you were wrong. What some people fail to remember is that, for example, several baby boys may have been born on the same day at any given hospital or maternity home. So finding the correct birth date, gender, and location doesn't guarantee a true match.

Passive registry

A passive registry is often called a *mutual consent registry*. This type of registry was established so that two parties who want to have contact can find each other. Both individuals register with the registry by filling out forms that allow the release of their identifying information to the other party. Only when both people have registered is the info released. The exchange of information is always a two-way exchange (hence the term *mutual consent*). When you register, you probably won't have any idea whether the person you're looking for has registered.

When a match is made, each party receives a letter with the name, address, and phone number of the other person. In some states, such as Indiana, you also receive some kind of legal document verifying that you've been connected with the right person. The adoptee gets an original birth certificate with the birthmother listed as mother, and the birthmother receives an adoption decree that states who adopted her child.

Active registry

With an active registry, your registration starts an actual search for the other party. You can find a lot of these registries on the Internet.

But before you sign on, keep in mind that, if the registry has no connection to your adoption or no access to state records, it has no more information to go on than what you already have. How can the registry find a woman if it doesn't know her birth date, name, Social Security number, and so on? Many people fork over a lot of money to these registries with very poor results.

A note on open records states

Some states — specifically Alabama, Alaska, Kansas, and Oregon — don't require that the birthmother consent to the release of her name and other identifying information. These are *open records states.* If you live in one of these states, you simply need to complete an application process to receive identifying information from your files. Contact your local Office of Family and Children for details.

States with registries

The following states have search registries:

Arkansas	Hawaii	Maryland	New Jersey	Tennessee
California	Idaho	Massachusetts	New York	Texas
Colorado	Indiana	Michigan	Ohio	Utah
Florida	Louisiana	Missouri	Oklahoma	Vermont
Georgia	Maine	Nevada	South Dakota	West Virginia

When registries don't work:
An out-and-out search

In some instances, signing up with registries doesn't yield the information you want. In other cases, your state may not have a registry. In either of these situations, you can continue your search by other means.

If your state has a registry (explained in the preceding section), you must register before you begin the search procedure covered in this section. If the person you're looking for hasn't registered, then some states allow you to go further in the search process.

Getting the ball rolling

The first thing you do to initiate an out-and-out search is to call your agency to find out whether it has someone on staff to do the searches. If it does, you must request a search in writing, usually with your signature notarized and accompanied by photo I.D. and the fee. Some agencies charge a flat fee, some an hourly rate, and some a flat fee for so many hours, with an hourly fee that kicks in after those hours are used up.

If your agency doesn't have a search person on staff or if the adoption was handled privately, then you must petition a judge to have a confidential intermediary (C.I.) appointed. A C.I. is an individual the judge appoints to do a search (usually someone who has experience in searches and whom the judge can trust to be neutral). If the judge accepts your petition, he'll send a court order appointing the C.I. to your case and giving the C.I. access to all the court records of the adoption that are needed to do the search. You have to pay the court costs associated with filing the petition for the C.I. and then pay the search fee as well. You usually don't have to request the search in writing because the court order takes care of that.

Note: Most people don't seek the services of a private investigator. P.I.s don't have access to the necessary records for the search; only the agency or the court has those records.

Tracking clues

Every search is different. Here's an example of how a C.I. may proceed, once she has the information she needs to begin the search for a birthmother (she would follow essentially the same steps to search for a birthfather).

First, she reads the file and looks for clues. Where did the birthmother live? Did she have any brothers? What would her parents' ages be? And so on. (Why look for brothers and not sisters? Brothers generally don't change their names.)

She'll follow all the leads available in the existing documentation. She'll search Internet phone listings and check Social Security death records and any other records she can find. If she discovers that someone died, she may get a copy of an obituary to see how the survivors are listed. For instance, if the birthmother's dad died, his obituary may say that he's survived by a daughter, Lisa Miller of Bowling Green, Ky. With that information — the birthmother's name and where she lives — the C.I. can now go to libraries and read old newspapers on microfilm to find newspaper notices that may be helpful.

If the C.I. finds a relative, she can't tell the person about the search, so instead she'll say something like "I have confidential information for this person and need to speak with her."

Making a connection

When the C.I finds the birthmother (or adoptee, depending on who is searching), she tells her who requested the search and what this person is hoping for. The birthmother basically has three options:

✔ **She can agree to a meeting.** In this case, she'll be sent the registry forms to fill out so that the state will release the identifying info.

✔ **If she isn't ready for a meeting, she can opt to correspond with the other person through the agency.** Similar to what people in semi-open adoptions do, the people involved can exchange letters and photos but no identifying information.

The C.I.s are never allowed to disclose the identifying information, unless the state has given them a release, which doesn't happen unless both parties have registered.

✔ **She can refuse any contact.** C.I.s must honor this request and report the response to the other party. I (Katrina) am a C.I. in Indiana. When the people I contact choose this option, I ask them whether they have a message I can give to the other party. If I'm contacting a birthmother, I ask her to give me an updated medical history.

Options for children adopted internationally

Many international adoption agencies that have been around for a while have their own programs established to help adoptees search or receive additional info. These programs generally entail your paying a fee to the agency that handled your adoption. Then the agency asks the agency staff in the other country to try to find the birthmother.

Some adoptees who decide to search on their own (because the agency search wasn't successful, for example, or doesn't offer the search service) post ads in newspapers in the country of their births. For instance, "I was a baby boy found on the doorstep of the xyz orphanage on January 12, 1976." We don't know how successful these ads are.

Specific registries have been established in the United States for internationally adopted children. Examples of such registries include

- ✔ **ISSR or International Soundex Reunion Registry** (www.isrr.net) is a nonprofit mutual consent registry.
- ✔ **Seekers of the Lost** is a free registry found at www.seeklost.com.

See the section "Registries and how they work," earlier in this chapter, for more information on registries.

My (Katrina's) daughter's search took place with the help of a Korean friend who took an interest in her situation. He made frequent trips to Korea. We supplied him with the name and address of the agency in Korea, and he made a personal visit. The agency staff told him they could only release info to my daughter in person. Soon after, she was able to travel to Korea and accompany this man to the agency office. Her presence was enough for them to generate a search on her behalf. She was united with her birthfather before she left to come back to the States. She was able to meet her birthmother during a later trip to Korea.

Happily Ever After? When the Search Ends

Your child has wondered about his birthparents most of his life. He's asked you question after question. He's fantasized about what his birthmother is like and how their first meeting will go. Maybe he's thought beyond the first meeting to the relationship they will (or won't) have. And now, he's found her.

Probably the easiest part of searching is the search itself. The hardest part may very well be actually making the connection. Regardless of whether your child is searching because of a deep desire to build a relationship with his birthparent or a simple need for more-complete medical information, the situation is a very emotional one — even for those who claim otherwise.

The honeymoon period and after

Many meetings between adoptees and birthparents begin with a sense of euphoria, what I (Katrina) call the *honeymoon period.* Everyone is thrilled. There are hugs, tears, and unbelievable coincidences. I hear, "She loves spaghetti!" or "Her favorite color is blue!" and no one seems to recognize that half the population loves spaghetti and blue.

This meeting is also a time when an adoptee may actually see someone with the same nose or long toes. These similarities are a longed-for reality at last. All seems right with the world. These are the moments you see on *Montel, Jerry Springer,* and *Oprah.*

After the initial euphoria, the relationship starts to develop, and differences may arise. Ideological differences, like "I am pro-life, and she is pro-choice," or core differences, like "I am educated, and she is uneducated," start to emerge. I don't know how many adoptees have told me, "We don't really have very much in common."

Some adoptees very quickly grow tired of the birthmother acting "motherly." They say things like "She is driving me nuts calling me all the time" or "I already have one mother telling me what to do; I certainly do not need another." Sometimes unexpected feelings of anger or resentment can emerge. A birthmother looking at old photos can say something like "I wish I could have been there for your second birthday," and the adoptee will be shocked when her first thought is "Well, you could have been if you hadn't given me away." These angry feelings can be quite confusing, especially when the adoptee has just dedicated the last six months to finding this woman so she could express her appreciation to her.

The birthmother may also struggle with her own feelings of resentment or rejection. After the initial meetings, she may find that she wants a deeper relationship than the adoptee wants to have. She may be jealous when she sees the loving relationship the adoptee has with her adoptive mother (even though she really wouldn't want it any other way). Looking at the photos of that second birthday party and realizing everything that she's missed may be quite painful. The birthmother is confronted with the reality that she will never have a typical parent/child relationship with this person because they are beginning their relationship as two adults with different experiences.

At this juncture, both parties have to make some choices. Just as after a honeymoon, when a wife realizes that her husband is always going to throw his socks on the floor and leave the toilet seat up, someone has to decide whether this relationship is worth the effort it will take to preserve it. If having a relationship is important to both parties, they can agree to work through their differences and remain in contact.

Sometimes both parties want a deep emotional attachment, and sometimes they both prefer a casual acquaintance. Curiously, some people who want a deep attachment never seem able to develop it, and some people who want a casual arrangement sometimes grow very close.

Tripping over great expectations

The adoptee-birthparent meetings that seem to work the best are those in which neither party has a list of expectations for the other.

Some of the most disastrous meetings have occurred when one party has different expectations than the other. For instance, a birthmother may think, "This is my BABY! I can't believe she has come home! Wow! She will be here for Thanksgiving, Christmas, and Easter and every weekend in between." At the same time, the adoptee may be thinking, "I hope I can get a complete medical history, and I would like to meet her once in person. It might even be nice if we exchange Christmas cards and letters every year." (These unequal expectations can happen in reverse, as well. The adoptee may want more of a relationship than the birthmother does.)

One reunion/relationship I (Katrina) was a part of ended abruptly when the birthmother demanded the adoptee call her "mom" and the adoptee refused. The birthmother stated she refused to be "disrespected," and the adoptee said that only one woman in her life had earned the title "mom." Clearly, these two people had different expectations for their relationship.

Good-bye, fantasy; hello, reality

Many adoptees and birthmothers describe their meetings as another type of loss. They say they have to give up their fantasies of how things might be. Nothing is ever quite the way they daydreamed about it. Next, each person has to deal with the reality of another flesh-and-blood person with her own set of expectations and ideas. Together, they have to find out how this relationship is going to work.

In addition, some adoptees who have felt an emptiness or void throughout their life may expect a meeting with their birthmother to fill that void. What they usually discover is that it doesn't. No matter how much time they spend with their birthmother, they're still persons who were placed for adoption. A meeting between the two never erases that original sense of rejection.

Having said all of that, I (Katrina) have never had an adoptee say he regretted his search. No matter what the result of the search was, at least the adoptee finally had some answers. When I called one adoptee to tell him his birthmother was deceased, I apologized for bringing him such sad news. He immediately said, "No, don't think of it that way. You brought me news. This is the first time I have ever had any news." After one birthmother tried to scam the adoptee out of a large sum of money, the adoptee discovered that her birthmother had a lengthy criminal record. The adoptee said she was so glad she had searched because she had spent her entire life imagining this warm, loving, and welcoming mother waiting for her. Now she realized that the woman she had dreamed of did not exist, and she could quit wasting time thinking about it.

Other adoptees have developed close friendships with their birthmothers. Many of their adoptive families have also welcomed the birthmothers into the fold.

And what about the adoptive family?

I (Katrina) have never had an adoptee desert or abandon her adoptive family after a search. Initially, in the rush and emotions of the meeting between an adoptee and the birthmother, an adoptee may be somewhat obsessed with her birthmother and the newly discovered answers. She may talk non-stop about the birthmother, saying, "She said this" and "She said that."

Bite your tongue till it bleeds but do *not* lay a guilt trip on your kid. Many adoptive parents call me during this time, concerned that they're "losing" their child. I always counsel them to be patient and give their child time. This is when your child needs your support and your blessing to explore the relationship. I guarantee you, when the car breaks down, you'll be the one your child will call. And, if the birthmother relationship fails to be all your child hoped for, your shoulder will be the one she'll cry on.

How You Can Help

Although you may feel threatened by your child's need to find his birthmother, you really are an important part of your child's search. Your support and love can help him through the emotional times ahead. You can also help him in practical ways, which the following sections explain.

Saving information

When you adopt your child, you get information. Maybe a little. Maybe a lot. All that info is like gold when your child begins a search. Your child's adoption information may be the only memento of her early life. What may seem inconsequential to you could very well be a treasure to your child. So make sure that you take proper care of this stuff. Save anything and everything, no matter how ridiculous it seems. Let your child decide later what is important.

If you're adopting internationally, save things like ticket stubs, hotel stationery, and the outfit your child was wearing when you first saw her. Take photos of the countryside, the agency office or the orphanage, and every person who had an impact on your child's life. Because searches are more difficult internationally, the mementos and documents that you save may be all the information your child will ever have.

Being the font of knowledge

If your child has a question about his birthparents or his history, you're the one he's going to ask. So, when your child is ready for the information and asks, be open and honest about the information you have. Don't hide the information or lie about it. If you do, your child will believe that he can't trust you, and your relationship could be permanently damaged. And don't hem and haw because you're uncomfortable. If your kid thinks that talking about his feelings or his desire to meet his birthmother makes you uncomfortable, he won't share this very important part of his life with you.

Remember, you want to be the *first* person your child feels like he can go to, because he trusts and relies on you for help when he needs it.

Supporting your child's decision

If you want to maintain a close relationship with your child and if you want to stay in the loop about his search, you must support his desire to search. Otherwise, your child may pursue a search without your knowledge. Many of the searches I (Katrina) conduct are done without the knowledge of the adoptive parents.

When your child is young, begin reassuring him that you're accepting of a search. As he grows older, let him know that you're willing to help him any way you can. Show him his adoption documents and let him know where you store them. Maintain an atmosphere of openness and full disclosure.

Do not push your child into doing a search (or try to "guilt" him out of it). A search must be his idea, and he must do it only when he feels prepared to handle the results.

Being there when the search is over

Whether the search ended the way your child wanted it to or not, she still needs you there for support. Searches generate a lot of emotions. The best way to help your child with her emotions is not to ride the emotional roller coaster with her. Try to be the stable and steady one in the equation. At the same time, don't discount or try to change her feelings. If she's angry, let her be angry. If she's happy, let her be happy. Your job is simply to be there for her, as you've always been there for her. After all, that's what parents are for.

Part V
The Part of Tens

The 5th Wave

By Rich Tennant

"Well, before you decide on what adoption agency to use, find out if they offer a service contract."

In this part . . .

*T*his part — a standard element in all *For Dummies* books — offers quick lists that you can use as resources for yourselves and your kids. You can find support groups, Web sites, and a list of great books to read to your children.

Chapter 20

Ten Great Books to Read to Your Kids

In This Chapter

▶ Animal stories that help children understand adoption

▶ Books to help kids answer questions about adoption

▶ Stories that reassure children that they're loved and wanted

▶ A workbook to let little kids express themselves

*I*n addition to telling your child his or her own adoption story (as explained in Chapter 16), you can use books as a way to broach sensitive topics and help your child understand adoption. A lot of great kids books are out there, and we list a few of our favorites here.

Before you read any book to your child, read it yourself first to make sure that you're comfortable not only with the story itself but also with *how* it's told. Some books sound great when you're looking at the title or reading the cover description, but then you get into the book itself and discover that the author uses language or deals with topics in a way that you're not comfortable with. This tip may sound like a no-brainer, but with books on adoption, insensitive portrayals or poor word choice is more than the writer's problem. It can become yours as well.

The Mulberry Bird: An Adoption Story

Written by Anne Braff Brodzinsky, Ph.D., and illustrated by Diana L. Stanley, *The Mulberry Bird* (Perspectives Press, 1996) is a poignant and beautifully told tale of a mother bird who decides to place her baby bird for adoption. Through the mother bird's struggles and love, the story (for ages 5 to 10) explains why a birthmother might make an adoption plan for her child.

A Mother for Choco

Written and illustrated by Keiko Kasza, *A Mother for Choco* (Scott Foresman Publishers, 1992) tells the story of a little bird who goes searching for a mother. After seeking out other creatures that share physical characteristics and being turned away by all of them, Choco finds a mother in Mrs. Bear and discovers that love, and not physical similarity, is what makes a family. This book is great for young children and beginning readers (ages 3 to 7).

The Day We Met You

Written and illustrated by Phoebe Koehler, *The Day We Met You* (Aladdin Paperbacks, 1990) uses simple words and images to describe the events on the day that adoptive parents meet their baby for the first time. The simple descriptions ("The sun shone bright the day we met you" and "We found some pacifiers that looked like butterflies and a mobile full of elephants") enable you to add your own special details as you read this story (for ages 2 to 5) to your child.

Never Never Never Will She Stop Loving You: The Adoption Love Story of Angel Annie

Written by Jolene Durrant and illustrated by children, ages 5 to 14, who've been adopted, *Never Never Never Will She Stop Loving You* (JoBiz! Books, 1999) is the true story of Annie, a birthmother, the things she did during her pregnancy to care for the child she was carrying, and the difficult decision she made to place that child for adoption. Although this book (for ages 3 to 10) shares Annie's story, its message is universal and helps to answer some of the questions that adopted children ask: Did she love me? Does she ever think about me? Was it hard for her to let me go?

When You Were Born In China: A Memory Book for Children Adopted from China

Written by Sara Dorow and with photographs by Stephen Wurow, *When You Were Born in China* (Yeong & Yeong Book Company, 1997) combines moving text and touching photographs to explain why and how children born in China came to their adoptive families. Sharing both the magnificence of China and some of its difficult truths (cultural "preferences" for boys, for example, or the restrictions on how many children are allowed in a family), this book (for ages 5 to 10) can help children understand why their birthmother chose an adoption plan, who cared for them and what their life may have been like as they waited for a family, and the process that finally brought their family together.

Zachary's New Home: A Story for Foster and Adopted Children

Written by Geraldine M Blomquist, M.S.W., and Paul B. Blomquist and illustrated by Margo Lemieux, *Zachary's New Home* (Magination Press, 1990), tells the story of Zachary, a little kitten who is removed from his parents' home after his father leaves and his mother, who is angry much of the time, sometimes hurts him. He moves into a foster home, where he feels unhappy and out of place. He is finally placed in an adoptive home, but being adopted doesn't make Zachary happy. He still misses his mother and father, and he's confused and angry and begins to think that no one loves him.

Written for children who've experienced numerous placements and the parents who love them, *Zachary's New Home* (for ages 3 to 8) introduces topics that may be difficult for kids to share on their own.

A New Barker in the House

Written and illustrated by Tomie DePaola, *A New Barker in the House* (G.P. Putnam's Sons, 2002) tells the story of the Barkers, a family of Welsh terriers. Mom, Dad, and twins Moffie and Morgie are preparing for the arrival of a new brother, 3-year-old Marcos, who speaks no English. As excited as the twins are to have a new brother, they soon discover that making Marcos feel welcome requires more than forcing him to play games he doesn't understand. When Marcos rebels — *"No Juego!"* ("No play!") — the children discover that they need to think about how Marcos feels and what Marcos likes to do. Soon, with Mom and Dad to guide them, everyone is learning English and Spanish together as they become a *familia* (family). The book is geared for children ages 2 to 7.

Tell Me Again about the Night I Was Born

Written by Jamie Lee Curtis and illustrated by Laura Cornell, *Tell Me Again about the Night I Was Born* (Joanna Cotler Books, 1996) begins with a little girl's request to hear the tale of the night she was born. Before long, however, it's clear that the little girl knows her own story by heart. The book focuses on the things a child would focus on and uses the insistent cadence of a child's request ("Tell me again. . . .") — "Tell me again how you and Daddy were curled up like spoons and Daddy was snoring" and "Tell me again how you got on an airplane with my baby bag and flew to get me and how there was no movie, only peanuts." The story (for ages 4 to 8) joyously and poignantly relates all the most important things about her birth and how they became a family.

W.I.S.E. Up! Powerbook

Adopted children face all sorts of questions (some general, some personal) about adoption from all sorts of people — friends, teachers, and even strangers. *The W.I.S.E. Up! Powerbook,* written by Marilyn Schoettle, MA, is a tool you can use to empower your child when he faces questions and comments that may make him uncomfortable. Instead of feeling like every question deserves an answer, this book explains your child's options (the first letters form the acronym used in the book title): Walk away, say It's private, Share something, or Educate. The book (for all ages) also includes scenarios to help kids practice and talk about their responses. It also provides guidance and instruction to parents.

All About Me

Written by Lynn Burwash and Cie McMullin, two adoptive mothers, and illustrated by adopted children, *All About Me* (PrintNet, 1998) is designed to be a workbook for younger children (ages 2 to 5) trying to understand the meaning of being adopted. With fill-in-the-blanks and extra space for drawings, children can use washable crayons and markers to create (and re-create) a story about themselves.

Chapter 21

Ten Support Groups for Adoptive Families

*T*alking with other people who've been in your shoes and have dealt with or experienced the same things you're experiencing (or likely to experience) can be a tremendous help. Whether you're facing a dilemma that you need advice on or are just looking for other families like yours, you can probably find a support group that meets your needs. Adoption support groups provide education, support, and social activities for adoptive parents and prospective adoptive parents. These groups are usually family-oriented and involve family activities or provide childcare for adult activities.

Adoption support groups don't benefit only you. They also offer one major benefit to your children: the opportunity for children to interact with other children who were adopted and to see that many families are similar to theirs. As the children grow older, these groups let them develop peer groups that have similar experiences and that may be dealing with similar issues or questions. In the same way, the adults can vent and support each other through the difficulties their children experience.

This chapter lists a few adoption support groups and explains their purpose. To find out whether these groups (or groups like them) are available in your area, ask the social worker at your adoption agency or attorney, contact your state human services agency, or look in your local Yellow Pages.

Latin America Parents Association (LAPA)

Latin America Parents Association (LAPA) is a support group for families who want to adopt kids from Latin America or who already have adopted from that region. Chapters are located in Connecticut, Illinois, Maryland, New Jersey, New York, Pennsylvania, and Washington, D.C.

For information, contact LAPA, P.O. Box 339, Brooklyn NY 11234; phone 718-236-8689.

The National Adoption Center (NAC)

The National Adoption Center (NAC) is a support group that focuses on families who adopt special-needs children (those who are school aged, in a sibling group that needs to stay together, or who have emotional, physical, mental, or developmental disabilities).

For information, contact NAC, 1500 Walnut St., Philadelphia, PA 19102; phone 800-TO-ADOPT.

The National Council for Single Adoptive Parents

The National Council for Single Adoptive Parents (a nonprofit organization formed in 1973 and formerly known as the Committee for Single Adoptive Parents) is an umbrella organization for single adoptive parent support groups. Through this organization, you can find information on how to adopt as a single person and how to manage as a single parent.

For information, contact National Council for Single Adoptive Parents, P.O. Box 55, Wharton, NJ 07885; e-mail: ncsap@hotmail.com.

North American Council on Adoptable Children (NACAC)

The North American Council on Adoptable Children (NACAC) is another umbrella organization for adoptive parent groups. This organization helps start new support groups, coordinates the sharing of information between support groups, and holds national conferences focusing on adoption issues. NACAC's database of parent groups includes a list of hundreds of support groups, enabling you to find support in your area.

For information, contact NACAC, 970 Raymond Ave., Suite 106, St. Paul, MN 55114-1149; phone 612-644-3036. You can find the database at www.nacac.org/pas_databasehtml.

Adoptive Families of America (AFA)

Adoptive Families of America (AFA) is a national parent group with chapters throughout the country. These groups provide support and information for domestic or international adoptive families. For information, contact AFA, 2309 Como Ave., St. Paul, MN 55108; phone 800-372-3300.

Families Adopting Children Everywhere (FACE)

Families Adopting Children Everywhere (FACE) is an adoption support group. Based in the Washington, D.C., and Maryland areas, this group also gathers adoption resource information for the mid-Atlantic region.

For information, contact FACE, P.O. Box 2805, Northwood Station, Baltimore, MD 21239; phone 410-488-2656.

Families of Children from Vietnam (FCV)

Families of Children from Vietnam (FCV) is a national support group for families who are considering or have already adopted children from Vietnam. This group currently lists chapters in 28 states plus 2 chapters in Canada.

If you're interested in starting a chapter in your own area, contact Allison and Rick Martin at 5martin@bellsouth.net.

For information, go to the FCV Web site at www.fcvn.org/fcv_chapters.htm.

The Korean American Adoptee Adoptive Family Network (KAAN)

The Korean American Adoptee Adoptive Family Network (KAAN) is an organization in which children adopted from Korea, their parents, and other Korean Americans work together to link individuals and organizations across the United States and Canada. Currently, this group has approximately 35 support groups in the United States, Canada, Switzerland, Denmark, and Sweden.

For information, go to the KAAN Web site at www.kaanet.com.

Families with Children from China (FCC)

Families with Children from China (FCC) is a network of parent support groups through the United States, Canada, and the United Kingdom. These chapters range from the formally structured, with by-laws and boards of directors, to the informal groups of families sharing activities. You can find a listing of all current chapters at the FCC Web site (www.fwcc.org/contacts.html). To find the FCC support group closest to you, click your state on the site's interactive map.

To Find Other Groups in Your Area

The National Adoption Information Clearinghouse (NAIC) has information about adoptive parent support groups in your own area. Just enter your state on its Web site (www.adoptivefamilies.com/support_group.php) to access a list of adoption support groups.

For more information, contact NAIC, 330 C Street, SW, Washington, DC 20447; phone 703-352-3488.

Chapter 22

Ten Helpful Web Sites

- -

- -

*T*o find adoption Web sites, you simply have to go to your favorite search engine and type in **Adoption**. For a more refined search, add any descriptors (like state name or subtopic: **Adoption Kentucky**, for example, or **adoption international**), and you'll get sites that match the narrower search. What we list here are specific sites that we've found helpful because of the information they contain and the links that they offer. Do not, by any means, consider this a complete list. It's about 999,999,999 entries short.

General Adoption Web Sites

Obviously, numerous Web sites are devoted to adoption. You can find sites of individuals looking to adopt or place a child, government sites, commercial sites, and more. As you peruse the various sites that you no doubt will encounter, remember a couple things:

✔ Not all sites offer accurate or trustworthy information; nor is any site's information absolutely complete or up-to-date.

✔ Some sites are out to attract clients or make money; others are out to provide information. Both types of sites can provide you with decent content, but you need to know the difference so that you can evaluate the veracity of the info.

National Adoption Information Clearinghouse (NAIC)

The National Adoption Information Clearinghouse (www.calib.com/naic), sponsored by the U.S. Department of Health and Human Services, offers a wealth of information and adoption resources. Examples of the links you can click for additional information include the following:

- **National Adoption Directory** to locate agencies, support groups, adoption services, and more in your area
- **Adopted Persons** for information on accessing vital records and adoption records, book lists for kids, and more
- **Laws** to find out what federal adoption laws are and to access summaries of each state's adoption code

Administration for Children and Families

The Administration for Children and Families (ACF) is a federal agency within the U.S. Department of Health and Human Services. Although the ACF home page (www.acf.dhhs.gov) contains a lot of general information, the Adoption & Foster Care link takes you to information that you may find especially helpful and interesting. Of particular interest may be the Adoption Topics link, which lets you access articles relating to adoption, adoption directories, laws and policies regarding adoption, and organizations that deal with adoption and adoption issues.

LII: Law about . . . Adoption

The pages of the Legal Information Institutes (LII) Law about . . . Adoption site (www.law.cornell.edu/topics/adoption.html) are prepared by LII student editors working under the supervision of a professor at the institute. Revised at least annually, the site contains links to primary source material — that is, the statutes themselves — and a little commentary. This is a good site if you're interested in the actual laws relating to adoption and are comfortable reading legalese.

Adoption.org

This easy-to-navigate site (www.adoption.org) offers general adoption information in a number of areas: law, crisis pregnancies, adoption professionals, and birthparent searches. You can also find lists of adoption agencies and attorneys by state, look at adoptive parent profiles, or link to online businesses that sell books, cards, announcements, and so on specifically geared to the adoptive family.

ABA Center on Children and the Law

Although not a site devoted specifically to adoption, the American Bar Association's Center on Children and the Law (`www.abanet.org/child/home.html`) focuses on improving the quality of children's lives by "advances in law, justice, knowledge, practice, and public policy." This is a good site to check periodically if you're interested in being an advocate for children or want to be informed of updates and changes in the status of child welfare laws and public policies in the United States. To find information specific to adoption issues, click the Issues category and then select Foster Care/ Adoption.

TransracialAdoption.com

TransracialAdoption.com (`www.transracialadoption.com`) is a good place to go for general information on transracial adoption. Although the site's content isn't greatly detailed, it does provide a launching point for those who want to gain a basic understanding of transracial adoption, access articles relating to the topic, or see some statistics and study results regarding how many adoptive families in the United States are transracial and how the children in these families fare.

AdoptionBooks.com

Affiliated with Amazon.com, AdoptionBooks.com (`www.adoptionbooks.com`) provides a list of categories that touch on all aspects of adoption. The site also includes children's books and fictional books that have adoption as a theme. You can buy books directly from the site, if you like, or you can just see what's available and head to your local bookstore with your list.

Sites for International Adoptions

Believe it or not, much of the best and most recent information regarding international adoption comes from government Web sites. Of course, being the government, it doesn't put all this helpful information at one site — or make it particularly easy to find. But it's there nonetheless. Other sites, devoted specifically to international adoption, combine a lot of relevant info — including overviews of the government info — all in one easy-to-locate place.

InternationalAdoption.org

At InternationalAdoption.org (www.internationaladoption.org), you can find a great deal of information about countries that currently have active international adoption programs. An on-site map links you to these countries. The information includes fact sheets, country-specific adoption information, information on the culture and heritage, travel information (such as maps and currency exchange rates), and so on.

The BCIS Online

The Bureau of Citizenship and Immigration Services (BCIS) contains all the information you've ever wanted (or not) about immigration and naturalization in the United States, including information on international adoptions. From this page (www.immigration.gov), you can find the official government rules and definitions of international adoptions, the labyrinthine process required to successfully manage it, and the myriad forms you must fill out. Although this site can lead you to lots of good information, it isn't for the faint of heart. But it *is* for those who want to double-check the information they receive from other sources.

The International Adoption Page

Although run by the U.S. government (specifically, the U.S. Department of State, Bureau of Consular Affairs, Overseas Citizens Services, Office of Children Issues), this site (http://travel.state.gov/adopt.html) actually has info that's easy to read and easy to find. Here you can access notices and updates posted by the U.S. government regarding adoption status in various countries, booklets dealing with international adoption, and fliers on specific countries, arranged alphabetically for your searching pleasure. If you're adopting from a country that may have experienced problems in its adoption program (such as Cambodia recently) or want to know whether the country you're considering is even open to adoption by American citizens, go to this site.

Index

• C •

• *D* •

FOR DUMMIES®

The easy way to get more done and have more fun

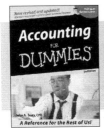

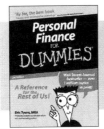

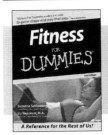

FOR DUMMIES®

A world of resources to help you grow

HOME, GARDEN & HOBBIES

Feng Shui For Dummies
0-7645-5295-3

Gardening For Dummies
0-7645-5130-2

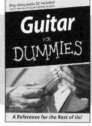

Guitar For Dummies
0-7645-5106-X

Also available:

Auto Repair For Dummies
(0-7645-5089-6)

Chess For Dummies
(0-7645-5003-9)

Home Maintenance For
Dummies
(0-7645-5215-5)

Organizing For Dummies
(0-7645-5300-3)

Piano For Dummies
(0-7645-5105-1)

Poker For Dummies
(0-7645-5232-5)

Quilting For Dummies
(0-7645-5118-3)

Rock Guitar For Dummies
(0-7645-5356-9)

Roses For Dummies
(0-7645-5202-3)

Sewing For Dummies
(0-7645-5137-X)

FOOD & WINE

Cooking For Dummies
0-7645-5250-3

Cookies For Dummies
0-7645-5390-9

Wine For Dummies
0-7645-5114-0

Also available:

Bartending For Dummies
(0-7645-5051-9)

Chinese Cooking For
Dummies
(0-7645-5247-3)

Christmas Cooking For
Dummies
(0-7645-5407-7)

Diabetes Cookbook For
Dummies
(0-7645-5230-9)

Grilling For Dummies
(0-7645-5076-4)

Low-Fat Cooking For
Dummies
(0-7645-5035-7)

Slow Cookers For Dummies
(0-7645-5240-6)

TRAVEL

Italy For Dummies
0-7645-5453-0

Hawaii For Dummies
0-7645-5438-7

Las Vegas For Dummies
0-7645-5448-4

Also available:

America's National Parks For
Dummies
(0-7645-6204-5)

Caribbean For Dummies
(0-7645-5445-X)

Cruise Vacations For
Dummies 2003
(0-7645-5459-X)

Europe For Dummies
(0-7645-5456-5)

Ireland For Dummies
(0-7645-6199-5)

France For Dummies
(0-7645-6292-4)

London For Dummies
(0-7645-5416-6)

Mexico's Beach Resorts For
Dummies
(0-7645-6262-2)

Paris For Dummies
(0-7645-5494-8)

RV Vacations For Dummies
(0-7645-5443-3)

Walt Disney World & Orlando
For Dummies
(0-7645-5444-1)

Available wherever books are sold. Go to www.dummies.com or call 1-877-762-2974 to order direct.

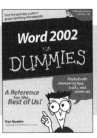
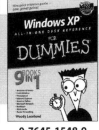

FOR DUMMIES®

Helping you expand your horizons and realize your potential

INTERNET

0-7645-0894-6

0-7645-1659-0

0-7645-1642-6

Also available:

America Online 7.0 For Dummies
(0-7645-1624-8)

Genealogy Online For Dummies
(0-7645-0807-5)

The Internet All-in-One Desk Reference For Dummies
(0-7645-1659-0)

Internet Explorer 6 For Dummies
(0-7645-1344-3)

The Internet For Dummies Quick Reference
(0-7645-1645-0)

Internet Privacy For Dummies
(0-7645-0846-6)

Researching Online For Dummies
(0-7645-0546-7)

Starting an Online Business For Dummies
(0-7645-1655-8)

DIGITAL MEDIA

0-7645-1664-7

0-7645-1675-2

0-7645-0806-7

Also available:

CD and DVD Recording For Dummies
(0-7645-1627-2)

Digital Photography All-in-One Desk Reference For Dummies
(0-7645-1800-3)

Digital Photography For Dummies Quick Reference
(0-7645-0750-8)

Home Recording for Musicians For Dummies
(0-7645-1634-5)

MP3 For Dummies
(0-7645-0858-X)

Paint Shop Pro "X" For Dummies
(0-7645-2440-2)

Photo Retouching & Restoration For Dummies
(0-7645-1662-0)

Scanners For Dummies
(0-7645-0783-4)

GRAPHICS

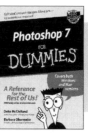

0-7645-0817-2

0-7645-1651-5

0-7645-0895-4

Also available:

Adobe Acrobat 5 PDF For Dummies
(0-7645-1652-3)

Fireworks 4 For Dummies
(0-7645-0804-0)

Illustrator 10 For Dummies
(0-7645-3636-2)

QuarkXPress 5 For Dummies
(0-7645-0643-9)

Visio 2000 For Dummies
(0-7645-0635-8)

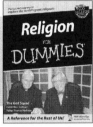

FOR DUMMIES®

The advice and explanations you need to succeed

SELF-HELP, SPIRITUALITY & RELIGION

0-7645-5302-X

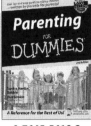

0-7645-5418-2

0-7645-5264-3

Also available:

The Bible For Dummies
(0-7645-5296-1)

Buddhism For Dummies
(0-7645-5359-3)

Christian Prayer For Dummies
(0-7645-5500-6)

Dating For Dummies
(0-7645-5072-1)

Judaism For Dummies
(0-7645-5299-6)

Potty Training For Dummies
(0-7645-5417-4)

Pregnancy For Dummies
(0-7645-5074-8)

Rekindling Romance For Dummies
(0-7645-5303-8)

Spirituality For Dummies
(0-7645-5298-8)

Weddings For Dummies
(0-7645-5055-1)

PETS

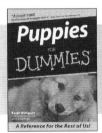

0-7645-5255-4

0-7645-5286-4

0-7645-5275-9

Also available:

Labrador Retrievers For Dummies
(0-7645-5281-3)

Aquariums For Dummies
(0-7645-5156-6)

Birds For Dummies
(0-7645-5139-6)

Dogs For Dummies
(0-7645-5274-0)

Ferrets For Dummies
(0-7645-5259-7)

German Shepherds For Dummies
(0-7645-5280-5)

Golden Retrievers For Dummies
(0-7645-5267-8)

Horses For Dummies
(0-7645-5138-8)

Jack Russell Terriers For Dummies
(0-7645-5268-6)

Puppies Raising & Training Diary For Dummies
(0-7645-0876-8)

EDUCATION & TEST PREPARATION

0-7645-5194-9

0-7645-5325-9

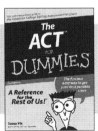

0-7645-5210-4

Also available:

Chemistry For Dummies
(0-7645-5430-1)

English Grammar For Dummies
(0-7645-5322-4)

French For Dummies
(0-7645-5193-0)

The GMAT For Dummies
(0-7645-5251-1)

Inglés Para Dummies
(0-7645-5427-1)

Italian For Dummies
(0-7645-5196-5)

Research Papers For Dummies
(0-7645-5426-3)

The SAT I For Dummies
(0-7645-5472-7)

U.S. History For Dummies
(0-7645-5249-X)

World History For Dummies
(0-7645-5242-2)

FOR DUMMIES

We take the mystery out of complicated subjects

WEB DEVELOPMENT

0-7645-1643-4

0-7645-0723-0

0-7645-1630-2

Also available:

ASP.NET For Dummies
(0-7645-0866-0)

Building a Web Site For
Dummies
(0-7645-0720-6)

ColdFusion "MX" For
Dummies (0-7645-1672-8)

Creating Web Pages
All-in-One Desk Reference
For Dummies
(0-7645-1542-X)

FrontPage 2002 For Dummies
(0-7645-0821-0)

HTML 4 For Dummies Quick
Reference
(0-7645-0721-4)

Macromedia Studio "MX"
All-in-One Desk Reference
For Dummies
(0-7645-1799-6)

Web Design For Dummies
(0-7645-0823-7)

PROGRAMMING & DATABASES

0-7645-0746-X

0-7645-1657-4

0-7645-0818-0

Also available:

Beginning Programming For
Dummies
(0-7645-0835-0)

Crystal Reports "X"
For Dummies
(0-7645-1641-8)

Java & XML For Dummies
(0-7645-1658-2)

Java 2 For Dummies
(0-7645-0765-6)

JavaScript For Dummies
(0-7645-0633-1)

Oracle9i For Dummies
(0-7645-0880-6)

Perl For Dummies
(0-7645-0776-1)

PHP and MySQL For
Dummies
(0-7645-1650-7)

SQL For Dummies
(0-7645-0737-0)

VisualBasic .NET For
Dummies
(0-7645-0867-9)

Visual Studio .NET All-in-One
Desk Reference For Dummies
(0-7645-1626-4)

LINUX, NETWORKING & CERTIFICATION

0-7645-1545-4

0-7645-0772-9

0-7645-0812-1

Also available:

CCNP All-in-One Certification
For Dummies
(0-7645-1648-5)

Cisco Networking For
Dummies
(0-7645-1668-X)

CISSP For Dummies
(0-7645-1670-1)

CIW Foundations For
Dummies with CD-ROM
(0-7645-1635-3)

Firewalls For Dummies
(0-7645-0884-9)

Home Networking For
Dummies
(0-7645-0857-1)

Red Hat Linux All-in-One
Desk Reference For Dummies
(0-7645-2442-9)

TCP/IP For Dummies
(0-7645-1760-0)

UNIX For Dummies
(0-7645-0419-3)

Available wherever books are sold.
Go to www.dummies.com or call 1-877-762-2974 to order direct.

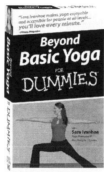
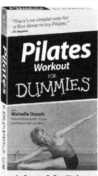

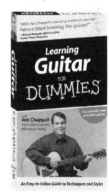

Made in the USA
San Bernardino, CA
20 January 2019